LOVE ON TRIAL

LOVE ON TRIAL

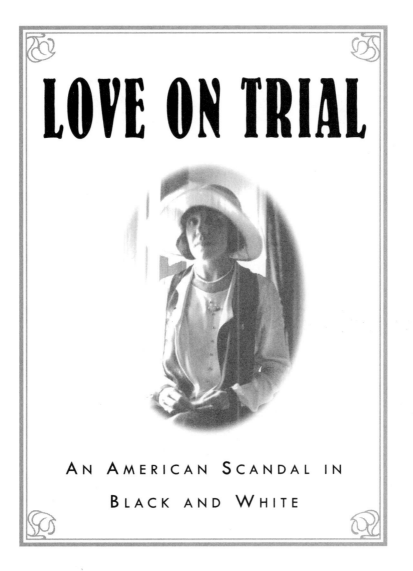

AN AMERICAN SCANDAL IN
BLACK AND WHITE

Earl Lewis and Heidi Ardizzone

W. W. NORTON & COMPANY

NEW YORK   LONDON

Photograph credits: Josephine Baker (Roger-Viollet); composite scene
in judge's chambers (*New York Evening Graphic*); former Jones house (Heidi
Ardizzone); all other photos (Bettmann/Corbis).

For information about permission to reproduce selections from this book,
write to Permissions, W. W. Norton & Company, Inc.,
500 Fifth Avenue, New York, NY 10110

The text of this book is composed in Electra
with the display set in Bernhard Bold Condensed and Twentieth Century Light.
Book design by JAM design
Production manager: Julia Druskin

Library of Congress Cataloging-in-Publication Data

Lewis, Earl.
    Love on trial: an American scandal in black and white / Earl Lewis and
Heidi Ardizzone.
        p. cm.
    Includes bibliographical references and index.
    ISBN: 0-393-05013-0
    1. Jones, Alice Beatrice. 2. Rhinelander, Leonard Kip. 3. Interracial
marriage—New York (State)—Westchester County—History—Case studies.
4. Marriage—Annulment—New York (State)—Westchester County—
History—Case studies. 5. Scandals—New York (State)—Westchester County
—History—Case studies. 6. Scandals in mass media—Case studies. 7.
Westchester County (N.Y.)—Race relations—History. I. Ardizzone, Heidi.
II. Title.

HQ1031 .L655 2001
306.84'6—dc21   00-067005

W. W. Norton & Company, Inc., 500 Fifth Avenue, New York, N.Y. 10110
www.wwnorton.com

W. W. Norton & Company Ltd., Castle House
75/76 Wells Street, London W1T 3QT

1 2 3 4 5 6 7 8 9 0

To my children, Suzanne and Max

E. L.

To the memory of Beveridge Webster, Frances Webster,
and Joseph R. Ardizzone, and to Dora Ardizzone,
who remembers hearing about the
Rhinelanders as a young girl

H. A.

CONTENTS

Introduction

❦

TIL DEATH DO US PART

STROLLING THROUGH THE Beechwoods Cemetery in New Rochelle, the astute observer will gain from the names on the headstones a quick glimpse of the ethnic patterns of settlement along the eastern seaboard for more than a century and a half. Surnames call to mind the ships that brought men, women, and children from Italy, Germany, Russia, Poland, and England. There, nestled among the others, one will find the Jones family—George and Elizabeth and their daughters, Emily, Grace, and Alice. In a far corner of the graveyard their flat, simple stones mark their resting places with only their names and dates.

Only a mile or so from the cemetery sits the home they shared and left, one by one. Set back from the street, their small home, now divided into apartments, sits between two larger, looming houses that face Long Island Sound on Pelham Road, which runs along the shoreline. Here George and Elizabeth raised their daughters, watched them grow, worked hard to provide for them. One by one the daughters married—Emily first, a local man named Robert Brooks. Her parents disapproved of the match, and the Brookses moved to a neighboring town and had a child. Grace married next, an Italian (despite his name), Albert "Footsie" Miller, and the couple moved into her parents' home.

Alice, still single, continued to work and live with her parents. Through Grace, Alice eventually met the man she would marry. The three met outside the sister's home on Pelham Road. For three years Alice had loved him while he came into and went from her life, waiting for him to return and marry her.

In the old downtown area on Huguenot Street stands the Pintard Apartments, in which Alice and her husband planned to live. Then new, modern, and exclusive, it is now a fading brick building, no doubt prized for its old-fashioned wood floors and high ceilings, no doubt still expensive.

They never occupied the apartment they had rented.

ALICE'S HUSBAND IS not buried beside her. Neither is Grace's: They divorced and Grace later remarried, moving to California. Emily's husband and child are both with her in the cemetery. But Alice's husband is interred in the "Second Oldest Organization in Bronx County"—the Woodlawn Cemetery. The Rhinelander plot is marked by a large marble building, in which the bodies of its family members lie in drawers, one on top of the other. It would be difficult to miss were it not surrounded by similar mournful architectural and stone-carved homages to passed souls. The entire graveyard is surround by high walls and guarded at the entrances against intruders. Once set in the countryside of northern New York City, Woodlawn now shares its neighborhood with bars, high-rises, and convenience stores with bulletproof windows and metal gratings across the doors. It harkens back to a time when the Bronx was a place of privilege and leisure, maintains its identity as a cultural organization and a rural cemetery, and provides the final resting place for such varied figures as Miles Davis, Irving Berlin, F. W. Woolworth, Fiorello La Guardia, Elizabeth Cady Stanton, Madame C. J. Walker, Herman Melville, Joseph Pulitzer, and Countee Cullen.[1]

Leonard Rhinelander's remains are there, with those of his mother, who died when he was a child, and his father, who outlived him by only four years. All of Leonard's siblings are there as well, including a brother who died in infancy and one who died during World War I, and a sister and brother who outlived him. The plot was owned by one of Leonard's grandfathers, also interred there, and was planned to provide for eighteen additional catacombs, if desired in the future.[2] Like Alice's, Leonard's remains are with those of his birth family.

ALICE OUTLIVED HER husband by almost sixty years. But that is not why they were not buried together.

ALICE BEATRICE JONES and Leonard Kip Rhinelander met in September 1921 and married in October 1924. Three weeks later their marriage made headlines across the country. Two weeks after that he left her, claiming that she had misrepresented herself to him and that he would not have married her had he known who she truly was. There are many ways to try to explain what happened to tear them apart so soon after their wedding—what had changed in those six weeks despite their having stayed faithful to each other for three years, often across long distances. Perhaps, most fundamentally, it simply came down to who their fathers were and what that meant in the 1920s United States.

Philip Rhinelander, an officer of the Rhinelander Real Estate Company, controlled millions both personally and on behalf of his well-heeled family. Listed in the *Social Register*, he was descended from several of New York's founding families, an American version of aristocracy. Given all that, it went without saying that he was white. George Jones was an English immigrant who had met his wife while they were both working as servants on a large estate in Leeds. Elizabeth was white. But George? Well, nobody was exactly sure *what* George was; some of the headlines announcing Alice and Leonard's marriage proclaimed him a colored man. What exactly *that* meant is something of a mystery, but if he was colored he couldn't be white. And if he wasn't white, then by American racial definitions Alice certainly wasn't. But even those who weren't sure about the Joneses' racial status could find sensation in the tremendous class differences between the lovers.

In New York, at least, the marriage became the scandal of the decade. By the time Leonard's annulment suit went into a public, juried trial, people throughout the country knew about the "Rhinelander Case." And the primary way they heard about it was through the newspapers.[3] With the aid of an extensive telegraph system and several national press organizations, including the Associated Press, daily updates on the Westchester County trial appeared on the doorsteps of Americans across the nation. Although some sought to censor or minimize aspects of the trial, none could completely ignore it.

The issues raised by the Rhinelander Case were of high interest and importance in America in the twenties. Was Alice black or white? What would make her one or the other? How could one tell? How much did it matter? Why was it such an outrage for Leonard to have married Alice? Was it that they were an interracial couple? Or that he had legitimized their relationship through marriage? Did a possibly black woman stand any chance of winning in court against the money and status of a Rhinelander? Other interests were less significant in social and political implications but equally important in explaining public obsession with the trial. What details of romance and sex would be revealed about the couple's courtship and marriage? What insights into the life of a Rhinelander? What were the emotional dynamics of this interracial, cross-class relationship?

Like their white counterparts, black-published newspapers across the country followed the trial with great interest. The Rhinelander Case offered numerous opportunities for African Americans to continue to challenge American racial stereotypes, racial discrimination, and the very idea of racial categories themselves. The disparity between white Americans' presumptions of racial, gender, and class superiority and the person of Leonard Kip Rhinelander provided perhaps the most fertile grounds. And black newspaper editors were particularly gleeful at being able to drive a deeper wedge into the American power base of whiteness, manliness, and money.

In 1925 interracial marriages were outlawed in more than half of the United States, and the segregation of the black and white races was the law in the south and general practice in other regions. Did that make Leonard and Alice's marriage a romantic triumph of love over class and race prejudices? Or an embarrassing, even dangerous, example of misguided youth ignoring the importance of their place within American hierarchies? And what would be revealed when the promised love letters and secrets of this couple's courtship were made public? This real-life love on trial promised sensational revelations and dramatic scenes. And it delivered: By the end of the trial women would be banned from the courtroom, both spouses' reputations would hang in shreds, and even the most sensationalistic tabloids would refuse to print full transcripts of certain episodes.

Behind all the headlines and the public displays, however, lies a story of two people, from two very different families, who chanced to meet and fall in love. The events that led to their estrangement and the annulment trial also provide an unusual entry into the everyday lives, dreams, and tragedies of Alice and Leonard Rhinelander. Though they never completely revealed their entire inner lives and shared experiences, the bright spotlights of public attention illuminated many aspects of their private world. Their love story became a media scandal, attracting attention across the country and crowds of curiosity seekers at their doorstep. Their behavior prompted outraged editorials regarding interracial mixing, racial definitions, white manhood, upper-class morals, working class respectability, and the place of racial and class hierarchies in a democratic society. Outside their families and circle of friends, Alice and Leonard became known primarily for the media frenzy that surrounded them between November 1924 and December 1925. But from the sensationalistic uproar emerges a story of two individuals and how these broader concerns came to define their lives.

LOVE ON TRIAL

1

≈

WAITING FOR LEONARD

ALICE BEATRICE JONES RHINELANDER, fashionably dressed, sat quietly in the hard wooden seat and smiled. Leonard was late and Alice was waiting. It was a familiar feeling. She had waited for him before, waited while he traveled the world and went to school. Waited in her bedroom in her parent's house, reading his letters and writing poetry and copying song lyrics that reflected the drama of her longing and uncertainty:

> Sitting alone at the window, watching the moonlit street,
> Bending my head to listen for the sound of your feet,
> I have been wondering, darling, how I can bear the pain,
> When I watch the signs with tear-wet eyes and wait for your
>   coming in vain,
> You will grow weary of sighing, you will long for a love
>   that is purer than we know;
> Remember me dear![1]

Waiting for the next letter, for the next visit, for the news that he was finally moving on . . . or finally coming back for good. And all those nights and months and even years of waiting had brought her here to the Westchester County Supreme Courthouse, where she sat, once again, and waited.

On this particular day, November 9, 1925, Alice did not wait alone. She sat between her lawyers, flanked by her parents, sisters, and brothers-in-law. Fully aware of the "white light of publicity," that illuminated this vigil, the Jones family sat upright, outwardly composed and calm.[2] They sat and waited together as journalists, photographers, and a crowded courtroom of curious onlookers occupied their time watching Alice and her family, scrutinizing their every movement, dress accessory, and facial expression. She wore a "tight-fitting tan gown, black silk stockings and black pumps, a cloth coat trimmed with gray fox fur and adorned with a gardenia." Her mother, Elizabeth Jones, a small, determined woman perched primly beside her daughter, plainly dressed, white hair pulled into a bun. Her father, George Jones, sat fingering his chin, a "long-faced, dark-skinned man, with long wavy hair."[3]

Everyone in that courtroom was waiting for Leonard. He had been expected, according to his own lawyers, early in the morning when the proceedings began. Twelve middle-aged and older white businessmen, a few retired, sat in the jury box and waited to be confirmed.[4] Leonard's own lawyers were waiting to begin the opening arguments. Everyone was ready for the event to begin, but where was Leonard? The trial could not proceed without its plaintiff. Perhaps he would not come; perhaps he had changed his mind.

It had been just short of a year since Leonard had filed the charges that led to this trial. A year of lawyers' statements, media speculation, and public debate. A long year for Alice to wait, unable to talk with Leonard about his feelings and motivations. The court recessed for lunch and reconvened. Leonard, however, was still missing. Yet all the onlookers knew that if there was to be a trial Leonard would have to show. Everyone in the courtroom watched Alice and wondered: What would she do when he arrived? How would they react to seeing each other for the first time in a year?[5]

Anticipation rivaled tedium. The morning of jury selection had passed slowly. Those inside had been privy to a relatively uneventful selection process. Leonard's lawyers had made sure that all the jurors were married and that nine out of the twelve were fathers. Meanwhile, Alice's lawyers had asked only one question of prospective jurors: "Do

Onlookers at the trial of Alice and Leonard Rhinelander, November 1925.

you feel that you can be absolutely fair to this girl?"[6] Alice and her family had sat silently through these hours, watched by the assembled crowd, everyone waiting for the real action to begin. Gathered outside the White Plains courtroom early in the morning, the eager crowd had jostled for entrance. Extra guards had been called in, as they would be many more times in the weeks to follow, to help control the court watchers. The audience, an estimated third of whom were black, whispered audibly as the prospective jurors were questioned about their jobs, families, and attitudes. At some points the black spectators were described as particularly enthralled by the courtroom transactions. At other times it was white women who seemed most invested in witnessing the proceedings. But all agreed that the trial had attracted an unusual mix of spectators.[7] Drawn by the hope of sensational testimony and a spilling of Rhinelander family secrets, New York City and Westchester County citizens vied with hundreds of travelers for admission into the small courtroom.[8] The Rhinelander case, after all, promised to be one of the most sensational legal battles fought in New York State that decade.[9]

Finally, at 2:30 P.M., the doors opened and Leonard Kip Rhinelander entered the courtroom, accompanied by a bodyguard. He appeared pale and drawn, "obviously," according to one observer, "wishing that he were anywhere else in the world than in the Supreme Court room at White Plains." Those expecting sparks or drama between the couple were disappointed: The young plaintiff studiously took no notice of her. She, however, searched his face intently as he entered, "as though expecting a sign of love, or recognition, at least, from him. It was not forthcoming."[10] Leonard walked past Alice without a glance and took his place at his lawyers' table. As the jurors were officially seated and the trial began, the young man sat unmoving, his eyes fixed straight ahead.

It had been almost one year since Alice and Leonard had been in the same room together. One year since they had last laid eyes on each other. One year and one month since their wedding day.

ON OCTOBER 14, 1924, Alice and Leonard had appeared at the New Rochelle courthouse and been married by Mayor Harry Scott. No descriptions remain of the brief ceremony, witnessed only by courthouse employees. No photographs tell us what the couple wore for the wedding, what mixture of nervousness, happiness, excitement, tension, or relief their faces revealed. We don't know why or how they chose that particular day. Leonard had reached legal maturity that spring; perhaps the paperwork on his trust fund took several months to clear; perhaps they were waiting for that money to be able to live independently. Perhaps he delayed, hoping he would be able to tell his family and include them in the celebration of his marriage.

The only direct record of the event was registered in the courthouse marriage license files that day. In an even, looping hand a city employee dutifully copied the marriage application information into the county books, filling in the form's blanks for groom and bride:

Full Name: Leonard Kip Rhinelander
Color: white
Address: . . . Pelham Rd., New Rochelle, N.Y.
Age: 22
Occupation: Real Estate
Birthplace: New York City
Father: Philip Rhinelander

Birthplace: U.S.
Mother: Adeline Kip
Birthplace: U.S.

The same clerk's hand recorded Alice's information:

Full Name: Alice Beatrice Jones
Color: white
Address: . . . Pelham Rd., New Rochelle, N.Y.
Age: 23
Birthplace: Pelham, N.Y.
Father: George Jones
Birthplace: England
Mother: Elizabeth Jones
Birthplace: England[11]

Both gave as their address the home of George and Elizabeth Jones.

At first glance, there was little here to distinguish this marriage from any other entered in the days and weeks of October 1924. The pages of New Rochelle's marriage records were filled with the children of immigrants and the native born, marrying within and across ethnic lines, coming from religious or civil ceremonies, starting lives with the promise of hard work and modest gains.

Their marriage duly recorded, Leonard and Alice Rhinelander returned to her parents' home in New Rochelle, where they quietly began making plans to move into their own place. They rented an apartment in the recently built Pintard, on Huguenot Street, one of the main roads in the older section of New Rochelle. Together they began ordering housewares and decorations for their first home together, into which they planned to move by Thanksgiving. They bought from a local furniture dealer, Joseph Rich, striking up a friendship with Rich and his wife, Miriam. Alice began to build a wardrobe fit for her new role as Mrs. Leonard Rhinelander, visiting several exclusive Westchester shops. She showed off some of her new clothes to friends and coworkers, who agreed that her selections were exquisite and expensive.

Separated for most of the three years they had known each other, Alice and Leonard no doubt luxuriated in being together, finally, despite the many obstacles their courtship had endured. For months, even years, "young Rhinelander [had been] seen by neighbors to park his sport roadster in the lane almost every evening and march up to the Jones's front door carrying flowers or candy or a book."[12] In those first few weeks after the wedding, little changed in outward appearances. Not yet ready to occupy their new apartment, the newlyweds continued to stay with her parents on Pelham Road, which Leonard had done intermittently since that spring. Leonard also continued to visit his father in Manhattan and sometimes stayed nights with either his father or his aunt, even after his marriage to Alice. According to some reports he was still working in the family's real estate company during that month. Apparently he told none of the Rhinelanders of his marriage.[13] The Joneses' neighbors themselves "were inclined to hold themselves aloof" from the family and therefore knew neither who Leonard was nor that he had married Alice until they read it in the *New Rochelle Standard Star*.[14]

It is not difficult to understand how the newlywed Rhinelanders were able to hide out for so long without great effort. George and Elizabeth Jones lived in a row of attached units at the end of a long driveway. Set behind two larger houses, theirs was physically secluded from their neighborhood. Although the building had three apartments, no mention was ever made of non–family members living in one. One of Alice's sisters, Grace, lived in one of the apartments with her husband, Albert Miller. The other sister lived in the neighboring town of Pelham Manor, New York, with her husband, Robert Brooks, and their daughter, Roberta. Exactly what the division of the row house was in 1924 and precisely where Alice and Leonard were staying is not clear.

This seclusion may have helped the couple keep a low profile during the first weeks of their marriage, but local reporters soon got wind of the news. Eventually someone divulged the secret: A local girl had married a Rhinelander![15] For professional newshounds, a quick check of the courthouse records confirmed it. Everyone knew who the Rhinelanders were, of course: They were one of the founding families of New York's economic and social elite. Leonard's grandfather William Rhinelander had married Matilda C. Oakley, daughter of T. J. Oakley and Matilda C. Cruger, two other proud families whose names were passed down the line along with their status and wealth.

Former Jones home in New Rochelle, New York, 1995.

These families, more than one newspaper hastened to remind its readers, had been rich and powerful when the Vanderbilts were still farming on Staten Island. The Rhinelander family made its fortune as provision merchants, shipping agricultural goods to the West Indies.[16] In fact Philip Jacob Rhinelander had originally settled in New Rochelle and Pelham Manor in the mid-1700s, owning an extensive tract of land just a few miles from the Jones home. Leonard's father (and his older brother, at least one cousin, and two uncles) were named for this particular Rhinelander. And the Rhinelander family continued to play a significant role in New York society and finance through the Rhinelander Real Estate Company and the philanthropic and cultural contributions of individual family members. Not surprisingly Leonard's mother came from similar roots. Adelaide Kip's family name was important enough to be given to each of her five children: Isaac Leonard Kip Rhinelander (who died in infancy), Philip Kip Rhinelander, T. J. Oakley Kip Rhinelander, Adelaide Kip Rhinelander, and Leonard Kip Rhinelander.[17]

In 1924 the first thing many middle- and upper-class Americans thought to ask about a prospective spouse was his or her lineage and social status. When it was a spouse of someone in the Rhinelander's social circles, the question became even more urgent. Who was Leonard Kip Rhinelander's bride? Who were her parents? What kind of woman had this heir to millions chosen? With what kind of family had he associated the Rhinelander name? Local reporters made it their business to find out.

Following the paper trail of birth certificates, immigration papers, and marriage licenses left by the Joneses in their forty years in the United States, New Rochelle reporters soon realized that they had more than a socialite's marriage announcement on their hands. By mid-November it was ready for press. Both the Rhinelander family and the newlyweds themselves seem to have tried to prevent its publication. Most reports identified the Rhinelander family, and Leonard's father, Philip, in particular, as the force behind these attempts. According to the *New York Daily Mirror*, the New Rochelle editor had been approached by agents representing the Rhinelanders, threatening "dire punishment" if he dared print the story.[18] *The Daily News* described Philip's secretary rushing to New Rochelle to examine the marriage record and phoning in his findings to Philip's lawyer, James Gerard. According to this story, witnesses at the clerk's office could plainly hear the father's sobs through the phone wire. Philip's secretary and a clerk from the county office then rushed over to the *Standard Star* building to try to "wrest [the article] from the presses." They failed.[19]

Money, some suggested, may have been offered, or even changed hands. In an interview reported by several New York papers, Alice's sister Grace maintained that "we were betrayed." She declared that the Joneses and even Alice and Leonard themselves had tried to dissuade the *Standard Star* editor from publishing the news of their marriage. Her sister and new brother-in-law, Grace complained, had "paid well to keep this out of the newspapers." She deemed it a "dirty trick for this story to get out now."[20] In a different version Harris Forbes, the publisher of the *Standard Star*, simply consulted legal advisers and then decided to print the story despite the family's protest.[21]

Whatever the circumstances surrounding it, Forbes's decision to publish the story set in motion what may have been an inevitable shift in the couple's future together. On November 13, 1924, a scant four weeks after the quiet wedding ceremony, the *New Rochelle Standard Star* broke the story. The front page article featured a large, bold, and capitalized headline: **RHINELANDER'S SON MARRIES DAUGHTER OF COLORED MAN.**

In this fateful headline both Alice and Leonard were reduced to the family lineage that defined them. Leonard's greatest claim to fame was his family name: He was, as the article pointed out, the "scion of a prominent New York family." And her family background, too, primarily defined Alice in the article: Her parents were both English immigrants but only one, Elizabeth, was white. Alice's father, George, was the "colored man" of the headline. What the *Standard Star* did not make explicit, but would be understood as such by most Americans, was that having one black parent made Alice black. The paper also reported that this was the first marriage for both, that they had apparently been involved for three years, and that the groom's father, Philip Rhinelander, attempting to end the relationship,[22] had sent his son away three times. The main sensation, however, was clear: A Rhinelander had married a black woman.

By evening at least one New York City paper had picked up the news. Having been unsuccessful in their attempts to reach the Rhinelander family for comment, the *Evening Post* could only repeat the information in the *Standard Star* article, even quoting it directly at times. But there was one crucial difference: Unlike the *Star*, the *Post* made no mention of the racial identity of the Jones family in its coverage of the story. Given the powerful financial and social connections of the Rhinelanders, they may have felt it prudent to wait until they could confirm the report that Leonard's father-in-law was not only a "cabby" but also a "colored man." Having read the earlier article, with its blaring headline, the *Post* must have realized that there was some evidence that Alice's father was "colored." But the *Post* editors did not have the sources the *Standard Star* used at their disposal. So they simply said George Jones was "a native of England, . . . said to be of West Indian descent" and Elizabeth was "an Englishwoman." This was an interesting choice of terminology. It might have been unacceptable to call George an Englishman because doing so would have carried a strong connotation that he was white. "West Indian" both avoided naming a racial category and implied the possibility of not being white.

Two themes thus emerged from this first day of news coverage of the trial: first that the racial status of the Jones family might be suspect but was not yet determined, and second that the families' disparate class standings alone made the marriage a news story and a scandal. The

marriage was a sensation for the *Post* simply because the groom was
the son of Philip Rhinelander, a member of New York's social elite,
and the bride was the daughter of a cabdriver who had a taxi stand at
the Pelham Manor railroad station.[23] By omitting all overt mention of
race, the *Post* chose to err on the side of caution—if she was black,
they could report that the next day. Even the *Standard Star*, which
repeatedly identified Alice's father, George Jones, as a "colored man,"
never directly referred to Alice as "colored," or for that matter with any
racial category or description whatsoever. This reticence to label her
"black" was very apparent in the way newspapers around the country
announced and reported on the marriage in the days and weeks that
followed.

In fact, the first round of stories breaking the news of the marriage
gave class as much—and in some cases even more—emphasis than
race in the headlines and articles through November 16. To take an
extremely cautious example, the *New York Times* printed a very short
article—"Society Youth Weds Cabman's Daughter"—never suggesting the possibility that Alice or her father might be anything other
than white. The only hint of any racial impropriety was that Alice's sister Emily had married a "negro butler."[24] The *Poughkeepsie News
Eagle* published a similarly brief piece—"Rhinelander's Son Marries
Nurse Maid"—with no mention of race.[25] The *Boston Daily Globe*
detailed the various working-class occupations of members of the
Jones family (nursemaid, taxi driver, gardener, and laborer) and the
"shock" to high society of their marriage into an "old New York family."[26] It also ignored reports of their racial status.

When Alice and Leonard woke up on the morning of November 14,
1924, they found that their quiet honeymoon was over. New Rochelle
was in an uproar. Through the night of the thirteenth, telegraph wires
had carried the story to newsrooms across the country, where it was
picked up immediately and usually carried the next day. As people
read their papers over breakfast in almost every major city in the
United States, they read that Leonard Kip Rhinelander, son of one of
the leading New York real estate families, had married Alice Beatrice
Jones, an "obscure" woman who had worked as a nanny.[27] Whether or
what they learned about her racial ancestry, however, depended on
where they lived and what paper they read. For although the initial
New Rochelle article had clearly reported that her father was "col-

ored," the more widely read *Post* had not. Nationwide, editors had to filter conflicting reports and decide what to believe—or at least what to print—regarding Alice's racial ancestry.

Most of the papers that opted to ignore the question of race ran only short two- or three-sentence stories reporting the marriage of a Rhinelander. Few details were revealed in these announcements; such details, one paper claimed, were "meager." What tidbits were available almost universally pointed to the wide class gulf between the Joneses and the Rhinelanders. Leonard Rhinelander was a "society youth" and a "clubman" from an old New York family of distinguished lineage. He stood to inherit millions from his father, and he had married a "nurse maid." The new Mrs. Rhinelander was the daughter of a taxi, cab, or bus driver; her sisters had married a gardener and a laborer, respectively. Her parents, with whom the couple had been living, owned a small, "humble" house at the end of an alley.[28]

This was quite a story in and of itself. As the *Philadelphia Tribune* noted, the class differences alone made Alice and Leonard's marriage "[f]ront page feature stuff."[29] Few New York Rhinelanders had ever crossed class lines to marry a domestic servant. Despite the ideological promise that the United States held for upward social mobility and democratic blurring of economic lines, class played almost as strong a role in social stratification as did race. At the same time, however, the peasant or working-class heroines of fairy tales and movie screens were applauded by audiences when they crossed these economic lines to marry their prince or capitalist aristocrat. Love across class boundaries was both a social transgression and the stuff of romance. For those not born into money, it offered one possibility of the upward mobility promised by the American dream. For working-class women, marriage to a middle-class or wealthy man offered a fantasy fast track in a world in which the mythical rags-to-riches journey through hard work and labor eluded even most men.

WITH HER MARRIAGE to a Rhinelander, then, Alice had traversed a broad social and economic span between her husband's world and her own family background. The breadth of her journey ignited the curiosity of the New York media and its readership, raising comparisons with other such cross-class marriages. As it turned out, they did not need to search very far. Leonard's own uncle, William Copeland Rhinelander, had shocked his family and society in the 1870s by marrying a family servant soon after he graduated from Columbia University and turned twenty-one. William's wife was white and claimed to be descended from royalty, but as an Irish working-class immigrant she was unacceptably below his station in the United States. Cut off from the family inheritance with the relatively "paltry" stipend of five thousand dollars per year, William was socially disowned as well, and his name does not even appear on a Rhinelander family tree.[30] (This stipend was paltry only in comparison to his expected inheritance from both his aunt Serena Rhinelander's two-million-dollar estate, as well as from the fifty-million-dollar estate of his parents, William and Matilda Cruger Oakley Rhinelander.)[31] William was arrested in 1884 and charged with attacking John Drake, a Rhinelander family lawyer whom he accused of "trying to alienate the affection of his [William's] wife and offering her money to go [back] to Ireland and never return." Although Drake died six months after being shot in the shoulder, William Rhinelander was never tried for the attack. Instead he left New York City, according to the terms of his father's will.[32] One of the lessons of William's story, then, was that a cross-class marriage did not always mean a rags-to-riches rise for the lower-class spouse; in William's case it meant a descent from riches to average stability.

William separated from his first wife and remarried in the 1890s, this time to a waitress. When interviewed by the *World Magazine* in 1914, still living with his second wife, the wayward Rhinelander vehemently denied any regrets at his decisions. "Do I regret what I did? . . . Not for one moment, sir. I'd do it all over again for a woman I loved. What is life without love? But if you prefer money to love, do not marry as I did."[33] Though Leonard also chose love over money, he was not willing to throw away all financial stability: He had been able to restrain his desire to marry Alice long enough to receive his trust fund at the age of twenty-one. We don't know whether he learned this from William's example (William was the older brother of Leonard's father, Philip) or simply wanted to protect his economic interests from expected repercussions. It does seem apparent from their newly leased Pelham apartment, however, that despite the media focus on Alice's ascent into the Rhinelander family, the young couple did not intend to live in high society. Rather, they hoped to live comfortably and quietly on Leonard's trust income, outside the elite circles of those listed in the *Social Register.*

Certainly Alice evinced great disdain for her supposed social betters. As the *New Rochelle Standard Star* suggested, Alice was more interested in Leonard than in high society. In March 1925, her name appeared in the supplemental issue of the *Social Register,* which noted her marriage to the already-listed Leonard Kip Rhinelander. A small ripple of reporters returned to her home for her reaction. It was biting: "I didn't marry Leonard to get my name in any book. I married him because I loved him. . . . What is society anyway? There isn't a single wholesome thing in the life of the so-called 400 as far as I can see."[34]

Apparently the feeling was mutual. The following month the "Negro bride who . . . sailed into the March supplement of the register for one fleeting cruise under her husband's colors, . . . was dropped overboard in the next edition."[35] As far as we know, this was the first example of a black person being named in the *Register.* Leonard's name was eventually dropped as well.

Yet Leonard's own behavior suggests that he may have sought a more than casual tie to the world of the social elite. Even after marrying Alice, he continued to frequent his father's home and to attend social functions. Conceivably Leonard intended to keep his two families separate, remaining true to both by not blurring the line between filial love and romantic love. Had the world ignored his marriage to Alice, it is possible to contemplate it as a convenience available to an elite white man. After all, white southern gentlemen had long ago maintained both black and white families. Of course, as often noted, few white men actually married their black lovers.[36]

And for Leonard, the difficult choice seems to have been less between love and money and more between Alice and his father. How much did he know about the Rhinelander's reactions to his uncle's marriage? Had he even known William? Had his father ever spoken of his feelings regarding his brother's actions and subsequent treatment? We don't know. Philip was clearly opposed to his son's involvement with Alice Jones. During the three years prior to their marriage, Philip had repeatedly sent the young man away from New York to try to break up the relationship.[37] With his mother and one brother dead, and his

remaining brother and sister married and away from home, Philip
Rhinelander was Leonard's sole family. By marrying Alice, Leonard
had made a choice, but he was still very concerned about his father's
reaction. As he told one reporter the day after the news broke, he had
not yet told his father of the marriage. His "dad," he worried, "would
probably disinherit me if he knew."[38]

Philip Rhinelander, Leonard's father, c. 1925.

Leonard was not the only one who was interested in his father's approval. Philip's reaction to the publication of the marriage was highly dramatized by the *Daily Mirror*, which described the "elder Rhinelander" spending a "sleepless night" with his staff of servants packing up his household and creeping out at dawn. "With him came the whole service staff and luggage . . . —as if he had contemplated ten years' [sic] in the South Sea Isles."[39] The next day, however, he had returned from this brief exile and called a family conference. Details from the meeting were vague—newspaper reporters never managed to invade the property and privacy of the Rhinelanders as they had the Joneses'. The privileges and practices of wealth kept Philip and his family out of the limelight to an astonishing degree.

On November 15, however, Philip did issue a public statement. Leonard, he pointed out, was over twenty-one, certainly far beyond the need for parental consent. In fact, Philip's remarks continued, he had been unaware of the marriage and had not yet met his new daughter-in-law, but he was "informed that she is of English parentage."[40] This was as close as Philip Rhinelander ever came to publicly addressing the question of Alice's race. It was also widely reported that privately Philip was "determined to sift the statements and reports that his son's bride had West Indian blood."[41]

Philip Rhinelander's announcement added that no other official statements would be made by the family. Nevertheless reports leaked through of other Rhinelanders' responses, usually through the dubious path of second- or third-party sources. Reporters at the *Daily News* claimed to have spoken to Kip's uncle T. J. Oakley, who said simply, "There's nothing to say." ("No comment" was not yet a standby of the media harassed.) A servant at Philip's house was more forthcoming:

> The old gentleman didn't carry on much . . . but you could see he didn't like the idea of the match. He shook his head and said it was too bad the young master didn't consult him before taking the step. And Mrs. Oakley [Leonard's aunt], too—she didn't like it either, but what could either of them do? It was all over. [Leonard] stayed here regular and not once did he tell anybody about the girl he was going around with. Thursday night was the last night he slept at home. He hasn't got in touch with his father since then, at least at home.[42]

The *Daily Mirror* reported a few days later that the marriage announcement had threatened "the most important social event of the winter season": the marriage of William Rhinelander Stewart, Leonard's cousin, to Laura Biddle. At thirty-five, William Rhinelander Stewart was a "supremely eligible Manhattan bachelor," who had already made his mark on New York philanthropic and civic endeavors.[43] The problem now, however, was that his intended bride was from Pennsylvania: "The horror of the Biddle family of Philadelphia at the negro-white alliance of Leonard is greater than that of the Rhinelander's [sic] by exactly the ratio of their nearer proximity to the Mason and Dixon line."[44] And so began a rather forced theme in the New York papers—the projection of white racist concern about interracial marriages onto the South. Here the task was made more difficult by the fact that not only was Philadelphia not in the South, but it had been a center of antislavery and civil rights activism.

Another unsubstantiated but not improbable report from the Rhinelander family conference involved the "minor, but annoying, matter of the Rhinelander family jewels with which young Leonard has endowed his negress bride." Other heirlooms were missing as well:

> A huge emerald ring and two diamond solitaires, also identifiable in the Rhinelander gallery of portraits of generations of pale-face brides, now decorate the dark digits of Mrs. Leonard. It is understood that the Rhinelanders would give pints of blue blood to redeem the heirlooms from their present fate.[45]

The contrast drawn between Alice and other Rhinelander brides was not subtle. In the public construction they were pale while she was dark; they were well-born, she was a "negress." Given this heavy-handed depiction, it is understandable that Alice was called not "Mrs. Rhinelander" but "Mrs. Leonard" in this passage, in stark contrast to accepted newspaper policy. Giving her the name "Rhinelander" put her in the same category with the "generations of pale-face brides," and, in this article anyway, the *Daily Mirror* was sure that she was black and therefore not an acceptable Rhinelander. The *Daily News* also demonstrated ambivalence about giving her the title "Mrs. Rhinelander." When quoting Alice's brother-in-law Albert Miller, that "everybody's jealous that Mrs. Rhinelander has captured a millionaire," writers for the *Daily News* then added, "Yes ma'm, they called her Mrs. Rhinelander."[46] Yet, in another article in the same issue, they wrote, "Mrs. Rhinelander was popular with young white men in New Rochelle and has been seen dancing at inns in that vicinity countless times."[47]

Did Alice deserve to be Mrs. Rhinelander? Did she fit the role? Would the marriage survive the scheming of the Rhinelander family conference and the publicity furor? For the media the answers depended on a complicated combination of her racial ancestry, appearance, community standing, dress, behavior, family, and material surroundings. In other words, in the week following the wedding announcement, whether Alice was considered more properly Alice Jones, Alice Rhinelander, or Mrs. Leonard depended on the evidence culled regarding her racial and class standing. And anyone who had relied on the newspapers for knowledge of her family background would have remained confused for quite some time.

2

WHO WAS ALICE JONES?

 WITHIN TWO DAYS of the publication of the *Standard Star* story, the focus of investigation had swung to concentrate squarely on Alice and Leonard Rhinelander and on the Jones family, with whom they were still staying. Throughout the following week, a crowd of reporters and curiosity seekers milled around the Joneses' home, creating a scene often described as a state of siege. In fact, all of New Rochelle was in an uproar over the reported interracial cross-class union. Westchester County white supremacist groups organized. Tenants at the Pintard Apartments complained to their building manager about allowing someone who wasn't white to sign a lease for one of their exclusive units. A New Rochelle women's group met and planned a protest to the mayor for his part in marrying the young couple. Alice and Leonard woke up from their scant month of married life and found their privacy shattered, their past under an unfriendly spotlight, and their dreams of sharing their lives in jeopardy.

In these early days of media coverage, the harshest lights were focused on Alice and her family. Reporters tracked down coworkers, neighbors, former teachers, employers—anyone with information about the Jones family's history and identity. While Alice's class standing alone may, as the *Philadelphia Tribune* pointed out, have made the story front-page news, that she was reportedly "colored" or a "Negro" made it "[f]ront page scandal stuff, crime, tragedy, unbelievable, awful."[1] These questions had had little significance in October 1924. In the comfort of her home, in the arms of her husband, she was Alice, and whatever her ancestry or identity, she was accepted and loved. In the headlines of the nation's newspapers one month later, however, her racial categorization and identification became the crux of her public reputation and future life.

In the context of the United States in the 1920s, when so many of the nation's social mores were in flux, the marriage became more than a story of ill-fated love. The Rhinelanders' stature, on top of the concerns raised about immigration, race, and color, made this a front-page story across the country. One of the clearest signs of the breadth of interest in this case was the immediate and consistent coverage by newspapers across the country. No newspaper could afford to ignore it—and none did.

This was in many ways a New York story, and New York papers followed it most loyally, supplying constant interviews, eyewitness accounts, and related stories for more distant papers and readers. The older, traditional dailies, like the *Times, Herald-Tribune, World,* and *Sun,* gave the developing story relative care, greater censorship, fewer front-page headlines, and only occasional photographs. The newer "picture papers" catered to a working-class, multilingual readership and counted on human interest stories such as the Rhinelander Case to bolster their circulation. The *Daily News, Daily Mirror,* and *Evening Journal* all competed for readership with front pages made up of nothing but photographs and headlines, and devoted pages to the unfolding story. These tabloids (with their distinctive small format) ran hundreds of pictures and cartoon depictions of news events in every issue, and were far more willing to speculate and sensationalize.[2]

But the Rhinelander Case was also an American story, and media and public interest was national. Every one of the more than five dozen papers and periodicals surveyed covered the story, whether tabloid or conservative city press, North or South, white or black published, American or British. The story of Alice and Leonard reflected many of the themes of social conflict roiling the nation. Laced with a juicy love story, the case became magnified, under curiosity and scrutiny, into an American scandal in black and white.

AS WITH THE initial coverage of the Rhinelanders' marriage, the most crucial question these newspapers grappled with was how to deal with and assess the *Standard Star*'s story that Alice and her father were black. Throughout the first week, as the *Standard Star*'s sources were sought and examined, other papers continued to choose different ways to report, hint, or ignore the question of Alice's racial identity. These approaches reveal much about the conscious and unconscious definitions of race, and of the ways to distinguish between black and white, in 1920s America. Some strategies followed clear patterns. Southern newspapers, for example, when they did run articles the week of November 14, seemed particularly adept at avoiding explicit declarations about race. Of the five that ran articles that week, not one explicitly labeled Alice or her father as "colored" or "Negro." The *Richmond News Leader* simply ran a photo of Alice with the caption "Weds Rhinelander" and no accompanying story.[3] The *New Orleans Times-Picayune* printed a photo of Alice that it placed next to a photo of a local white woman; in this context Alice appeared slightly darker or tan. The *Birmingham Age-Herald* said only that Alice's brother-in-law Robert Brooks was "swarth-faced," emphasizing instead the class differences in their announcement that "Taxi-Driver Father-in-Law is Rhinelander Choice."[4]

But the question of whether Alice was black or white was highly relevant in the United States in the twenties. This decade saw the rebirth and ascendancy of the Ku Klux Klan, the hardening of segregation in the South, and a national commitment to quieter racial times after the summer of race riots in 1919. In many quarters, as a result, whites paid even more attention to the policing of racial boundaries. In any southern state and many northern and western ones as well, marriages between blacks and whites were illegal. Depending on the specific state law, Alice and Leonard's marriage would have been automatically nullified, and one or both might have been subject to a fine and/or imprisonment if she was indeed black.

Furthermore, it was a delicate move in 1924 publicly to call any person who might be white a "Negro." Time and time again, light-skinned African Americans reported that whites were often hesitant to challenge them for fear of offending, which could lead to libel suits. "Inevitably a colored man knows but usually keeps his mouth shut, aided by a generous tip. But a white man fears to insult another in the South, and when in doubt, he lets you alone,"[5] boasted an anonymous writer in the *Independent*. Insulting a Rhinelander could prove more than a faux pas; it could lead to financial ruin. On the other hand, if Leonard had unknowingly married a black woman, he could in turn sue her. Neither situation had any direct relevance to the New York marriage, however: While never openly accepted, interracial marriages had always been legal in the state of New York.

Some newspapers felt they could report the full story and avoid liability by simply reporting the reports that the new Mrs. Rhinelander had black ancestry. Refraining from offering a determination itself, for example, the *St. Louis Argus* carefully headlined that the "millionaire's wife" was "said to be colored," while readers of the *New Orleans Times-Picayune* learned that Alice's father was "said to be a negro."[6] The *Detroit Times* questioned the "rumor" that Alice had "negro blood in her veins," stressing Leonard's initial loyalty to her in the face of these reports. The *Times* also gave a fairly detailed version of William Rhinelander's experience, suggesting that a Rhinelander marrying a "servant girl" was enough to cause the current furor.[7] Even the *Chicago Defender*, a black-published weekly that did not pick up the story until November 22, highlighted class difference as the defining issue, with the front-page headline MILLIONAIRE'S MARRIAGE TO POOR GIRL STARTLES WORLD.[8]

Eventually, however, most newspapers had to decide how to describe or categorize Alice and her family. In this endeavor both southern and northern newspapers faced a similar set of problems and contradictions in trying to explain to their readers who Alice Beatrice Jones Rhinelander was. The definition of who was black and who was white seemed on the surface to be a very simple one. But as journalistic coverage of the Rhinelander marriage reveals, the simple answers hid the very deep, very complicated tangle of American definitions of race, and of blackness especially. Some of the specific knots in this tangle will be examined again as the events of the Rhinelander Case unfold. Here, however, the basic question is: What assumptions and information would American newspaper readers and journalists have relied on to determine the racial identity of Alice and her family?

The most straightforward definition of blackness was simply that someone is black who looks black. This was, of course, a circular definition, but one with great popularity and power. Across time many have played the racial guessing game, looking at hair, skin color, and other phenotypic characteristics to assign racial membership. Scores no doubt did so as they surveyed the nation's newspapers for confirmation of Alice's pedigree. Pictorial or verbal descriptions of Alice's appearance, or that of her family, were the easiest means for newspapers to alert their readers to the issue of race. It was particularly useful in these initial reports as a way to hint at the question of blackness without actually calling Alice or George Jones black. Early descriptions of her or her father's physical appearance often suggested but didn't specify that they weren't white. Again and again papers tried to describe Alice, an endeavor that actually painted a range of images of her appearance: She was "dark"; she was "of light complexion"; she was "dusky"; she was "a pretty girl of the Spanish type"; she was "of medium height, dark and of a Spanish or Latin type of features. Her straight black hair is worn in a long bob"; she was "a comely young woman with bobbed black hair and a complexion of Spanish tint."9

In addition, photographs—almost all the papers carried them—sometimes stood in for physical descriptions, allowing and even overtly challenging readers to judge for themselves what she was. New York City's Yiddish-language *Jewish Daily Forward* printed a photograph with the caption "Does she look like a Negro?"10 Furthermore, the collection of published photos, all in black and white, of course, showed a range of skin tone. It is highly likely that some were retouched for publication—several actually appear to have been lightened. Newspaper photos of the time were routinely "doctored" in ways that were not considered misrepresentations. Framings were painted in, backgrounds rubbed out, cheeks highlighted, circles under the eyes lightened or even accentuated.11

Through this combination of "said-to-be's" and coded descriptions, even papers that did not explicitly discuss race still managed to convey the distinct impression that all was not white in the Jones family. Other clues to Alice's racial identity drew from descriptions of her father and her sister Emily's husband, Robert Brooks. Her brother-in-law was "dark skinned" or, more blatantly, a "black man." Brooks's employer said "she had always regarded her butler's wife as also col-

Alice poses for reporters, November 1924.

ored."[12] Her father was "a bent, dark complexioned man who is bald, except for a fringe of curly white hair." Her father was said to be of West Indian descent; he had a "swarthy complexion." But did that leave, as one paper put it, "no doubt" that George was "colored"?[13]

These reports used descriptions of family members to suggest or assert that they were not white, but also relied on additional definitions of blackness to suggest or assert that Alice was not white. Having a black brother-in-law does not in and of itself make one black, of course. By that criterion, papers should have been suggesting that Leonard might be black by association. But having a sister who had married a black man and whose own marriage license had identified her as "colored" seemed to suggest that Alice was therefore more likely to be black.

Although legal in New York State, interracial marriages were rare. Around 1 percent of the registered marriages in New York City during this period were black-white unions. By contrast, between 10 and 13 percent of the marriages in Boston were between blacks and whites — mostly between black men and white women.[14] The implication? It was far more likely that Alice's sister was also black. And that was far more crucial to the question of Alice's race. Outside the United States, some racial systems recognized dozens of racial categories based on color, ancestry, behavior, occupation, religion, and other criteria. In such cases it would not be unlikely to find full siblings falling into different categories. Within the United States, however, there were only three possible categories for Alice and her sisters, and since they all shared the same biological parents, they all would occupy the same category.

THE BALTIMORE SUN was the epitome of circumvention. In a fairly detailed article, the Sun managed to include every element used to demonstrate or imply the Joneses' racial identity without once even suggesting the rumors that they were not white. With the headline L. KIP RHINELANDER WEDS OBSCURE GIRL, it reported that her father was "spoken of as a taxi-driver" and that she was "described as dark . . . with straight black hair." Even the element of her sister's black husband was mentioned, but without racial categories. Instead, her sister was the "wife of [a] butler." The Sun was clearly aware of the report that she was black — it went out over the wires from New York — and it included all the pieces of evidence used to support that report, only with the racial explicitness removed.[15]

Other papers, particularly in the Northeast and Midwest, were quite happy to follow the New Rochelle Standard Star in declaring that Alice and her father were "colored." The early-morning pink edition (so called because it was traditionally printed on pink paper) of the New York Daily News announced "nuptial news" complete with a lot of speculation about the racial identity of Alice, Emily, and George. Readers of the later home edition, however, only had to glance at the front-page headlines to see that Leonard's wife was a COLORED GIRL.[16] And the Daily Mirror simply blared out on the cover page that Leonard had married a "Negress." Both the News and the Mirror followed the same format, reserving the front page entirely for photographs and headlines, following up with the stories inside. The Des Moines

Register reported on the first page that the "Young Blue Blood's Bride is Colored," citing her father's citizenship application as proof.[17]

Whatever their assertions, none of these approaches actually addressed the question of what would make Alice black or white. All these criteria—appearance, family ties, presumed identity—rested on other definitions of blackness in early-twentieth-century America. The modern idea of races as distinct physical groups defined by inherited biological, intellectual, and moral characteristics developed in the nineteenth century in the context of slavery and postemancipation attempts to maintain white supremacy. With the rise of scientific racism (the use of scientific methods to "prove" that one race is superior to another) by the second half of the century, this belief in discrete biological categories merged with preexisting assumptions of white superiority in the United States and European colonial outposts. Yet, as early as the 1920s, anthropologists and other scholars were beginning to question the scientific validity not only of the doctrine of racial superiority but also of the idea of race itself.

By 1924, however, the energies of white Americans had been focused for some time on the project of maintaining racial inequality through a legal and social system of segregation. This project required, among other things, that people of mixed black-and-white ancestry be placed in one category or the other. The most common solution to this problem was to simply define as black anyone of any known black ancestry. Known as the one-drop rule, this definition of blackness included people whose physical appearance was other than black. Thus the peach-skinned, light-haired, blue-eyed Walter White, a black man and secretary of the National Association for the Advancement of Colored People (NAACP), was able to capitalize on his appearance to travel in the South investigating cases of lynchings in situations in which a physically obvious or known black man would have been in great danger. Walter White was black, according to the one-drop rule, according to most state legal definitions, and according to his own self-identification.[18]

What Alice and her sisters were, then, would be based on George Jones's racial identity, since Elizabeth's whiteness was never questioned. If George was white, or if he was determined to be white enough, then his daughters could be white. (This possibility was raised briefly later in the case.) If George was not white, and particularly if he was black, then his daughters could not, by definition, be white. Two questions then arose: First, was George Jones black or white? Second, at what point, if any, could one draw the line between black and white in people of mixed ancestry? In this situation appearance was beside the point: According to the one-drop rule, a person was black if any of his or her ancestors, no matter how remote, had been black. One-drop racialism ignored physical appearance as the ultimate marker of race in favor of ancestry.

This is not to say that white and black Americans had never perceived social or physical differences between people of mixed black and white ancestry and other blacks in the United States. Quite the contrary. The wide use of the term "mulatto" as a category for people of mixed ancestry itself attests to a perception of difference between mulattoes and blacks. And in the scientific and popular projects of tracking the differences between blacks and whites, the characteristics of mulattoes were of great interest. But discerning the dominant American perception of people of mixed ancestry is a confusing task. By the early twentieth century, two opposing images developed as strong legacies of the theories and assumptions of nineteenth-century scientific racism and the growing social sciences. One school, based historically in "scientific" arguments that "hybrid" or "mixed" races were often physically weak, infertile, and so on, continued to assert the inferiority of the mulatto, even in relation to the Negro. African Americans of mixed white and black descent were, to paraphrase the view of this school, more devious, more emotionally unbalanced, and more rebellious and untrustworthy than "pure Negroes." The opposing school, more prevalent by the 1920s, countered that mixed races were physically and intellectually superior—at least to the lower of the pure races they descended from. In other words "mulattoes" were between whites and pure blacks—superior to blacks by virtue of their "white blood" and/or greater access to education, economic opportunities, and the like; inferior to whites by virtue of their "black blood." This perspective led white reformists to look to mulattoes for the salvation of the Negro race rather than its destruction. But both schools also believed in the superiority of whites.

Social scientists and popular white (and sometimes African American) fiction writers portrayed mulattoes as torn between loyalties to the two races, internally torn between their two "bloods" and two resulting natures, doomed to a tragic ending, liable to use both their connections with other African Americans and their light-skinned privileges to stir up trouble. Earlier white theories of physical weaknesses, however, shifted to visions of mulattoes as emotionally or psychologically unbalanced, at worst liable to insanity, at best doomed to "marginality." While true Negroes might be expected to accept their lower position in U.S. society, mulattoes were moody, overly sensitive to imagined injustices, and envious of white privileges. In romantic melodrama the inevitable downfall of the tragic mulatto warned even the most liberal sympathetic audiences of the dangers of racial mixing.

The female version of the tragic mulatto looked very similar to the male one, but accentuated her sexual beauty; her desire to gain power, wealth, or whiteness by sleeping with white men; and her astonishing tendency to die, perhaps at the hands of a jealous black or white lover, or at her own at the discovery of her black "blood" or general despair at her plight.[19] In fact it was the figure of the female tragic mulatto that received much of the dramatic attention in the late-nineteenth and early-twentieth-century United States. Though lacking in subtlety, descriptions of the physical beauty of these characters, with an attention bordering on obsession, became stock.[20]

DISTINCTIONS BETWEEN BLACKS and mulattoes sprang in part from real historically grounded situations in which color both divided and united black communities across the country between 1860 and 1920. By the 1920s African American writers of the Harlem Renaissance were documenting more realistic portrayals of the positions of mixed-race African Americans. African Americans, regardless of ancestry, had long shared a common history and experience but in some places and contexts had formed separate communities, in part on the basis of color and heritage. One of these places was New Orleans, Louisiana, whose residents spoke several languages, combined Catholicism and other beliefs, and blended diverse architectural styles to create a city like no other in the country. Moreover, it was one of the few places where Europeans—be they Spanish, French, or English—freely associated with Africans, although retaining a keen understanding of the differences among them. On this racial frontier and out of this social interaction a new people, called Creoles, emerged.

Although socially black after the Civil War, members of Louisiana's Creole community were often lighter than many olive-complexioned Europeans. Many valued their light skin and elevated social position. After all, some had owned slaves before the Civil War, fought on behalf of the Confederacy, and distanced themselves from the affairs of the more observably black population well after the war concluded. Beginning in the 1870s, the social gulf between blacks and Creoles narrowed somewhat. A number of citizens of color—Creoles, because of prior access to better education—assumed important leadership positions in Reconstruction-era black communities. The end of Reconstruction and the introduction of racially restrictive legislation in the last years of the nineteenth century deepened the connections. Opposition to marriage between the groups and to some forms of socializing remained, however. In Charleston and other communities, distinctions between black and tan meant something. Nonetheless, stopping the introduction of segregated seating on public transportation was an area for common cause—and a project in which both the intention of segregation and the coalition needed to fight it required a strengthening of the association of people of mixed ancestry with blacks.[21]

By 1890 numerous cities and towns practiced racial segregation in theaters, churches, and other places of public congregation. Buttressed by pseudoscientific teachings and the history of unequal race relations, more and more whites, regardless of station, believed in the logic of white superiority and devised strategies to protect their privileges. In California this general sentiment took the form of anti-Asian legislation. Laborers and state legislators worked together to curtail Chinese immigration. Texas officials adopted similar measures for Mexicans and Mexican Americans. And whites in the South and North rigorously policed the social activities of African Americans, which included all those with any African ancestry, restricting housing, educational opportunities, and social relations. In states as diverse as Illinois, Pennsylvania, Maryland, Georgia, and California, railroad officials attempted to segregate black and white passengers as early as 1868. Prior to the 1890s, most courts ruled such actions unconstitutional.

Many were nonetheless startled when southern states, as the first step in the near total disfranchisement of African Americans that occurred by the turn of the century, began separating the races on public conveyances. Louisiana enacted such legislation in 1890, forcing the railroads into the unenviable position of social and racial brokers. The period's typical train offered first- and second-class travel accommodations. First-class cars prohibited smoking, sheltered middle-class women, provided drinking water, and offered a quieter, cleaner, and safer place for those with the funds to purchase comfort. By contrast the smoke-filled second-class cars, whose passengers used the floors as spittoons, could turn even the most disciplined stomach. Situated behind the coal-fired engine, where each belch of smoke caused passengers to squint and become dusted with soot, second-class cars became America's most democratic site—a place where people of all races with modest resources sat together. The belief in American democracy did not extend to first-class accommodations, however.[22]

In an organized attempt to challenge the practice of segregation, an interracial civil rights organization, the National Citizens Rights Association, chose Homer Adolph Plessy to provide a test case they hoped would force the U.S. Supreme Court to rule segregation unconstitutional. A New Orleans native, Plessy was seven-eighths white and one-eighth black. His physical appearance was white. So, in a conscious attempt to void the new statute barring blacks and whites from riding in the same first-class cars, Plessy informed the conductor of his background, whereupon he was instructed to retire to a "separate but equal" second-class car for blacks. Homer Plessy refused and was arrested and charged with violating the state law. By the time Plessy mounted his challenge, the law had been in effect for three years, and the Louisiana courts had already ruled that segregated seating on interstate trains violated the Fourteenth Amendment's guarantees of equal protection and due process. Plessy and his associates correctly believed that intrastate travel was the key problem. It was on such a train that Plessy entered, confessed his racial identity, and set into motion a series of legal maneuverings that shaped key aspects of American life for more than half a century. Albion Tourgée, a white lawyer, author, and veteran civil rights fighter, defended Plessy.

The case reached the U.S. Supreme Court on appeal after Louisiana's highest court found racial separation on intrastate trains to be entirely permissible. Drawing a clear distinction between inter- and intrastate commerce and movement, the state court ruled that the Constitution was not violated if the state ensured separate but equal facilities. In 1896 the U.S. Supreme Court agreed. In a seven-to-one decision the Court, with only Justice John Harlan, a Kentuckian and former slave owner, dissenting, ruled that separate but equal did not violate the Constitution.

Although legal scholars and historians have questioned Harlan's racial views because of his background, and his willingness to validate the legitimacy of school segregation in a case three years later, there is little doubt that Harlan understood the implications of the *Plessy* decision for a nation undergoing profound change. He wrote in his dissent:

> The destinies of the two races, in this country, are indissolubly linked together, and the interests of both require that the common government of all shall not permit the seeds of race hate to be planted under the sanction of law. What can more certainly create and perpetuate a feeling of distrust between these races, than state enactments, which in fact, proceed on the ground that colored citizens are so inferior and degraded that they cannot be allowed to sit in public coaches occupied by white citizens? That, as all will admit, is the real meaning of such legislation as was enacted in Louisiana.[23]

In many ways the decision marked the final retreat from the promise of a truly "reconstructed" United States.

IRONICALLY THE LAWYERS for *Plessy* had also tried to challenge the definitions of black and white that designated Homer Plessy as black. They pointed out that Louisiana did not have a legal definition of blackness, and that there was no logical reason why a person who was seven-eighths white should not be defined as white. The Court upheld the larger issue of segregation and refused to answer the question of whether Plessy was, or should be considered, black. Both the definition of segregation and the definitions of race that underlay them were turned over to the province of the states.

By 1924 twenty-nine of the forty-eight states in the Union had provided legal definitions of blackness. Twenty-eight of these definitions were embedded in anti-intermarriage laws. Taken together the twenty-nine definitions provided no consensus on the amount of black ancestry required to make a person legally black in the United States. About half gave vague definitions or cited the one-drop rule, and three of those simply gave circular definitions such as "African" or "of the negro race." Seven more specified that black included people of mixed ancestry: "negro and mulatto."[24] Arizona, Georgia, Louisiana, Oklahoma, and Virginia decreed that any black ancestry, no matter how remote, made one legally black. Homer Plessy, then, became legally black in Louisiana; in fact this law was enacted only a few years after the *Plessy* decision. The remaining fourteen states with legal definitions, however, provided specific blood-quantum boundaries that established the amount of black ancestry that made a person black. In Alabama, Florida, Indiana, Maryland, Mississippi, Missouri, Nebraska, North Carolina, North Dakota, Tennessee, and Texas, Homer Plessy would also have been black, but if he had had children with a white woman, those children would have been legally white. In those states a person with one-eighth or more black ancestry was black.[25] Only in Kentucky, Michigan, and Oregon would Plessy have been clearly, legally white: The definition of blackness in those three states was one-fourth or more black ancestry.[26]

These blood-quantum definitions corresponded with two well-known terms denoting mixed racial ancestry: "octoroon" and "quadroon." Alice would be called both by newspapers. Although not always used with great precision, "quadroon" meant that she was one-quarter black (implying that her father was half black), while "octoroon" meant that she was only one-eighth black (implying her father was a quadroon.) "Mulatto" was an even vaguer term. Anthropologically it meant someone whose ancestry was half white and half black. Colloquially, however, it referred more broadly to anyone of mixed black and white ancestry. The states that defined blackness as "negro or mulatto" probably meant to include anyone of mixed ancestry in that category. Alice was often called "mulatto," as was her father, whose own mother was white. But, as these definitions suggest, "mulatto" was largely a subcategory of "black" by 1924.

Legal definitions, then, provided another way to determine an individual's racial identity. In addition to looking at Alice and her family, reporters and readers could turn to legal documents for evidence of their racial status. New York State, as noted, did not have legal definitions of "Negro" and "white." Therefore, as it probably did in many of the above states as well, the task of determining who was black and who was white fell to medical personnel, government employees, and, in some cases, to the individuals in question themselves.

Unfortunately for newspapers trying to determine the "true" racial identity of the Jones family, the legal documents provided conflicting evidence. The newspapers repeatedly turned to birth certificates and census data, despite their contradictions, for evidence of the family's racial identity. George Jones's naturalization papers listed him as colored, and Emily Jones's marriage license listed both herself and her husband as colored. These were the foundation of the first reports that George and his daughters were colored. On the other hand, the *New York Evening Journal* noted that Alice and her family had all been designated "white" in the 1915 New York State Census. This, the paper suggested, contradicted reports that the marriage "was inter-racial." Alice's birth certificate said "mulatto," as did a census taken during World War I. Her marriage license, like the state census, said "white."[27]

Who wrote these various categories down, and on what basis? Was such categorization legally binding in a state without official definitions of racial classifications or official policies regarding differential treatment or discrimination on the basis of race?

Actually two pieces of information entered on the marriage license would return to haunt Alice Rhinelander. Of lesser significance was the age Alice gave—she was actually several years older than she said she was. In the 1920s it was hard enough for a woman to admit to being a year or two older than her husband; the four years between Alice and Leonard were a violation of convention that would have caused many women great embarrassment. Although no one made much of the fact, Leonard listed his age at the time of marriage as twenty-two, when the *New York Times* noted that he turned twenty-one just that spring (1924). Far, far more serious, however, was her color, which was listed in the clerk's hand as white. Had she made that claim? The two witnesses who signed the license told reporters that they did not have the "slightest suspicion that Miss Jones was not a white woman."[28] Had the clerk also looked at her and assumed she was white? If she had come in with a dark-skinned black man, as had her sister Emily, would they similarly have assumed her to be colored?

Few thought to question why New York State was monitoring the race or color of its citizens at all. The state did allow interracial marriages, although there had been a 1910 attempt to modify the state constitution to bar such unions. The following year, in fact on the very day that Alice sat in the courtroom awaiting Leonard's arrival, the *New Rochelle Standard Star* noted another marriage registered in City Hall: Lewis Kelly, twenty-two, white, and Norma Garlick, twenty-one, colored, received their license in the same office where Alice and Leonard had obtained theirs. Kelly and Garlick, however, had traveled from Richmond, Virginia, where their application would have been refused. Their marriage would not have been newsworthy if not for its coincidence with the events of the Rhinelander Case. Nevertheless it suggested that there was no barrier to the marriage of self-proclaimed interracial couples in New York State, or at least in New Rochelle.[29] If not intended to prevent interracial marriages, then, these questions — like those on the current census and other government forms that ask for race — were probably used to track the demographic patterns of New York's marriages.

So the fact that some of her legal documentation declared her white led to two major questions regarding Alice's racial identity: Did she claim to be white? Was she "really" white? By the evening of November 14 and throughout the next few days, many New York papers variously quoted Alice, her sister, mother, and father as directly contradicting the published reports that she and her father were not white. Most New York papers reported that Alice denied the "taint story," banking on her English ancestry to support this contention. The *New York Herald-Tribune* reminded readers that Alice challenged reports that she was other than white, and further stated that "[Leonard's] bride is white, according to the information given at the marriage license bureau, and of English parentage."[30]

The *Chicago Broad Ax* reported in its first article on the marriage that Alice had "indignantly" denied having "Negro" blood, but that her father and sister were listed as "colored" in official records. The *Broad Ax*, an African American–focused publication, also supplied a description of her niece, Roberta Brooks, whose father, Robert Brooks, was a dark-skinned black man. Roberta was "red-headed, but dark of skin."[31] The *Los Angeles Times*, meanwhile, simply led with, "Wife Denies Charge of Negro Taint, Leonard K. Rhinelander's Humble Bride Declares Father English."[32] The *Daily News* and the *Standard Star*, on the other hand, reported that Leonard was "happy" to be married to his wife and did not deny reports that she had colored blood.[33]

Was Alice seen by her neighbors and community as black or white? With conflicting descriptions, contradictory legal documents, and clashing reports of the Joneses' self-identifications, journalists scoured New Rochelle for neighbors, friends, and acquaintances to tell them what they had assumed the Joneses to be. How had Alice and her family represented themselves to friends, neighbors, coworkers, and church members? With whom did they socialize? The stories flew thick and fast and added up to no simple narrative. Former schoolmates, "little girls, now grown to womanhood," remembered that Alice was "always exquisitely dressed" and that they had thought she was Spanish. Her former principal said that he had believed her to be white until an attendance officer visited her home and reported back that George Jones was "colored." Even then "I could scarcely believe him," recalled the principal. Her teacher, on the other hand, said she had always considered "little Alice" to be "a colored child, . . . a nice little girl."[34]

Neighbors reported that the Joneses were "generally known" as "colored persons," but that the three daughters, Alice, Emily, and Grace, "did not associate with Negroes." Ironically the same story also noted that Emily's husband was black, which no doubt led discerning readers to question the credibility of the claim that the sisters avoided social contact with black people.[35] Alice herself had reportedly worked several times in homes where her employers had an expressed preference for hiring "colored help" only.[36] The *Daily News* summed up the conundrum: "Some thought her colored. Some did not."[37] Although Alice may not have frequented black churches, clubs, or other community organizations, she had certainly become friendly with many coworkers, white and black. Soon after she left school, Alice apparently went with a black man, Ira Morris, whose mother and sister worked with her. According to Morris their friendship ended when "she told him she was 'white' and would have nothing further to do with him."[38] When reporters asked him "what attitude Miss. [sic] Jones had assumed, he said, 'She said she was a white girl, so I said to her, 'Aw right. Go 'long, then.' "[39]

Like many families of mixed ancestry and interracial families in the Northeast, the Joneses seemed to live in an ambiguous space in the American system of racial classification. They seemed to be neither denying nor actively claiming a black racial identity. Sociologists of the time and current historians have documented a number of cases—indeed a pattern—of mixed-race or mixed-marriage families living quietly in small "white" towns. Unlike the model of "passing," in which formerly black-identified individuals or families would become white-identified, many of these individuals and families simply lived in the spaces between absolutes.[40] Less consciously a political act of affirmation or denial of self, racial ambiguity enabled such individuals and families to embrace the multiple histories that constituted them. They were black and white and other. They understood that American society lacked a suitably dexterous category for those who defied the conventions of perception and boundary. Former Kentucky politician Mae Street Kidd, born to a black mother and white father in 1904, summarized the sentiment of many when she wrote, "I never made an issue of my race. I let people think or believe what they wanted to. If it was ever a problem, then it was their problem, not mine."[41]

Unlike most American mixed-race families, however, Alice's parents were both immigrants from England. The Joneses' English origins, then, placed them outside the patterns of interracial families in the United States and patterns of immigration as well. Even at the height of the U.S. anti-immigration movement, emigration from England was never limited or restricted. English nationals were assumed to be Anglo-Saxon, or certainly at least white—"safe" immigrants whose culture, language, and politics were not seen as threatening the vision of American society held by those who opposed immigration from Asia, Mexico, and southern and eastern Europe. Nativism, in fact, reached its legislative height in 1924 with the passage of the National Origins Act (or Johnson-Reed Act), which established national origin quotas for immigrants based on 1890 census data. The yearly levels amounted to 2 percent of the foreign-born nationals from each country in 1890. Racial concerns were not the only motivation behind nativism, but they were an important and explicit part of the campaign. Asian immigration was highly limited, even completely restricted in many cases. Southern and eastern European immigration was cut to stem the flow of Jews, Slavs, Italians, and other non–Anglo-Saxons to America. Some critics of the 1924 act, in fact, complained that it did not do enough to protect the status of the United States as a white nation because it ignored immigration from Africa, South and Central America, and Mexico.[42]

As a mixed-race family, however, the Jones family challenged the ideals of America as a white society linked to a glorious Anglo-Saxon past. The apparent discrepancy between the image of an Englishman as an ideal of whiteness and high culture and the figure presented by George Jones was a constant source of comment, confusion, and even amusement. Many of the Joneses' English cultural behaviors were perceived as proof of their whiteness or as a shocking contrast with their nonwhiteness. There was, for example, the "surprising fact" that the Jones family attended the "exclusive" Christ's Church, just down the road in Pelham Manor. The Episcopalian church, one of the oldest in Westchester County, was described as "a handsome stone building attended by fashionable Pelham Manor's smartest residents." Mrs. Jones and her daughters were members, George attended regularly, and granddaughter Roberta was enrolled in its Sunday school.

The *Daily News'* contention that the parishioners had never protested "when the Jones daughters knelt at communion with their white church associates" was borne out by statements made by the pastor.[43] The Reverend J. McVickar Haight observed:

> There is no color line in Christ's Church. I have lately noted that George Jones, father of Mrs. Rhinelander, has been lax in his attendance, whereas he used to be most faithful in worship. But his granddaughter, Alberta [sic] Brooks, is one of the brightest little girls in our Sunday School class. She and all her folk are welcome. I believe in the brotherhood of man.

Although Reverend Haight misremembered Roberta Brooks as Alberta, even that error suggested a familiarity with the family. Roberta was presumably named for her father, Robert, Emily's husband. Albert was Grace's husband; they had no children. Furthermore, other people connected with Christ's Church said that "there never had been any pretense on the part of Mr. Jones, who frequently attended the church, nor on the part of his daughters, that they were not of negro blood."[44]

That the Joneses' black background was assumed in some instances and wholly ignored in others highlights the tension between different definitions of racial identity and status. Fellow church members judged the family on what they did and achieved as much as on race.

Of course the ambiguity in parentage in part made this possible. Those readily identified as black in New Rochelle lived a much more circumscribed life. Language, nationality, and demeanor secured a more sequestered space for the Joneses, a space they claimed and at times guarded.

The early difficulty in labeling Alice as black or white had long-lasting ramifications for the development of the trial and for media coverage of Alice and of the Rhinelander Case. The pretrial confusion over her race foreshadowed the major issues of the trial and stirred up an already contentious set of concerns for white America: What defined the difference between white and black? How could one tell? The trial took place at the height of white American obsession with determining the physical boundaries of race. Whites, and to some extent blacks, were intensely preoccupied at the turn of the century with the challenge posed by racial mixing and by people of mixed descent to "scientific" classifications of race and social segregation.[45]

However, in the year separating the announcement of Alice and Leonard's marriage and their appearance in the Westchester County Courthouse, the waiting reporters and onlookers had learned a great deal about the love story that first captured national attention. Surely this was a scandal in the eyes of some. But it also gave a very personal face to the hierarchical racial system. Whatever their perspectives on the marriage, whatever their thoughts on the feelings and motivations that had brought these two individuals together, those who sat waiting for the Rhinelander trial to begin knew that it held a tragic tale of the ramifications of race, class, behavior, and family background on the lives of two now well-known people.

3

BROKEN PROMISES

SITTING IN THE WHITE PLAINS courtroom, Alice was probably not immediately concerned with the challenge her existence and her marriage may have posed to American racial and class hierarchies. A tangle of emotions must have gripped her as she faced the man she professed to love in a setting designed to make one the victor, the other the loser. Clearly he had not decided to end these proceedings. Circumstances had altered the bonds of love and affection that brought the two together and fed Alice's hope of reconciliation. Instead Leonard had elected to follow his father's lead and end his marriage to the woman he claimed to love. He was there seeking an annulment of their marriage; Alice was there to preserve it. And now the trial would begin: opening statements, examinations and cross-examinations, and painful revelations.

A trial, however, was not preordained. In fact, in the media frenzy that immediately followed the public announcement of their marriage, Leonard remained loyal to his wife. He stood by her side in interviews and defended her against the rumors about her family and racial ancestry. In some interviews he reportedly declared that she was white. In others he said that she was colored but maintained he did not care, although he worried what his father would think. In all he said it did not matter what the papers said or who his wife's family was: He loved her and he would stay with her no matter what.

As further proof of his initial loyalty to his beleaguered bride, the young Leonard remained sequestered with the Jones family for the first week after the marriage became national news. As reporters and curiosity seekers surrounded the house, the couple remained hidden within, giving a few scattered interviews but mostly allowing Grace and Alice's parents to speak for them. At one point during that period of "siege," visitors were warned off the Jones property "on penalty of death."[1]

What happened, then, to change Leonard's mind? To bring him to the point of leaving Alice and signing this annulment suit? Suspicions that he had done so under duress from his father, made these tricky questions in the trial, and each brought different interpretations to the events in question.

As reporters unearthed more and more information suggesting that Alice and her father were not white, the crowds surrounding the small building became more menacing. Finally the threat became physical: Rocks were thrown at the Jones home, breaking a window. Later a letter arrived signed by the Klan. Alice recalled that these events propelled Leonard to send her into hiding, while he and his father's attorney, Leon Jacobs, sought safer accommodations. Leonard, however, recalled that it was Alice who had feared bodily harm, which precipitated their exodus.[2]

At the same time rumors circulated that the Rhinelander family's hopes for a quick dissolution of the embarrassing marriage might soon be realized. Under the headline KIP UNHAPPY, the *Daily Mirror* reported on November 21 that a conference between lawyers in New York hinted at a break.

> The dusky bride will be offered a large sum in cash to allow her husband to return to the Rhinelander home, while she remains at the home of her father in New Rochelle. She is said to be in a receptive mood. . . . The plea for annulment will be made on the grounds that the bride swore falsely to her color in her application for the marriage license.[3]

By November 22 New Rochelle buzzed with rumors of an imminent annulment.

The Jones family rushed to counter the rumors. Elizabeth emerged from the besieged home to "belligerently insist . . . that there would be no annulment." The only person who could bring an annulment suit was Leonard, and she was sure this was "not among the possibilities." Elizabeth continued, "This talk of annulment is all newspaper talk. It is just the newspaper trying to put notoriety upon us. Isn't it an outrage? If he wants her, and she wants him, whose business is it anyway?" Answering her own question, Elizabeth spurted, "I think that they should be left alone to live their lives as they choose. There will

George Jones throwing stones at reporters
and others besieging his home, 1924.

be no settlement and no annulment and my daughter has everything she needs."[4] In fact Elizabeth had every reason to believe her own words. Until this point Leonard had seemingly swayed little from his devotion to Alice. Thus what happened next at first appeared routine and not a cause for alarm.

The couple knew they had to escape the oppressive scrutiny of the reporters. And as the attention grew more threatening, it seemed reasonable for Leonard to leave with his family's longtime lawyer Leon Jacobs the morning of November 20, 1924. Jacobs and Leonard had spoken several times over the previous week, and now Jacobs was there to collect the media-bashful Rhinelander. Leonard's father wanted to speak with him, he was told. Actually Philip Rhinelander had desired his son's presence since the first reports of the marriage reached him, but his summons had been ignored. According to Alice's first lawyer, city judge Samuel F. Swinburne, lawyers had called at the Jones home "seven or eight times, . . . before they could persuade him to go with them. And then he went most unwillingly, promising to meet his wife at the Rich home in Mt. Vernon."[5]

Thus Alice had been married for one month and six days when her husband left her. Expecting the separation to be fleeting, she encouraged his departure, hoping that he and his lawyer would find a quiet place for the two of them to live. He would call that evening, he said; he would send for her in a few days. Leonard kissed his wife good-bye and left in the company of Jacobs.

Secure in Leonard's promises that he would return to take her away from the unwanted attention, Alice bade her husband farewell and packed a few bags to stay with the Riches, the furniture-store-owning couple who had become friends, in nearby Mount Vernon. Alice seemed to have good reason to expect her husband to return. Leonard called her at the Riches' that night, according to plan, telling her he was safe and she was "not to worry as he would soon have her join him." Furthermore, during the preceding week, Leonard's attorney had been in frequent contact with the couple. Alice understood that he was arranging for them to leave New Rochelle to "go to some place where they could live quietly until public interest in their matrimonial affairs should have subsided." Leonard had left, she thought, to finalize these plans.[6]

Most assumed that Leonard's departure signaled a breach between the couple.[7] Others, however, believed that the two were escaping together. A reliable source revealed to the *Standard Star* on November 21 that the couple "were happy together and that they were fleeing from any possible conference which might be arranged by Philip Rhinelander, father of the groom." Word surfaced again that the senior Rhinelander wanted the marriage annulled. This was no surprise. Yet, few expected Leonard to waiver in his resolve to be with Alice, least of all Alice's family. The Jones family, not knowing all the details of Leonard's whereabouts, also seemed to believe that the couple had disappeared together. Elizabeth proclaimed that no one would ever find out where they had gone. "We've all stopped talking," she told reporters, "and no one will find out another thing from any of us."[8]

Alice, meanwhile, remained with the Riches. Leonard, who stayed away, still called to reassure Alice of his love and his expectation to return eventually. But Leonard's father had not surrendered his fierce determination to end the marriage. On the contrary, a representative of the Rhinelander family had approached Alice and offered "any sum of money she might name within reason if she would allow Leonard to get the marriage annulled." Alice continued to refuse all offers of money. She told the representatives and Mrs. Rich that she and Leonard were in love with each other and money meant "absolutely nothing to her."[9]

As Leonard's absence grew so too did speculation about his whereabouts. The *Evening Journal* suggested that he had been kidnapped from his bride and sent away "on the high seas on a forced tour of the world."[10] On November 25 the *New York Times* reported that Leonard was gone and no one seemed to know where he was. Manhattan's paper of record did note that "Mrs. Jones says that the couple see each other frequently, and that they will soon leave together for a place where even Mr. Rhinelander's parents [*sic*] will not be able to locate them, probably for Europe."[11]

Despite all public pronouncements, Leonard never sent for Alice. One month and thirteen days after they wed, Leon Jacobs served Alice with a summons for the annulment suit. He also brought a letter from Leonard, which he permitted Alice to see but not to read or keep. Instead Jacobs read it aloud. Alice later recalled that the letter, in Leonard's unmistakable handwriting, directed her to get a lawyer and "fight this case as hard as she could." Jacobs later testified in a sworn statement that Leonard's letter said he wanted her to fight the annulment and prove that she was white, since that was what she claimed to be.[12] Perhaps he was hoping she could defeat the suit in a way that would force his family to accept their marriage.

AS IT TURNED out Leonard had already signed the suit the day he left Alice, although he did not mention it in any of his subsequent phone calls. On taking his young charge from his in-laws, Jacobs presented him with an annulment suit, already drawn up and compiled by Jacobs and other Rhinelander family lawyers. After several hours of discussion, persuasion, and traveling around, Leonard finally capitulated, signing the complaint in a subway station.

On November 27, 1924, the annulment was officially filed at the Westchester County Supreme Court in White Plains, New York. Newspapers jumped on the annulment story without hesitation, eager for a new twist to the popular tale. The *New York Times*, for example, ran the full text of the complaint on their front page. Others, such as the *Daily Mirror*, sermonized about the duplicitous actions of the senior Rhinelander and weak acquiescence of his son in succumbing to his father's pressures.[13]

The papers were so efficient that they broke the news before the Jones family received official notification of Leonard's action. With Alice still at the Riches', the Joneses were initially skeptical of these reports. Rumors of separation, after all, had been flying for a while. Elizabeth Jones, who opened the door briefly to address questioning reporters, proclaimed somewhat indignantly: "Nonsense. It's a lie. He loves my daughter and she loves him."[14] Although they seemed to know that Leonard was with his father, they claimed that Alice's only concern was "that Rhinelander will be kept away a long time, and that distorted accounts of her behavior, and what she says in his absence will gain circulation and he will be warned away from her."[15] Very soon thereafter Alice returned to the warm embrace of her family. With the aid of these stalwart supporters and protectors, she planned her defense.

The decision to file an annulment suit thrust Leonard and Alice into a larger world of innuendo, speculation, criticism, and idle curiosity. For some, of course, the news of the annulment suit promised to restore the imbalance of race and class alliances to their proper state. In an article reporting that the never-occupied Pintard apartment had been cleaned out and the lease canceled, the *Standard Star* commented:

> Kip Rhinelander has gone back to his clubs and his town-and-country life; but his bride is living once more in the humble home on Pelham road where, for over a quarter of a century, her parents have lived in respectable comfort—her mother an English white woman, and her father an Englishman, who insistently denies that he is "colored" despite sworn statements in his citizenship papers.[16]

Others saw "young Rhinelander" as a betrayed hero. "He denied his wife was colored," explained one commentator, "preferring to take her word to that of all the world. Later, however, the weight of evidence was too great and two weeks ago Thursday the young millionaire left the home of his bride . . . apparently never to return." The problem, for this reporter, was simple: He had been deceived.

> The young heir, whose answer to questions was always that his wife was white, had been told by her that she was of Spanish descent, which accounted for her dark skin, and for that of her father, George Jones. Jones had already been known about New Rochelle and Pelham as a colored man.

Similarly, other papers also used the announcement of the suit to point out the unreliability of the Jones family claims.[17]

There is little doubt that Alice, distraught over the end of her marriage, blamed her father-in-law, Philip Rhinelander, for the annulment suit. Her surprise at the suit and her suspicions as to its true source were clear in even the least dramatic renditions of her story:

> She insists he is not remaining away from her of his own free will, but is being restrained. Her belief is fostered by the declarations of her husband, repeated many times in the first days when their marriage became public, that he would not leave her and that anything that might be said about her family would not influence him. It is declared, too, that since their separation last Friday she has received daily messages from him.[18]

Other papers described Alice's bafflement at the "sudden change" in Leonard. He was with his father, she thought, for nearly a week after leaving her. For three days, she said, he called and made no mention of problems. Then, silence for a few more days until she was served notice of the annulment suit. She speculated that it was his father's influence that had prompted the change. Under the legal conventions of the time it was a crime to interfere in a marriage. If Philip had persuaded his son to file this suit, perhaps, the *New York Daily Mirror* suggested, she could file her own lawsuit against him for alienation of affection.[19]

The decision to seek an annulment also ended any hope for a quiet settlement of a deeply personal affair. Once Leonard signaled his intentions to invoke the courts, Alice saw no recourse other than to proclaim her own innocence. This matter would be settled in public, in court, in full view of a local and national community obsessed with a marriage that violated social prohibitions on cross-class and interracial relations. Once lovers — and deeply in love — they were now cast as combatants in a legal drama about truth, love, honor, status, and justice. Their marriage was now on trial. But so were conflicting American values pitting love, democracy, and freedom against race and class distinctions, family pride, and public morals.

4

⤜

THE VAMP AND

THE DUPE

IN THE AMERICAN legal tradition, trials provide an arena
for resolving conflicting stories. Opposing counsel present
their sides and attempt to persuade judges and juries
through argument and evidence that their account is the correct one.
Opening statements provide the first opportunity to hear each version
of the events in question, as attorneys lay out the substance of their
argument and the steps they will take to convince the jury that theirs is
the correct story. Evidence is crucial but, as any good trial lawyer
knows, the substance of the tale itself can carry great weight. What is
the best explanation that fits the evidence, fits acceptable social expectations, and makes your client appear sympathetic and even innocent?
As the trial opened, two basic questions were before the court: Was
Alice black or white, and had she deceived Leonard by claiming to be
white? As the opening statements made clear, however, there was far
more to the stories that would shape the trial and public debates over
the Rhinelander Case. The interpretation of how the couple had met
was also in conflict: Who had pursued whom? What was the nature of
their relationship? What were Leonard's and Alice's motives and strategies for continuing it? And who had pushed for the marriage? The
answers and explanations that each side highlighted were both simple

and strong, and both hid layers of cultural meanings and historical resonances that the subsequent days of the trial unveiled. Even after the first statements, however, it was clear that this trial was going to challenge not only American definitions of race and expectations of class behavior and standards, but sexual mores; family dynamics; notions of identity, respectability, and masculinity; and the meaning of marriage, love, and commitment.

WITH LEONARD SEATED and the jury confirmed, Isaac Mills stood to give his opening statement. Mills, a former New York Supreme Court justice himself, was an extremely well-respected and well-known attorney in Westchester County. Hard of hearing, on the verge of retirement, he started his opening statement. Lee Parsons Davis, Alice's lawyer and a former student of Mills, would address the court the next day. Both lawyers, of course, had a tale to spin, both based on the events of Alice and Leonard's relationship and marriage. Their desires, motivations, and conflicts—their family's lives—all were now to become a matter of public record and the topic of conversations across the nation. Or at least certain versions, for surely some of the most important events remained private from even the couple's legal representation. So for the next four weeks the nation would find itself caught up in the Rhinelander story almost spellbound. But which story?

A practiced attorney who understood the value of carefully crafting a legal narrative, Judge Mills began to introduce the main characters and outline the marriage and events leading to the annulment suit. He spoke slowly in a low voice, forcing his audience to strain to hear his

Mills begins opening remarks as other principals look on.

words. Leonard leaned forward in his chair watching through "balloon tire" spectacles. He gave the appearance of a big overgrown "kid," torn with emotion but bravely trying to look grown up, in his polka-dot tie and his Valentino hair, slicked back and glistening. Mills pointed to Leonard and then to Alice: "This young man and this young woman are aligned against each other." With this lead-in, "Kip turned at right angles, for the first time looking directly at his wife." Alice couldn't avoid making eye contact, but the intensity of feelings proved too much. "She shot one pathetic glance toward him, and again dropped her eyes to her shoes, a dull blush staining the olive duskiness of her face."[1]

Had Mills even noticed this display of emotions? Methodically and professionally he went on with his opening. "The law in this section is important." he instructed the court. "It is this: 'Any material misrepresentation of a material fact of a matrimonial relation which would prevent the marriage, is sufficient ground for an annulment.' " His case, he promised, would prove that Alice was in fact colored, that she had misrepresented herself by pretending to be white, that Leonard had married her believing she was white and that he would not have married her if he had known her to be otherwise. The jury would have six questions to decide:

1. At the time of the marriage was the defendant colored?
2. Did she ever represent that she was white?
3. Did she make such a representation in an attempt to defraud the plaintiff?
4. Was the plaintiff induced to marry her under the representation?
5. Did the plaintiff marry her with the full belief that she was white?
6. Has he lived with her since?

Mills next turned to the most basic element of his case—that Leonard was white and Alice was not. He could certainly prove, he declared, that Alice had a "substantial strain" of "black blood," and that Leonard and his family were of "pure white stock." As evidence of the Jones family's ancestry, he was prepared to draw on "several suitcases full of bulky documentary evidence and had marshaled a dozen witnesses for the express purpose of proving that colored blood flows in her veins." He cited the well-known examples of George Jones's immigration papers and driver's license application, which listed him as colored; and his three daughters' birth certificates, which listed each as "black," "mulatto," or "negro mixed." Mills did report substantial frustration in chasing George's paper trail back to England. None of the information he furnished had led to the discovery of any documents regarding him or his parents in England. "'I deemed it incumbent to try to trace his ancestry—I hadn't seen the father until today,'" charged Mills, implying that George's physical appearance alone was enough to substantiate charges he was black. The audience's titters seemed to indicate agreement.

Investigators had unearthed other tidbits, some salacious. They delved into the origins of Elizabeth's and George's relationship. They found evidence of an earlier indiscretion that would cause Elizabeth much suffering and embarrassment later in the trial. They looked everywhere for information on Alice's previous relationships that supported the evolving narrative crafted by Mills. Yet no matter how much they tried, George's own family background remained a mystery, one Mills tried to exploit. Mills called on the jurors to observe that "[a]s you can see by looking at her the trace of Negro blood in Mrs. Rhinelander is almost imperceptible."[2]

Mills described the Jones family as desperate to merge into white society. The sisters, he declared, sought to hide the evidence of their mixed racial ancestry with the collusion of their white mother, who encouraged them to marry white men. So intent had Elizabeth been on that goal, Mills explained, that Emily's marriage to a dark-skinned black man had caused turmoil in the Jones household. Her choice of a husband had alienated her from her parents until reconciliation following the birth of her first and only child.[3] Grace had managed at least to marry an Italian, but Alice had hit the jackpot in her "catch." In short Leonard was, Mills explained to a fascinated crowd, the innocent dupe of a manipulative gold-digging vamp.

To explain his client's unfortunate marriage, Mills pointed out that Leonard was four years younger than Alice and suffered from a severe lack of self-confidence, among other things. His mother had died a decade earlier, when the boy was only twelve. While dressing for an evening out, Adelaide had knocked over a kerosene lamp, igniting her clothing. Doctors, no doubt leading medical practitioners, soon responded to urgent calls. Today a person suffering such severe burns faces painful but often successful treatments, including liquid immersion and skin grafts. If the burns are too extensive, however, even nearly a century later there is little to be done. In 1916 no amount of money or social connections could save Adelaide Rhinelander. Sixteen hours after her accident she died in her own bed.

Leonard was actually thirteen years old and at home on the evening of his mother's immolation. We do not know for sure what he saw or heard—no doubt as the youngest he would have been protected from the situation as much as possible. Family lawyers later implied, however, that the incident had left deep psychic scars on the young boy. It is hard to imagine that it would not have: The loss of a parent at a young age under any circumstances would have been traumatic. And the circumstances of Adelaide's death were horrifying. Nor was this the last of his losses. A few years later the United States entered World War I, and both of Leonard's older brothers left home within a year and a half of their mother's death to fight in Europe. Before leaving, the younger Philip Rhinelander quickly married Helen Alexander at St. Thomas's Church in Manhattan. He returned to her several years later, raised two daughters with her, and joined his father at the Rhinelander Real Estate Company. T. J. Oakley Rhinelander, however, did not return. He died in 1917 of a fever while stationed in France. By 1918, then, Leonard Rhinelander had lost his mother and one brother to death, while another brother left home after he married. His sister had already left home for school and eventually her own marriage. When Leonard met Alice Jones in 1921, he was the only child still emotionally and financially dependent on his father.

But Mills's depiction of his client went beyond this image of a lonely abandoned child. The crowded courtroom gasped as Mills described Leonard as a "brain tied," feebleminded boy on whom no woman, or at least no woman "of his kind," had ever smiled before. When he met Alice he was a patient at an institution for nervous disorders in Stamford, Connecticut, from which he had some freedom to come and go. While there he fell under the influence of a "miserable wretch," an older, married man named Carl Kreitler, who led him astray and directly to the New Rochelle street where he met Grace Jones and then Alice.

In Mills's scenario Alice and her sister Grace were sexually experienced women who walked the streets preying on gullible young men.

Emily, Alice, and Grace's calm demeanor contrasts
with Mills's depiction of them.

Not quite daring to call them prostitutes, Mills instead emphasized the facts that Alice had once dated a black man and had had a serious romantic and physical relationship with a white man, which she had confessed to Leonard in a letter. Mills knew that even this much information would cast aspersions on Alice's character, and by extension on her parents' ability to offer moral guidance.[4] In fact, he continued, Elizabeth taught her daughters to pursue white men by any means necessary. Under her mother's coaching, Mills charged, Alice had seduced a naive and unsophisticated boy, taking advantage of his innocence and forcing him to fall in love with and eventually marry her.

Plotting, calculating, and devious: That was the image Mills sought to convey. A woman of the world, Alice had lured Leonard to the Marie Antoinette Hotel within a few months of their first meeting. On at least two occasions, the young couple had spent several consecutive nights in the hotel—the last time Leonard's father had taken him from the room and sent him to school in Arizona to separate the two. While

Leonard was there Alice used love letters to maintain her control over his mind and heart. This physical seduction, Mills surmised, was only part of Alice's malicious plot to ensnare her wealthy lover into marriage by destroying him mentally and morally.[5] Throughout his three-year courtship of Alice, Mills emphasized, Leonard had been aware of the Joneses' "inferior social position" but not of their racial position. Alice was willing to use her written expressions of love and her sexuality to vamp her dupe into supporting and marrying her. Lying about her age and race were simply additional means toward that end.

Giving a taste of the testimony to come, Mills read from a few of Alice's letters in which she alluded to their sexual relationship: "Do you remember the night you and I were in the [Marie] Antoinette [Hotel] and I was lying in your arms"; "You will always be welcome to put your shoes under my bed, dearie"; "I have never let a fellow love and caress me the way you do, Leonard, because you make me feel so happy and lovable toward you dear. But wouldn't it be awful if you had me, myself, alone? What you would not do to me I cannot imagine." Even when they were physically apart, such "knockout" letters, Mills asserted, made him her slave, body and soul.[6] The stages of her seduction shifted from asking for an apartment, to a ring, and finally to marriage.

Here, on the very first day, was all the sensationalism and scandal the Rhinelander Case had seemed to promise. Throughout the dramatic attack Alice sat between her lawyers, smiling demurely. She and her husband listened unflinchingly to an hour and a half of Mills's accusations and defamations. Neither could have been very pleased with his version of their motives and characters. Leonard sat with arms folded while his attorney painted him as a simple-minded dupe. Not once did he glance at his wife, who sat staring at her shoes, sometimes hiding her face behind a handkerchief. (Some were sure she used it to hide her audible weeping; others claimed she mostly tried to mask her amusement.)

Both Alice and Leonard had their own memories and knowledge of their courtship. And though bound in part by the shifting historical events and cultural conflicts, their story was also an individual one, determined as much by their personal histories and dispositions as by the tides of social patterns. In this courtroom, however, their story of love and marriage was often lost. Instead, their individual experiences were seen through the judgments and interpretations provided by the competing lawyers, each drawing on the class and race perceptions they expected would be familiar to the average American represented by the jury—and those who tried the pair in the court of public opinion.

Since the startling disclosure of their marriage in the fall of 1924, nationwide attention had been focused on the star-crossed lovers.[7] Front-page news again, the trial promised scandal, editorial opportunity, and sales. It had been a long spring and summer, with only occasional interviews and court postponements to keep the story going. Now a third set of narrators emerged to rival the attorneys: the press. In an attempt to balance the need to sell papers against claims of objective journalism, papers across the nation took a keen interest in the details of this case. In the process they perpetuated the scandal.

That afternoon newspapers had a juicy first day to mull over. Even before hearing Davis's version of the events, local and national newspapers raced stories to the presses weighing in on Mills's opening. Mills, the *Daily Mirror* summarized, had "dealt out sensational detail after sensational detail in a story of how the scion of one of New York's wealthiest and most aristocratic families, a descendant of the first French Huguenots to land in this country, was 'inveigled' into an alliance with a girl of colored blood whose own father does not remember his parentage."[8] The headlines screamed and the commentary began: KIP'S BURNING LOVE LETTERS FROM COLORED BRIDE READ topped the front page of the *New York Daily Mirror*, tempting passersby to purchase and read the story on page three.[9] Readers in Philadelphia were informed: WIFE ATTACKED IN RHINELANDER MARITAL SUIT. GIRL HAD MANY AFFAIRS BEFORE MARRYING SCION OF NEW YORK FAMILY, COUNSEL SAYS.[10]

For the more circumspect papers, the subjects in question had to be handled carefully. Certainly many kept these more sensational details from the headlines, telling scanners only that RHINELANDER BEGINS SUIT FOR MARRIAGE ANNULMENT or RHINELANDERS MEET IN COURT, TRIAL OF HUSBAND'S SUIT FOR ANNULMENT OPENS. PAIR IGNORE EACH OTHER AS HEARING BEGINS.[11] Many stories omitted the information about the Marie Antoinette Hotel and the letters referring to Kip and Alice's activities there—at least initially. Some deemed them unfit for print or left out the offending sections. Others used terms like "vamp" or alluded to the "sensational and stunning details" to suggest what they could not specify—that the couple had had a sexual relationship and that Alice, according to Mills, had been a willing, perhaps initiating, partner in it.

INDEED THE PORTRAITS painted by Mills were summed up by the media in two oft-cited images: Alice as the vamp and Leonard as the dupe. The female vamp, or vampire, was a popular icon of stage and screen in the 1920s. Although related to contemporary images of male vampires with pointed teeth and a thirst for human blood, the 1920s female vamp had a much less supernatural background. Popularized by silent-movie star Theda Bara, the female vamp was overtly sexual and always dangerous. The cultural historian Lary May has pointed out that in film the female vamp represented the fear that sex, particularly uncontrolled female sexuality, might destroy the social order.[12] While not literally sucking the blood out of men's bodies, she did deprive them of their power and the predatory role of their social privilege. Men, not women, were expected to be the sexual aggressors. Women, not men, were expected to subordinate their desires and needs to those of their partner. On film and in Mills's tirade, the vamp reversed these roles and conquered her desired mate through seductive manipulation.

Film star Theda Bara, movie model of the female vamp.

First popularized during the second decade of the twentieth century, at the height of popular support for the women's suffrage movement, the vamp films represented both a response to and an acknowledgment of shifting gender roles. Victorian standards, in which women's sexual nature was seen as essentially passive, were now under attack from more modern perspectives. The movie vamps had real-world counterparts in the high-living flappers, who exposed their shoulders and knees in shockingly skimpy dresses; cut their hair short; and drank, smoked, and danced to fast, jazz-influenced rhythms. Both a stereotype and an indication of rapidly changing youth culture and gender behavior, the flapper also had a male counterpart, called a "sheik" or "cake eater." Both, although particularly the flapper, threatened an American self-image based on the conservation of the social order, female domesticity, and racial segregation.[13] And the connection between flapper and vamp was more than ideological. Into the early 1920s, the vamp provided a fashion trend for young women, who emulated her deathly pale skin and dark eye makeup and lipstick and tried to mimic her sinewy, sexualized movements.

Alice and Leonard's marriage clearly did pose a threat to a social order based on both racial and class stratifications. And the image of Alice as a "vamp" who had seduced and destroyed a poor unsuspecting elite white man added an additional threat to gender hierarchies. As a nonwhite working-class woman, Alice was willing to abandon the pedestal of true womanhood to break into America's higher economic strata. Such women, of course, had never been intended to occupy a pedestal that was designed for white middle- and upper-class women alone. In fact historians of race and gender have argued that the very development of the image of the respectable, white, passionless woman depended on the concurrent ideological development of the oversexed enslaved black woman.[14] Certainly Alice's presumed race and class placed her on the wrong side of this Madonna-whore duality. But the duality was being challenged from several angles, and for many onlookers premarital sex and female sexual aggressiveness or pleasure were not shocking or unusual behaviors.

For the New York dailies the supposedly outrageous behavior of the vamp was in fact unremarkable. The *New York Evening Journal* was inspired to publish a brief history of vamping in response to Mills's contention that Alice's behavior as a vamp was unusual. Folks in the big city, the copy implied, would know better than to consider female sexual desire a new and unusual phenomenon: "Up in Westchester County, where men are men, where the great open spaces are dotted with towns . . . it has been [said] . . . that such a thing as a woman pursuing a man is new to lawyers and other inhabitants."[15] To edify the small-town lawyers, the *Journal* provided several historical examples of "vamps," with accompanying photos and paintings next to a picture of Alice. While making fun of the shock Mills expressed at this young woman's behavior, the *Journal* capitalized on the vamp image and used the classical artistic renderings of other women who seduced or destroyed their male victims to print images of female nudity. In addition, their comparisons of the Rhinelander Case with well-known biblical and historical figures emphasized the dramatic content of the current trial and heightened its symbolic importance for readers.

A painting of Venus and Adonis by Titian depicted Venus as "the vamp of mythology," trying to keep her love from going out to hunt. The caption noted that she failed in this endeavor, and Adonis died on the hunt. Between photos of Alice and Leonard the *Journal* placed a portrait of Madame de Pompadour, who "vamped right and left," the power behind the throne during the reign of Louis XV. Finally one depicted Cleopatra, who "saved her throne for a time by her vamping, and . . . made a love slave of Anthony."

However, the combined imagery of "vamp and dupe" proved irresistible and captured, if not in words then in spirit, most of the headlines reporting on Mills's opening. Even the staid *New York Times* picked up the language in its headline: CALLS RHINELANDER DUPE OF GIRL HE WED.[16] So pervasive, in fact, was this image of Alice and Leonard, that it appeared even in papers that seemed to have no interest in publishing any substantive details of the case. One of the lightest coverages of the case came from the *Jacksonville* [Florida] *Times-Union*, which buried isolated pictures and two brief articles on relatively unimportant moments in the trial in its back pages. A week after the opening statements, the *Times-Union* published photos of the couple titled "Vamp and Dupe"—a vote for Mills if there ever was one. Buried in the middle of ads in the real estate section, the accompanying caption summed up the case in a few sentences.[17]

Indeed, Mills's image of his client as enslaved and helpless before Alice's physical and emotional seductions was compelling even to some who rejected it as a serious defense of Leonard's actions. "A white aristocrat enslaved by a black girl!" exclaimed the *Evening Journal*'s Margery Rex, reporting and commenting on Mills's opening statement. "Slowly, insidiously the attractive young woman drew in her net. And how!—as they say on Broadway." Both reveling in and ridiculing the image, Rex then turned to the question of love. Even if Alice was manipulating Leonard, was this love affair different from any other? Wasn't Alice to some extent acting the only way women were allowed to act when they were attracted to a man who was perhaps a little shy? "Is this then some magic that transcends the color line and makes a white man love one not of his race? Or is it simply the ancient formula of all Alice Jones's sex regardless of color, creed and previous condition of servitude? Of honeyed words and clinging persistence?" Rex also followed Mills's reasoning, suggesting that Leonard was particularly susceptible to hearing these "honeyed words" because he had heard them so seldom, because even his mother was no longer there to embrace him and tell him he was loved.

> How could the backward youth, left motherless at fifteen [*sic*], the blushing diffident boy who has such an impediment in his speech that he flees rather than seeks the society of women, how could a youth with such a sense of personal inferiority help but succumb to and be delighted in the company of an adoring attractive girl— whose social inferiority was, in a way, a charm?[18]

For Rex and Mills, then, Leonard's lacks explained his choice of Alice. But Rex was not as sure as Mills that Alice had coldly exploited that vulnerability; she thought it might also have been true love.

Rex reduced the question to whether Leonard loved Alice because of her status or in spite of it. Her final question suggests that, for an insecure man, an attractive but "socially inferior" woman might appear less daunting and therefore more approachable. It was not unknown for middle-class white families to explain their children's wayward behavior by accusing them, quite literally, of being insane or otherwise damaged. White women in particular might find themselves committed to a lunatic asylum by horrified parents to prevent them from marrying or continuing a relationship with a black man. Mental deficiencies, of course, were the only acceptable explanation of why otherwise rational people would marry so far beneath themselves. Several newspapers' coverage of Mills's opening also focused on the juxtaposition of these two claims: that Alice was black and that Leonard was "physically defective."[19] Was the latter the explanation for Kip's marriage to the former?

Further, Leonard was not the only white person whose interracial marriage required explanation in the press. Descriptions of Mrs. Jones, this one from the same article by Margery Rex, constantly buzzed around the question: Why had Elizabeth married a black man?

> Little Mrs. Jones, a tiny, plump, white-haired woman, well-dressed, black coat, brown fur collar, and with a no-expression face. A typical country housewife whose deepest thoughts never come to the surface. She looks down at her white silk muffler that has a design of black rings scattered upon it. Black and white! Beside her, George Jones, her second husband—her first was white, and from that first union came a white child, Ethel, now a Mrs. Moore, who will be called in, Mills said, dramatically, to testify. She will say that Jones, after he married her mother, always held up his thin brown hand to shade his brown face from her scrutiny. Whatever made Mrs. Jones marry a colored man?[20]

Interestingly Rex offers no actual description of George here. He is described only through Mills's secondhand story, which depicts him as shamefully hiding his dark skin from his wife's white daughter.

This focus on Elizabeth's marriage centered Alice herself as both the product of and a participant in an interracial marriage. In the same passage here she is described as "a quiet little figure at the end of the lawyers' table. Fluffy tan fur about her face, a black hat casting it into deeper shadow. Obviously, a nice looking, well bred mulatta, a casual glance would deceive you." Although the phrase "well bred mulatta" was an interesting one given the stigma Margery Rex attached to interracial relationships, her ambivalence toward Alice herself was quite common in coverage of the trial. It is just as likely that Rex's phrasing was designed to suggest that Alice wasn't as well bred upon closer inspection. With little discernible pattern the New York papers all see-sawed back and forth between describing Alice as very white looking (and not coincidentally very nice looking) or describing her as darkened or, here, cast in deep shadows. At this point Rex and northern white reporters in general had not yet made their judgment on Alice or the case.

Neither had the nation's black-published newspapers, which also presented an array of perspectives on the case amongst them. Most combined an interest in the SPICY TESTIMONY presented in court, as the front-page headlines of the *Richmond Planet* proclaimed, with a serious concern for the social and political ramifications of the arguments, particularly those of Mills. In reports of Mills's opening statements, many took a different stance on the "vamp and dupe" portrayal. The *Norfolk Journal and Guide*, for example, reported that the Rhinelanders wanted to prove Alice to be a "designing vampire" but described her themselves as

> a beautiful young woman of the modestly circumstanced family [who] has been lifted into the gilded society of the wives of millionaires, and had bestowed upon her the luxuries that millions can buy. She and her family are fighting that she may retain the Rhinelander name and the prestige that goes with it.[21]

Similarly the *Baltimore Afro-American* reframed the "public issue" from whether Alice had "a few drops of colored blood" or not to "why the Rhinelanders with their culture and wealth did not train young Kip to be a useful citizen instead of a 'tongue tied, brain tied' cake eater, dabbling in money, automobiles, and flappers."[22] The failure, they implied, was not Alice's racial ancestry but in what Leonard (quickly dubbed "Kip" by the press) had failed to make of *his* supposedly privileged and superior upbringing.

Others were more subtle in expressing their perspectives: The *Amsterdam News*, one of two New York–based black-published papers, referred to the BEAUTIFUL ALICE RHINELANDER in its headline and throughout the article, which repeated the summary of the first few days of the trial without comment.[23] Similarly, the *New York Age* topped a very dry report with the subheadline "Annulment Suit Based on Color Prejudice Attracts Widespread Interest."[24]

The *Chicago Defender* was even more explicit in its response to Mills's opening, comparing it to "the flimsy fortification of a cobweb." It also suggested that Leonard's delay in arriving the first day was due to the "great difficulty" his companions had "forcing him into the building," repeating rumors that the whole trial was proceeding against his wishes. When reporting Mills's claims that Alice had hidden her black ancestry from Leonard, the *Defender* pointed out that he had known her father and must have seen that he was dark-skinned.

MILLS'S OPENING HAD mesmerized his courtroom audience: a fatally flawed would-be hero . . . forbidden love, illicit sex . . . a dark, predatory seductress to rival any Hollywood icon . . . deception and a moral downfall. This was the stuff of movies with the lure of real-life drama. "The proverbial pin . . . if it had been dropped, would have sounded like the Wall Street explosion. Breathless the court spectators . . . waited for more."[25] And more was exactly what they would get. Clearly everyone was transfixed at Mills's rendition of the Rhinelander story. But Davis was up next. The vamp and the dupe provided an enticing framework around which to mold the story of Alice and Leonard. The story was not, however, a universally compelling one. Would the lure of Mills's rendition survive the onslaught of Davis's rebuttal? And how would Davis restructure the events laid out? What new information or interpretation would he offer to counter Mills's assault? Those who could flocked to White Plains early the next morning to jostle for a seat; the rest of the interested public waited to hear the results at the end of the day.

5

CONCESSIONS OF RACE

ON THE SECOND day of the trial Leonard managed to present himself on time and sat again with his lawyers and bodyguards. Alice was back in her seat, accompanied by her family and dressed in a black taffeta dress trimmed with white lace at the collar and cuffs. The crowd of onlookers had also reconvened and sat waiting for the defense's opening response to the annulment complaint. All assumed that Alice would claim she had not deceived her husband-to-be about her racial identity. But what would she claim that identity to be? And how would her attorneys answer Mills's claims that she had seduced and "vamped" a naive, defective boy into marriage?

Lee Parsons Davis, joined at his table by Swinburne and Richard Keogh, stood up and began with a bombshell. "The defense counsel," he announced calmly, "hereby withdraws the previous denial as to the blood of this defendant, and for the purpose of this trial . . . admits that she has some colored blood." Alice was no longer refuting Leonard's allegations that she was not white. Although Davis was careful not to say that Alice was black or Negro, his official declaration that she had "colored blood" was synonymous with blackness in the eyes of white America. To all intents and purposes for most onlookers, he settled the question of what Alice's racial identity was.

Onlookers gasped upon hearing the declaration. Alice bowed her head and cried, drying her lustrous brown eyes with a white handkerchief. Leonard's attorney's started in confusion and began shuffling papers. This had been, as Isaac Mills was later to complain to Judge Joseph Morschauser, a major part of the suit's original claim and therefore of their legal strategy and preparation. Mills and his team of lawyers and researchers had amassed a pile of documents to disprove Alice's marriage license designation as white. The defense's concession had rendered that time wasted and the documents useless—a point Mills emphasized later in the day when he insisted on introducing each one into evidence anyway.[1]

Now Alice's only defense to the annulment suit was to argue that she had not misrepresented her race to Leonard; that he had known she was of mixed ancestry when he married her.[2] But her admission of "colored blood" did not end speculation about the significance or even the nature of her racial ancestry—far from it. There was still the problem of whether Leonard Rhinelander—or any white American, for that matter—should have known that Alice had black ancestry? And if so, how? That is, now the main concern of the trial was what information and clues Leonard had had to indicate that Alice wasn't white before he married her. As has already been seen, the available clues were contradictory. And much of the difficulty in determining the Joneses' racial identity resulted from the ambiguity of American racial definitions and, ultimately, the arbitrary nature of the racial categories themselves. These questions of how Americans defined and recognized physical distinctions between black and white would continue to haunt the Rhinelander Case throughout the trial and beyond.

Giving onlookers little time to ponder the significance of his first admission, Davis quickly moved on to what would become the main issue of the trial—had Alice deceived her husband regarding her racial ancestry? Had she, in effect, tricked him into marrying her? Not surprisingly, in addressing these points Davis painted a very different portrait of his client and her estranged husband than had Mills. She was no vamp; he was no dupe. No, they were simply two people from very different worlds who had chanced to meet and fall in love. They married with full awareness of the social obstacles and probably of Philip Rhinelander's reaction. And had it not been for the interference of publicity and family pressures, they would still be living happily together instead of battling over the validity and fate of their marriage in a public court.

It was the Rhinelander family, not Leonard, Davis charged, that had brought this suit against Alice. "This is an effort to save an ancient name trailing back to the Huguenots and to crush a humble New Rochelle family." Rather than try to prove Leonard weak minded, he continued, his attorneys should claim him to be color blind. How else could he have failed to notice that Alice and her family were not all white? If Mills himself seemed to imply that George Jones was obviously not white in appearance, should not Leonard also have been able to "tell" her race on seeing her father? After all, as a suitor, he had called on Alice's parents many times, spending countless evenings and numerous weekends at their home during their engagement. He had been very friendly with her sisters and their husbands, including Robert Brooks, who was "obviously Negro." He had a close relationship with Alice's niece, who was, by some accounts, "nearly black." In other words, according to Davis, Alice's color, and that of her sisters, father, and niece, was clearly visible in their physical appearance. The

*Alice's attorney Lee Parsons Davis (7) identifies Alice during
a heated moment of cross-examining reporter William L. Lawby.
Also identified are Alice Jones (1), her mother, Elizabeth (2),
father, George (3), co–defense counsel Samuel Swinburne (4),
brother-in-law Robert Brooks (5), co-counsel
Leroy Keogh (6), and Leonard (8).*

family had not tried to hide its racial status from Leonard—indeed *could* not have hidden it. The young heir, then, had pursued Alice with full knowledge of her ancestry.

At the same time that he confessed that Alice was in fact not white, Davis continued to emphasize the ambiguity of the Joneses' racial status. As a colored man in England, George Jones had been accepted as an equal by whites, Davis explained; George's white mother had told him that his father was an East Indian rather than the West Indian often reported. He had never thought of a "taint in his blood" (black ancestry) until they arrived in the United States and realized that he was considered black here. Davis further pointed out that the plaintiff's own collected evidence of the presence of colored blood in Alice Jones's veins was also proof of the obviousness of that nonwhite ancestry. In compiling overwhelming evidence that George Jones and his daughters were not white, the Rhinelander lawyers were undermining their own argument that Alice's identity was hard to determine.[3]

Davis also took the opportunity to chastise Mills for his charges against Alice and her family. Mills's accusations were "vicious and unAmerican," and if the opposing side continued to drag Alice's name through the mire, Davis warned that he had the means to do the same. "If that's the kind of case Judge Mills wants—mud and dirt—he's going to get it. If they want to throw slime, I'm going to wreck the boy." Not only, he suggested, were Leonard's letters "infinitely more intimate" than Alice's, but they revealed the young man's ardent love and active pursuit of her. Following Mills's lead, Davis also read excerpts from Leonard's letters as part of his opening statement: "Be true and faithful to me alone, dearest. I love you and only you"; "There are many society girls on board the ship that I could have, but they are all cigarette-smoking, highball-drinking flappers, and I like you, darling, because you are not like that." Just as selective as his opponent, Davis obviously chose letters that shed a positive light on his own client, here described as of higher character and behavior than the upper-class women Leonard was expected to court. By the end of the trial, Davis promised, the jurors would have heard much more, and he would challenge them "as Americans" to "give this girl a square deal in the face of the assault backed by the Rhinelander millions."[4]

Full of slang and wit, the younger lawyer drew laughs and smiles from the audience as he ridiculed Mills's description of Rhinelander as the innocent victim of a vampire's wiles. Reported as "fine satire," Davis's opening continually referred to Leonard as a "papa's boy," "this stuttering nut," and "this brainstormed Rhinelander." To the jury he joked that Mills's speech marked "the first time I ever heard of a girl criminally assaulting a man." He also promised to show that records from the Orchard School indicated that Leonard's acquaintance with Alice had improved his stutter and self-confidence. Rather than preying on his impairments to manipulate him, her influence had been healing.

Finally Davis promised to show that Leonard's first reaction to news stories that he had married a woman of negro descent was to reassure her, in front of witnesses including journalists, that he did not care.[5] The suit, he concluded, had been drawn up by Rhinelander family lawyers and signed after the fact by Leonard, sight unseen and under pressure by his father. It was based on family pride and prejudice, not facts.

ALTHOUGH CONSIDERED LESS vicious than those of his opponents, Davis's dramatic announcements and sarcastic jibes rang hollow for at least two listeners. It had been a harrowing day for both plaintiff and defendant, and neither seemed pleased with Davis's acknowledgment that Alice was colored or with his continued references to Leonard as a "papa's boy" who drank wine and played cards with his "coal-black negro" brother-in-law. Of course neither was eager to be in that courtroom at all. Regardless of what the testimony would bring, regardless of the outcome, the experience of sitting across the aisle from each other must have been excruciating. And they did so under the constant gaze of the many onlookers while their lawyers recounted different versions of their romance, their characters, their motivations and their family backgrounds. This, as much as the events of the trial itself, provided a constant dramatic tension in the courtroom.

As the court recessed between Davis's statement and the beginning of the testimony, this tension came to a head. In a brief encounter noted by many and elaborated on by a few, Leonard strode toward Alice on his way out of the courtroom. She reached out her hand to touch him but was spurned as he brushed past her. Several newspapers printed this version of the interaction, but a sidebar in the *Mirror* claimed

that there was more to the encounter. In melodramatic tones this article reported an overheard wail between Alice and her mother, "Oh
Mamma, Mamma, to think that Leonard could have sat so close to me
in that courtroom and never even looked at me." The description of
their encounter here was heavy with added detail and commentary:

> At recess Rhinelander almost stumbled over the disconsolate New
> Rochelle beauty.
> "Leonard," she breathed in pleading low tones as he passed her
> chair.
> When Rhinelander refused her proffered hand she almost fainted.
> This incident had been unnoticed save to those who had watched
> for some such failure of the girl's boast that Rhinelander would nev-
> er be able to resist her.[6]

The main theme of this article was that Leonard's indifference, as
much as the publicity surrounding the trial, was driving Alice "to the
breaking point . . . [on] the verge of collapse."[7] But they were also fascinated with the details of Alice and Leonard's reactions during the
trial itself.

As the lawyers presented their opening statements, the newspapers
were the first to weigh in with their stories and interpretations.
Journalists, and perhaps the jury as well, also watched the young couple and to a lesser extent the Jones family.

> As she listened to the long legal battle and heard the lawyers flay and
> ridicule what ordinarily are the sacred relics of any family the girl
> toyed with the wedding ring Rhinelander had placed upon her fin-
> ger a year ago.
> At times she would remove the ring as if angered to a point ready
> to hurl it across the court room. Then again she would fasten a gaze
> upon Rhinelander with eyes obviously not unkind.
> Rhinelander continues the apathetic attitudes he has displayed
> from the commencement of the action. Not once has he conferred
> with his attorneys.[8]

In fact it quickly became a tabloid obsession to find evidence of the
true story in the reactions of Alice and Leonard themselves.

The newspapers had a field day after Davis's rebuttal to Mills. Finally the outlines of the upcoming battle had been laid out. Which story was more accurate? Who was to be believed? The "red hot shrapnel" Davis shot in his opening argument collided with Mills's charges of the previous day, swaying some onlookers and providing further scandal to sell papers. Davis seemed to have several advantages: He was able to respond directly to Mills's statement; he used sarcasm and humor to ridicule both the veracity and the tone of his opponent; and he could claim the sympathies of the underdog against the Rhinelander millions.

The *Daily News*, for example, seemed to accept Davis's story as more convincing, or at least more fun to parrot in content and tone. In a series of excerpts from the two statements, the *News* adopted his patronizing tone toward Mills and Leonard's case, and invited readers to join in.

> She came into contact with a stammering nut and that's why she should be released, they would have us believe. . . .
>
> Although she frankly admitted relations with another man, they try to show that she deceived Rhinelander. . . .
>
> He wrote letters, scores of them. One contained the sentence, "Promise me you won't see or speak to another man."[9]

The *Daily Mirror* emphasized the tit-for-tat nature of Davis's rebuff. "Into the same tub of suds in which attorney Isaac N. Mills began Monday the laundering of the 'linen' of the Jones family of New Rochelle, [are] to go the bedraggled Huguenot ruffles of the Rhinelanders of New York."[10]

The image of Leonard's relations with the Jones family was too much for Davis, or news coverage, to resist. His language, repeated across the nation, juxtaposed the plaintiff's ancestral standing with that of his in-laws. It was "the descendant of the Huguenots" who played with the nearly black daughter of Alice's oldest sister; it was "the bluest of the bluebloods" who wrote more than a thousand letters to a lover he knew was colored; it was the "bearer of a famous name" who became an unofficial and then official member of the Jones family and drank wine with his "negro brother-in-law," knew his wife was colored, and "cared not a button."[11]

For most papers, however, the headline of the day was Davis's admission that Alice was not white: YES, SHE'S COLORED, shouted the one-inch bold-type front page of the *Daily News*. Across the country, from the *New York Times* to the *Reno Evening Gazette*, the story was clear: "Rhinelander's Wife Admits Negro Blood," "Mrs. Rhinelander Admits Her Color," "Colored Blood Admitted by Mrs. Rhinelander's Counsel," "Mrs. Rhinelander's Counsel Admits She Has Negro Blood," "Girl Is Colored," "Admit Wife of Rhinelander Is of Negro Blood."[12]

A few newspapers had predicted that, once in court, Alice's lawyers would finally confess that she was black. But most saw it as a "great legal turning of tables," one which certainly rendered pointless a vast amount of the preparation to which Leonard's lawyers had devoted the previous months. The *Herald-Tribune* predicted in that morning's issue that Davis would admit that George Jones was "a Negro," endeavoring to demonstrate "that young Rhinelander knew it all along, but refused to let it make any difference." The previous night's *Evening Journal*, on the other hand, expected that Mills's primary tasks would be to "discredit whatever defense that may be interposed by . . . Davis that his client is not a negress, as charged by her husband."[13] In admitting through her attorney that she was colored, Alice threw a veritable bombshell into the legal preparations of Leonard's attorneys.[14]

WHY WAS THIS revelation such a surprise? Definitions and categories of racial identity and racial deception filled newspaper coverage of the affair between November 1924 and November 1925. During that time a less public legal skirmish was also developing. Between November 26, 1924, and December 3, 1925, Leonard submitted three versions of his annulment complaint, and Alice and her lawyers submitted three replies, only the first of which predated the trial. All of Leonard's affidavits contained the general allegation that the marriage was fraudulent because Alice had deceived him regarding her racial ancestry, by not telling him of her father's background, by claiming to be Spanish, or by outright denying that she had any black ancestry. His original complaint also charged that "the defendant (Alice) represented to and told the plaintiff (Leonard) that she was white and not colored, and had no colored blood."[15] Alice and/or her lawyer simply denied "each and every allegation."[16] It is not completely clear whether this meant she was denying that she had any black ancestry or just denying she had deceived him. In general the media assumed it meant she was claiming to be white, which they equated with a claim to have no black ancestry.

However, in the year between Leonard's filing the annulment suit and the trial's opening, the speculation and confusion over Alice and her family's racial status had continued. And as hints of her defense preparations began to filter into the newspapers, a dizzying array of possible explanations of her racial ancestry, identity, and legal status had emerged. Even Davis's divulgence of Alice's colored ancestry fell far short of a clear answer to the question of what Alice's race and iden- tity were. In fact Davis's admission of Alice's race served to maintain the ambiguity of her racial standing in the United States as much as, or perhaps even more than, to resolve it. In this light it is particularly crucial to note Davis's own continued attention to the multiple possi- bilities of the Joneses' self- and public racial identity even as he made his announcement. For one thing Davis specified that their conces- sion was only for the purpose of the trial. And in the next breath he suggested that George's father was East Indian, not black, and that George and Elizabeth Jones had had no idea that they would be received as a mixed-race couple in the United States.

So who were George and Elizabeth Jones? How had they arrived at their anomalous place in early-twentieth-century New Rochelle? Elizabeth Brown Holloway Jones was born in 1862 in Lincolnshire, England. She was white, by all accounts. George Jones was born in 1856 in Leicestershire, England, to a white mother. His father, who died when George was two years old, was reportedly from one of the British colonies, which most took to mean the West Indies, although researchers at the time and since have not been able to identify George's father or his place of birth. George and Elizabeth met while working as servants on the same estate in Bradford. They married in Leeds and, along with millions of Europeans, moved to the United States in 1891, settling almost immediately in Westchester County. (She was not the only member of her family to emigrate to the United States. On several occasions during the media spectacle she and Alice visited Elizabeth's relatives in Connecticut.)

Although his wife continued to work in domestic service, by 1924

George Jones had achieved a relatively comfortable retirement from his primary job, managing a cabstand at the New Rochelle train station. In retirement he owned and co-owned several local buildings that gave him a modest income. Indeed, he became increasingly frustrated with newspaper reports that refused to acknowledge this rise in his fortunes, continuing to describe him as a humble cabdriver and odd-jobs man. Jones had the connections to hire New Rochelle city judge Samuel Swinburne as his daughter's first attorney. Although a silent member of the defense team by the time of the trial, Swinburne was the family's primary spokesperson between December 1924 and November 1925.

As Davis suggested, George and Elizabeth Jones may have brought their own definitions of racial identity with them, definitions that lay in stark contrast to American racialism. The usually staid Elizabeth Jones gave at least one interview to a local paper in which she complained bitterly about the media coverage of her husband and daughter's racial identity:

> I don't care a bit for myself or what they say about Mr. Jones, but it's awful for the girl. The papers said that her father was a colored man. He isn't. He's a mulatto. The papers said, too, that he swore in his citizenship papers that he was colored. He didn't. The only thing asked was his nationality and that is English. His forefathers and my forefathers for generations were English. But nothing anyone says about him can make a difference with him and me.[17]

Elizabeth's contention that her husband was "mulatto" but not "colored" would have seemed nonsensical to most American readers in 1924. Even more so than "black" and "Negro," which could both include and be used in contrast with "mulatto," "colored" incorporated all people of black ancestry and, in some states, anyone who was not white—as in, "the colored races."

Furthermore, the distinction Elizabeth drew between colored and mulatto turned less on British conventions and more on the amalgam of racial positions the family occupied by virtue of moving to the United States. By the time Elizabeth and George left for America, Great Britain had colonial possessions all over the world. This empire complicated simple divisions into black and white. Yet if George had

The Jones family, c. 1925.
(Note the overexposure of Elizabeth, far left, and Emily, far right.)

one nonwhite parent, even in England his status as white would have been questioned, whether that parent was Indian, Caribbean, or African. The term "mulatto" had some currency as a marker of difference on both sides of the Atlantic, but insufficiently so. The United States and Britain shared more than a colonial past; they shared a history of slavery and racialization that exposed the difficulty but not the impossibility of instituting the distinction Elizabeth offered. Although the tendency to apply it was more pronounced in the United States, the one-drop rule was not unknown in England. In fact, if anything, the term "black" was used even more broadly there to include those of Indian or Asian ancestry as well as African.[18]

Nevertheless, soon after the annulment suit was filed, Swinburne suggested to reporters that George Jones's non-English lineage came not from the West Indies but from India. "In this event," he pointed out, "they would be members of the Aryan race, which is collateral with the Caucasian."[19] The origins of peoples of the Indian subcontinent had long presented a problem for the endless project of dividing humanity into discrete biological categories. Only one of many such challenges, the question of whether Indians were Asian or Caucasian entered American legal history in the 1920s. Bhagat Singh Thind, an Asian Indian national, sought to overturn his inclusion in the category "Asian." Asians were under special restrictions in American immigration and citizenship policies. Thind had contended, as did Swinburne, that Asian Indians were Caucasian and thus white. In 1924 the Supreme Court rendered its decision in a marvelous example of the tortuous job of defining and manufacturing race, including whiteness. The Court ruled that scientifically speaking Thind was indeed Caucasian. But he was not "white." According to the Court, it was enough that Americans did not generally consider the darker-skinned Indians to be white, despite their scientific designation as Caucasian.[20] Whiteness, the Court ruled, was determined by the viewpoint of the average citizen and thus based on phenotype, or physical appearance. Undoubtedly Swinburne and Davis were aware of this finding and the impact it would have on any attempt he made to claim that George Jones was Indian and therefore white, rather than black. It is possible that the legal decision to acknowledge that Alice was not white was influenced in part by the *Thind* decision.

George Jones himself did have the opportunity to give his statement regarding his race and ancestry. In an affidavit filed at the Westchester County Courthouse on December 23, 1924, Jones swore that he did not actually know what his father's national or racial origin was:

> I have no relatives in this country and have not been in communication with any of my people abroad since my arrival here. My mother was a caucasian of pure English descent. The only information which I have about my father is that he was a native of one of the British Colonies.
>
> . . . I am informed by counsel for the defendant herein that the information which may be obtained from the registry of births, deaths and marriages in England will not be sufficient to establish the race of my father but that further investigations must [be] and are being made.[21]

Jones acknowledged that because he was able to give so little information, that investigation might be long and costly. In fact it was the searches for George's family records in England, as well as Leonard's continued absence, that had postponed the trial for nearly a year.

Was George Jones telling all he knew about his background? He was, of course, under oath in this sworn affidavit. But the wording was careful enough to suggest that he was hardly trying to provide any more information than was strictly necessary. In the midst of legal skirmishes over the payment of counsel fees just a few weeks before the trial's opening, Isaac Mills did accuse George of lying in this statement. Mills believed the family information George gave must be "untrue" because "investigations have revealed the fact that in the locality stated the defendant's father was never known, that is to say, no trace of him or of his alleged father or mother there could be ascertained." According to Mills, George had caused great expense for researchers, essentially leading them on a wild-goose chase, for which they should be reimbursed.[22]

The possibility that George's father was Indian received relatively little attention in the press, which continued to debate the question of Alice's racial identity primarily in terms of black and white. Perhaps this was in part because Asian racial identity was not as salient an issue on the East Coast at this time. But, more important, it seems highly suggestive that neither Elizabeth nor any of the Joneses ever publicly claimed or even mentioned India as the origins of George's darker skin. Certainly they had plenty of opportunity to do so, but even on those few occasions when they addressed the issue of racial identity, they did so only in terms of whether or not Alice and her father were black, white, mulatto, colored. George's sworn statement that his father was "a native of one of the British Colonies" certainly did not rule out India, but it was only Alice's lawyers who specifically suggested that George's nonwhite ancestry was Indian, not African.

And, in fact, the dominant theme from Alice's lawyers in this intervening year was not that she was part Indian at all: It was that she was legally white. And the most common argument was that she was white regardless of George's race. Although often evasive in answering reporters' questions about how this could be possible, Swinburne repeated on several occasions that "[u]nder the laws of the State of New York Mrs. Rhinelander is white because her mother is white."[23] Swinburne was no doubt referring to colonial laws under which the status of a child of mixed ancestry followed that of its mother. If the mother was enslaved, the child was enslaved regardless of the father's status. If she was free, the child was free, regardless of the father's status. In other words, the mulatto children of white mothers had a different legal status than the mulatto children of black mothers.[24]

The possibility that Alice could be legally white even though she had some distant "colored blood" did receive marked attention in the press. According to the *New York Times*, Alice's primary legal objective would be to prove that she was white because her mother was white.[25] *Chicago Defender* editor Roscoe Simmons, writing after this first round of affidavits was filed, commented:

> In the Rhinelander case the question presented is the quantity of African blood in the bride. We infer from what her attorneys say that they are prepared to prove, according to the uniform standard, that *she is unquestionably white, although she may have a few drops of African blood in her veins.*
>
> The interesting part is how and who can determine the exact proportion of the different bloods. Her mother is pure white, and as to her father—who knows? . . . Before this question is settled it may be necessary for the court to bring to its aid a number of scientific ethnologists; but since according to the Bible all races are made of one blood, we cannot see how these scientists can come to any definite conclusion.[26]

In this editorial the *Defender* disputed the one-drop rule as arbitrary, challenging the very idea of race itself. The black-published *Houston Informer* also pointed out that Alice was not the only "'light-colored' Negro" to be living as white. This situation had gotten "so 'balled and mussed up' that it is quite difficult for an expert ethnologist to draw the line or differentiate between members of the 'colored' and white races."[27]

Once the trial actually began, the black press continued to use the case to comment on the illogic of American ideas about race. One editorial pointed out that Kip and Alice "were about the same complexion," concluding "We call all persons white who are the color of Mrs. Rhinelander." But "white" was often used as a description of a person regardless of his or her race, which would be "Negro," "White," or "Caucasian." Hence the term "white Negro."[28] A few weeks later the *Defender* told readers to ignore Alice and the Rhinelander Case. It had nothing to do with the black community, editor Simmons argued, because Alice Rhinelander was not black, having claimed to be white. In other words, if she didn't want to be black, she wasn't.[29] Similarly the *Richmond Planet,* in an editorial on the Rhinelander Case, charged that "Negro whites" who want to be white should be. "We don't want them" in the race.[30] She was white because she looked white. She was white because she identified herself as white. She might as well be white because the whole idea of race was unfounded anyway.

The press's coverage of the question of Alice's race prior to the trial also commented on the moral implications of her supposed racial transgressions. The *Richmond News Leader* lectured that Alice should have realized her husband would be "repulsed" upon learning of her "negro blood," and that the secret would get out eventually. They also suggested that she should be pitied as well as condemned, "for she has glimpsed a world she may not enter, and if she has sensibilities, she has been turned back with memories that will taunt her to the end of her days."[31] Several black-published papers also printed similar editorials, condemning Alice for trying to hide her racial ancestry. William Pickens, a former college instructor, field secretary for the NAACP, and author, wrote a commentary on "The Taint" about "the boo-hooing of sapheads and idiots who are easily frightened into asserting: 'I ain't colored!'" when "'accused' of being a Negro." Like other black authors, however, Pickens used the example of Alice to remind readers how many "white" Americans were actually colored by U.S. standards, their ancestors "forced by racism to cross the line."[32]

LEONARD'S REVISED CHARGES also suggest that his lawyers feared the defense that Alice might be "unquestionably white" despite her "few drops of African blood." Filed after Davis's announcement, the amended complaint elaborated the charge regarding Alice's racial status into three separate charges: that Alice "was colored and with colored blood," that Alice "had colored blood in her veins," and that Alice "was not entirely of white blood and ancestry."[33] In offering so many definitions, his attorneys may have sought to avoid the necessity of scientific testimony as to Alice's specific racial classification, or to "the quantity of African blood." They may also have noticed the continued slipperiness of Alice's racial claims, which had not been laid to rest with Davis's confession that she was colored.

In some important ways, then, Davis had closed the question of what Alice's race was. Certainly he had answered the question of what her legal argument would be regarding her race. And certainly the white press no longer questioned whether Alice was black. But in refusing to make her race a contested issue, and in the careful wording in his admission, Davis allowed some of the ambiguities of Alice's racial status to remain. These ambiguities would return to play an important role in the outcome of the trial.

In the meantime, the testimony of the assembled cast of witnesses, featuring Leonard Kip Rhinelander himself, promised far more juicy details about Alice and Leonard's affair and marriage. The opening statements were only the outlines of what was to come. They promised sensation, and they would deliver. Alice and Leonard were in for a difficult week; American readers were in for a vicarious melodrama.

6

JUST A COMMONPLACE

LOVE AFFAIR

 THROUGHOUT THE OPENING day and a half of the trial, the main actors in the Rhinelander Case had all assembled but sat silently. During the jury selection, the wait for Leonard's delayed arrival, and the dynamic opening statements, the responses of these central characters could only be inferred from body language and facial expressions, or lack thereof. Now upcoming testimony promised to introduce some new faces and expose those who had previously eluded the public gaze. And the most dominant figure for the first week of the trial would be the reclusive Leonard Kip Rhinelander: Alice wasn't the only one who had waited a year to see her vanished groom. She and her family had emerged from time to time since her marriage made headlines, usually to give interviews or chase off reporters. Leonard, however, had completely disappeared from public view. In 1924, his had been the familiar name, if only by virtue of his family connections, while she was a cipher. By the time of the trial the situation had become oddly reversed. Although both were now household names, it was she who was the more familiar figure while he was the relative unknown quantity. Everyone knew her version of their separation: They had been deeply in love and only the influence if not physical force of his father could have taken him from her. What would his story be? Would he support the claims of his lawyers that he had been duped by a vamp? Or would his love for Alice overcome the pressures of family and name?

The anticipation ended when Leonard, his light brown hair slicked back, took his seat on the witness stand. Adorned in his trademark tortoise-rimmed eyeglasses and dressed in a brown suit, handkerchief in left pocket, black patent leather shoes and gray spats, the well-heeled young man settled uneasily into his chair. His eyes blinked anxiously from behind the glasses as Alice and others in the courtroom fixed their gaze on him. He struck all that watched as nervous and unsure of himself.[1] But as soon as his lawyer started his examination, it was clear that Leonard was not quite the feebleminded youth portrayed in Mills's opening argument. He commanded an impressive recall of events and dates, as well as of the couple's developing intimacies and terms of endearment. Over the course of the next few days he revealed that his relationship with Alice had been commonplace in one important sense: Like others before him, Leonard had simply met a woman unlike any he had known before and fallen in love with her. While talk of color, class, sexuality, and race had grabbed headlines nationwide, those courtroom watchers straining in their seats for a better view witnessed in splendid detail the joys and travails of a love affair. For it was the nature and details of Alice and Leonard's romance that consumed the lawyers' attention in the first week of this case. It was their love that was on trial.

ON THE AFTERNOON of November 10, after a late-morning recess following Davis's opening statements, Isaac Mills called the first witness for the plaintiff: Dr. L. Pierce Clark. Clark had attended Leonard at the Orchard School, an exclusive inpatient clinic for nervous disorders in Stamford, Connecticut. With this testimony the experienced counsel tried to establish the limits of Leonard's faculties at the time he met Alice. After confirming that Philip Rhinelander had sent his son there in search of a cure for stammering and shyness, Mills asked the doctor for his medical diagnosis of the young man. Initially Clark confirmed Mills's assessment: "The main difficulty was his speech, his stammering. In addition to this, I found his trouble was based on a great sense of inferiority and incomplete mental development of judgment, memory and the power of attention."[2]

Yet the medical reports recovered for the trial show that Clark
didn't end his assessment there. He kept close tabs on Leonard
throughout his stay and kept copious notes recording the young
man's progress. Despite reports that Leonard "shows a lack of [under-
standing of] everyday affairs" or that "the patient can form no mental
pictures of what he wants to say," he did in fact make progress. In an
interesting revelation that Davis singled out, even Clark noted that
Leonard's verbal difficulties abated after he met Alice. The doctor
recorded that Leonard had "met some young girls on the street yesterday and talked well without stuttering. He talks well on the telephone
in the evening and when given freedom does well with his friends."
Clark went on to note that Leonard seemed especially fond of talking
with one girl in particular and had frequently absented himself from
affairs at the Orchard to be in her company. That girl, of course, was
Alice Jones.[3]

The highlight of the day was Leonard's testimony, but Mills also
called two other witnesses. The first was Joseph J. Strong, notary public and acting secretary to State Supreme Court Justice Fawcett of
Brooklyn and the man who had picked Leonard up from the Rich residence and served Alice with the annulment papers a week later.
Despite the insistence of Alice's attorney, Strong vehemently denied
working for Philip Rhinelander, Leonard's father, or of trying to persuade Leonard to end his relationship with Alice. Strong did confess
that he had worked for Rhinelander family lawyer Leon Jacobs, and
that he had visited the couple a week before delivering the annulment
papers. The purpose of this questioning was to establish that Leonard
had not been held against his will and that Philip was not the force
behind the suit.

And later in the day, Leonard's testimony was interrupted by that of
one Julia Despres, a former governess for Leonard's sister, Adelaide. In
her testimony Mrs. Despres recalled that, despite her valiant attempts,
the young man failed to master the French language. Both witnesses
aided Mills's strategy of portraying a helpless, perhaps mentally deficient, yet wealthy young man preyed upon by the worldly Alice
Beatrice Jones.

At exactly 2:30 P.M. Leonard was sworn in. "Are you the plaintiff in
this action?" he was asked. "I am," he replied. "Your age at the present
time?" Mills inquired. "Twenty-two," the young man answered. The

youthful aristocrat settled into the witness chair, glanced furtively around the room, and prepared himself for what followed. Over the next few days as Leonard testified, the mixed crowd of onlookers who jammed the courtroom were treated to a detailed and conflicted outline of how he and Alice had met, become involved, and eventually married. Over objections and legal squabbling, the nation would hear and read dozens of letters written between the two, documenting their developing relationship between 1921 and 1924. Throughout his narrative, guided alternately by Mills and Davis, the lawyers read from the more than four hundred letters they had collected from their respective clients.

Mills began his questioning with a focus on the Orchard School facility, reminding listeners of Leonard's problems by having his client repeat the information already provided by Dr. Clark. During this opening salvo Mills tried at every turn to present Leonard as mentally lacking. He clearly sought to portray a sympathetic, somewhat innocent lad, who quickly became derailed because a woman had taken an interest in him. Since neither the jury nor the witnessing public knew Leonard, save for his famous name and claims to wealth, the deft old lawyer realized that this was his chance to support his image of the young man for them. Thus he started the examination of Leonard with this reminder of Leonard's deficiencies.

To some extent Leonard did fulfill Mills's portrayal of him. He did stutter, a behavior that most Americans associated with nervousness. One Des Moines, Iowa, editorial described him as "[s]tuttering like a big horse fly caught on sticky fly paper."[4] Several papers devoted entire articles to his apparent flaws. The New York Daily Mirror highlighted "Defects of Youth Listed by Doctor," including an inferiority complex, stammering, and being "tongue-tied." And the New Rochelle Standard Star provided readers with a phrenological reading of Leonard's character weaknesses from his facial features and structures. This diagram pointed out how the physical measurements, angles, and placement of Leonard's facial and cranial features revealed his inner characteristics. Like the theories of race and racial differences outlined in chapter 2, this analysis reflected a commonly held belief that physical attributes determined behavior, character, and intelligence. Here Leonard's thin lips were read as showing his lack of assertiveness and dignity; the cleft in his chin, desire for approval; the shape of his head, vacillation. These physical traits, in other words, revealed "the currents of action that brought about the hectic events of his recent life" as well as what might be expected in his future.[5] In other words, by the time he came to the topic of Alice, Mills seemed to have successfully made his point: Though wealthy, Leonard had clear limitations, presumably the kind that would limit his attractiveness to most women. As the *Reno Evening Gazette* noted: "Even a very, very rich young man, with the proudest blood of the Huguenots in his veins, can acquire an 'inferiority complex.'"[6]

Next the seasoned lawyer turned to the moment the young man first encountered a member of the Jones family. Leonard explained that he first met Grace, Alice's older sister, in early September 1921. It was a clear, warm early autumn day in the quiet suburbs of New York City. Leonard, then eighteen years old, was out for a drive with a new acquaintance, Carl Kreitler, who worked as an electrician at the Orchard School. Carl was considerably older than Leonard and married. Nevertheless, as Leonard later recalled, Carl's marriage did not stop him from pursuing other women, and in this art he was apparently tutoring the sheltered and inexperienced Leonard.

On this particular day the two men and another friend of Carl's were out motoring in Leonard's new car, a recent gift from his father. A new car, beautiful weather, pretty scenery, nothing else to do—what better way to spend such a day? They drove the twenty miles from Stamford, Connecticut, to Westchester County, New York, following the northern shore of Long Island Sound until they reached a stretch of road between New Rochelle and Pelham Manor that boasted a gas station and a small eatery—and a young woman by the name of Grace Marie Jones who lived nearby. "We had trouble on the road with the car," Leonard recalled, "and Grace hailed us on the sidewalk and asked us what was the trouble and Carl got out and went over to her." Grace had apparently also been spending a leisurely afternoon looking for something to do, for she joined the group for a while, introducing herself simply as Marie.

With his hands betraying his anxiety, moving from knees to a strained clasp to knees again, Leonard spoke haltingly from the witness stand, often pausing with visible difficulty in formulating his memories. Prompted by his lawyer, he continued his labored tale.

The four young people drove around into the evening. They then split up for a while, Grace and Carl going for a drive together and Leonard and the third man stopping for something to eat. Afterwards the threesome drove Grace back to the block where they had met her, near her home. This was, according to Leonard, his first experience "picking up girls."[7]

Grace and Carl made plans to meet a few days later, but Carl sent Leonard instead to make apologies for him. Did it strike Leonard as curious that Carl, a married man, had agreed to meet Grace in the first place? Exactly how naive he was was yet unclear. Yet there was something about the chance encounter that the eighteen-year-old found intriguing enough to repeat. Whether out of sexual curiosity, adolescent high jinks, the thrill of a new adventure, or some combination, Leonard consented to be Carl's messenger.

Leonard explained to the packed courtroom how he retraced his path along the shore drive. Before too long he saw Grace very near the spot where he and the others had met her a few nights before. "I was traveling along and Grace, walking on Pelham Road, called me over," he told the court. The two began a conversation about Carl's absence, with the young man telling Grace of Carl's unavailability. "I was telling Grace about Carl and Alice walked up," he continued. "Grace introduced me to Alice and I suggested a ride." The sisters accepted the invitation, with Grace immediately suggesting that they pick up another fellow, making it a more balanced foursome then their previous outing.[8]

Leonard's recounting of events revealed that he was hardly a completely passive player in meeting Alice. He could have easily declined Carl's request for help. He certainly didn't need to drive the sisters and one of their companions around town. While Mills tried to conjure up images of dangerous women lurking on street corners, Leonard's words betrayed another likelihood: He was attracted to the sisters and wanted to impress them. Perhaps unable to do so with words alone, his shyness and lack of experience were offset by the material marks of his wealth: a new car and money for gifts and entertainment.

The quartet made its way to Mount Vernon, a short drive from New Rochelle, and took in a movie at the Proctor Theater. Afterward he returned the girls and their male friend to their home, leaving without approaching the house. On that second meeting Leonard gave Grace a ring, but she soon gave it back at her mother's urging—she was already engaged to marry. By that time the young man's attentions seemed to have turned to Alice anyway, and she soon wore the same ring.

In fact, only three days after meeting Alice, he returned to New Rochelle, this time looking for her, not Grace. Leonard explained that he had received a postcard from Alice, asking him to visit. But when Davis demanded to see the actual postcard neither Leonard nor his attorneys could produce it. Davis used the opening to raise doubts in the minds of all about the actual existence of the postcard: "I believe that Rhinelander went there without an invitation," he sternly informed the court.[9]

After the interruption Leonard continued his soliloquy. On that third visit he called on Alice at her home and met her mother, Elizabeth. He thought Grace was there as well, but clearly she was not the object of his attentions. He stayed for a few hours, sometimes in the presence of Grace or her mother, sometimes not. At one point he and Alice took a ride around the town for about an hour. The two apparently hit it off immediately, for at her invitation he returned the next evening and the next, and again a few days later.[10] Soon after their introduction, then, Alice and Leonard were seeing each other steadily, usually in her parents' home or in the company of other young people. In those first months, as the courtship heated up, Leonard delighted in spending long evenings with Alice. In response to one of Mills's questions, he noted that he often returned to the Orchard well after midnight.[11]

Between meetings they exchanged brief letters that, many having been read into the court record, remain to document their growing attachment to each other. Telephones became increasingly common throughout the 1920s but had not yet replaced letters as the primary method of communication. Today few of the day-to-day concerns of a romantic relationship would survive in the form of written letters. But this couple, separated by only an hour's drive, wrote often and used the telephone sparingly.[12] Barely two weeks after their first meeting, for example, Leonard wrote to apologize for missing a date Alice had proposed in writing.

Most of the first day of testimony centered on the letters Alice wrote Leonard. Over the course of the trial Leonard's letters were highlighted as well. As evinced by the ones he crafted in the early days of their romance, he pursued her as vigorously as she pursued him. In one of his earliest letters, written only a week or so after they first met, Leonard suggested new plans and asked her to confirm them by phone.

Sept. 28, 1921

My dear Alice,

Your postal has just reached me this minute and I cannot tell you how glad I am to hear from you and to know that you have not forgotten me. You, no doubt, will think that I purposely "stood you up" last night, but I swear I couldn't help it or else I surely would have been there. Your postal which you sent Monday afternoon did not arrive here until this morning, so you see I didn't know anything about the date. I hope, dear, you will forgive me as it was really not my fault. Last Friday when I left your Mother's and on my way to Stamford, I ran into a motorcycle cop. I immediately took him to the hospital and saw that he was made comfortable.

If it is convenient for you, I will see you at your Mother's Friday Sept 30th or Sat Oct 1st. However, don't forget to ring me up and tell me which night. Well, dearest, I must close and go down to mail this to you.

Much love,
Leonard.

P.S. I know you are taking good care of my ring and pin. I am glad you have them no matter how much I miss them.[13]

Clearly this method had its disadvantages, particularly in the first weeks of their relationship. Other letters between the two mentioned missed meetings and confused dates, as well as difficulties with Leonard's car—possibly a result of the accident with the motorcycle cop. At the same time, within three weeks of their friendship, Leonard was already calling her "dearest," closing with "much love" and had given her a pin in addition to the ring.

There were still problems, however. Leonard questioned the depth of Alice's commitment to him, and perhaps more important, wondered if she took him for granted. In October he complained about coming down and finding her not at home.

Do you think it's quite fair when I take all the trouble to come down to see you and then find you out? I wonder if you still care for me, or, as a matter of fact, ever did? Don't think, dear, that I am angry with you but just a little upset. You can't blame me, can you? . . .

Perhaps if you really want me to come down Monday night I will do so. Only, dear, if you promise faithfully that you will be there. This short letter is just to tell you how disappointed I was last night when you did not show up and I hope it will never happen again.[14]

Leonard closed by asking her to write and phone, reminding her of his phone number at Stamford.

At this point theirs had all of the features of an average romance: worries about faithfulness, commitment, and exclusivity punctuated by the showering of gifts and the exchange of endearments. But these letters of day-to-day events and a developing mutual closeness between the couple were not the ones Mills chose to focus on in his questioning. Instead he submitted as evidence a cache of letters written by Alice to Leonard—private thoughts, spirited in tone, but obviously intended as words shared between lovers, not for public display. Even these did not always support the impression of the manipulative temptress Mills hoped to cultivate in the jurors' imaginations. Still, he might convince some that her letters were not true expressions of love but written as ploys, tools of manipulation and seduction. Was her interest more in the money or the man?

Alice's earliest letters were short, simple affairs that mirrored Leonard's in focusing on daily events and gentle expressions of affection. In the earliest one available, penned about six weeks into their relationship, Alice invited Leonard to visit that coming Saturday and suggested a ride up the coast to Stamford:

Oct. 27, 1921

Dearest Leonard:

Received your welcome letter and very glad to hear from you.

But awful soary you got home so late, dear. Well how are you[?] Carl called me up, and he asked me how I were. But listen, you come down Thursday eve and I shall go to Stamford with you. Well dear, you must of been very busy shopping.

I only wished I had been with you. I bet you had some sport. Well, dear, I hope you are well and hope to hear from you real soon.

Love,
ALICE[15]

As most observers pointed out, some with sympathy, others with disdain, Alice's spelling and grammar reflected her limited education.

Not surprisingly these early notes gave little indication of deep emotions or long-term intentions. But over the next few months, the couple's developing attachment was clearly reflected in their correspondence. In a letter written only a week later, Alice professed her love for Leonard in several different ways: mentioning his "sweet letter" and her willingness to retire early to save her energy for him and their pending date. She wrote that he had been "lovely to me, just like a sister," and that she was forgoing a dance and an invitation to Hartford in order to be "true to you." At the same time she insinuated that she was a woman with the ability to go out alone and have fun, to perhaps pursue others and be pursued. No doubt she sought to woo Leonard, but her words suggest that in their private exchanges, Leonard also pursued and sought to woo her.[16]

This "sisterly" affection lasted only a few more weeks. In a letter dated November 17, Alice recalled the nice time she had had with her new beau and hinted at the sexual nature of that date. Like many of their contemporaries the couple had progressed to petting and kissing by November, and both habitually referred to these caresses in loving and teasing passages in their letters to each other. The presentation of this letter in particular led Judge Morschauser to clear the courtroom of all women, since he deemed the contents inappropriate for them. The reading of the letters and the judge's actions sparked a strong rebuke from Alice's lawyer, who worried that the entire drama might prejudice the jury against his client. Nonetheless the judge allowed this and the other letters to be entered as evidence, prompting Davis's steadfast objections at each submission.

Thursday.
(Nov. 17, 1921)

Dearest Lenard,

I am sitting down for a few minutes, to write you a few lines, what I promised you dear. Well sweet heart how did you get home, after such a wild excitement with me. But I would love Leonard to be with you day and night, but I feel terrible lonesome for you, when I do not see you, and to think I cant see you every night any more, as often what I am doing to do in the evening alone, no one hear But father and mother, And my self, and most of the time, I am hear alone, when I do not see you. But you will after give me Len, one of your picture, because thats what I want in my room, and I no that you want me to think a great deal of you. Listen Lenard, I have had some sweet hearts, but I have not loved them, like I have taken to you so. I have never let a fellow love and carress me, the way you do Lenard, because you make me feel so happy, and loyable toward you dear. But would it be awful if you had me my self alone. What you would not do to me. I can imagine.

> *Good bye Dearie,*
> *Love Best Wishes,*
> ALICE[17]

On the witness stand Leonard tried to explain the "wild excitement" mentioned by Alice. "I believe that was an evening that Alice and I and Carl and someone named Kitty Walton went to a café. We had

A magazine cutout that Alice sent Leonard
with her own message.

several drinks and we began feeling rather frisky and Carl took us back to Alice's home."[18] At Mills's instigation, Leonard identified this Kitty Walton as "an intimate friend of Alice's" who was white.[19] More inflammatory was Alice's sexual teasing about what Leonard could do if they were alone—which no doubt they were on other occasions.

Another typical letter read into the court record on the second day of testimony:

> 763 Pelham Road.
> New Rochelle.
> Friday 9th. 1921

My Own, Dearest Lenard:

Just think of me, this evening being hear alone, mother and father and sister Emily, and hear husband, as gone to the Westchester. . . . And I am hear alone, thinking of you, dear heart. I said to myself when they were going out, of the front door. I only wished Lenard was coming down this evening. How I could carress, you dear. Because you no you love for me to carress you dear. But my heart, feels very lonesome, this Eve. But what can I do dear because you are so far from my sweet heart.

Each day seems to get more lonesome. But Lenard I feel terrible lonesome for you dear and you no it.

But Lenard dear, at times you make me happy—I hope Len you arrived, home safe last evening and also made your train, dear heart after when I went home. I went to bed, and stayed in my room, until five minutes to twelve, and got in bed, at twenty-five after I hopped in bed, and layed there, thinking of you dear heart.

At this minuet I am thinking I am looking in your blue eyes.

So Good night, Lenard dear sweet-heart Sweet Kisses, Honey Bunch,

> *Love,*
> ALICE.[20]

Interestingly, another paper published a slightly different version of the same letter, including an extended description of Alice alone in her bedroom getting ready for bed and listening to music, thinking about Leonard doing the same in his room. "Can you imagine me, being hear alone, what I would never do before. Well dear, I will try and forget, about it, and I will live, in hopes, to see you early Saturday, dear heart."[21] It was quite common for newspapers to print only selections of the letters, omitting phrases they thought might be too explicitly, or in this case too implicitly, sexual.

More than anything the second day revealed that Alice was not simply a manipulative, gold-digging vamp. Even the *New York Times,* which constantly referred to her as a "Negress," acknowledged that Alice cared for Leonard. Her letters showed that she prayed for his well-being and counseled him to take care of himself and not to squander his money on frivolous things. While the cynical may have attributed the latter advice to a woman well aware of what she stood to gain if Leonard had means, it is just as likely that the working-class Alice understood the value of a day's labor and careful financial planning, and wished to share this with her wealthy boyfriend. "No one who heard today's recitals," insisted the *Daily News,* now had "any doubt of the genuine affection which flourished between the two."[22] And the *Detroit Times* suggested that the reading of Alice's letters might be backfiring on Mills by building "a great deal of sympathy for the wife among the auditors," including, presumably, the jury.[23] Some even hoped that now the two would end their separation before the eyes of the world. The setting would have been perfect for a dramatic happy ending. As the letters were read, women in the courtroom were sobbing, Alice's face was buried in her hands and handkerchief, and Leonard, according to at least one observer, "looked as though he was about to fly from his high perch . . . and gather his broken (up?) bride into his arms."[24]

Not all were so moved by her letters, however. Her writing style alone brought dismissive scorn from many newspapers. The letters revealed Alice, who had had only an eighth-grade education, to be a poor speller, indifferent to or unaware of certain conventions of grammar and syntax in standard American English. The *San Francisco Chronicle* dubbed her letters "illiterate and crude," while the *Detroit Times* called them "pitiful little mis-spelled letters" whose publication could only be an embarrassment to all involved. Several papers provided lists of her habitual misspellings and other writing errors, including "after" for "have to," "soary" for "sorry," and "latter" for "later."[25]

Her inclusion of poems and song lyrics in some of the letters inspired a variety of responses. Some of her poems apparently prompted gales of laughter from the courtroom audience.[26] On the other hand, the *New York Times*, perhaps looking for further "evidence" of her black ancestry, praised them with a rather backhanded compliment. Her poetry, it reported, had "a natural negro rhythm that was so superior to her ordinary forms of expression that it seemed as if she must have copied the lines from a popular song." Actually she may have. Several other papers noted that a few of her verses bore a marked resemblance to well-known songs.[27]

Nor did Leonard's writing escape criticism; his own attempts at romantic verse received little praise. And when a school paper submission resurfaced, there were more than a few harsh judgments on his decision to rhyme "farmer" with "mama"

> Old man Hutch, the sweet-pea farmer,
> Regularly meets his music mama;
> Practices diligently all the time,
> To equal and rival friend Rubenstein.
>
> He is an incubator fan of the rarest sort,
> He hatches chickens and calls it sport;
> Dirty old Dinty with his kinky rope,
> He's got ambition, but there is not much hope.

And, as the *Des Moines Register* pointed out, both Leonard and Alice ought to have realized by this point "how silly love letters can sound when read in court." (Of course the decision to air the letters in court rested with their attorneys and not solely with them.)[28]

But beyond these critiques there was little in the letters that titillated readers or condemned Alice. The "immoral inquisitiveness of the feminine crowd that stormed the court doors for hours in an attempt to hear the revelations [sic] of the miscegenous romance" went largely unsatisfied.[29] As a *New York Times* writer editorialized, "[N]one of the [letters] was of the lurid sort which the spectators had anticipated."[30] But there was more to come.

AFTER MILLS'S SELECTED reading of several of Alice's November letters, Leonard realized he was about to move into more treacherous territory. He knew what had happened in December. Sure enough, Mills soon began a new line of questioning: the Marie Antoinette Hotel. Leonard steadfastly maintained that his relationship with Alice had remained appropriately chaste in the first four months—that is, from early September 1921 until December 23, 1921. Then, two days before Christmas, the couple set out for New York City and a show. According to Leonard, on the way into the city Alice informed him that she planned to spend the night at the Marie Antoinette Hotel rather than make a late trip back to the suburbs. Mills asked his client, "Had anything been said before about staying there?" Leonard answered, "No, I expected to take her back to her home."

With his next questions Mills inched closer to his underlying contention that Alice had corrupted poor Leonard: "What happened after that?" After all, once Alice had admitted the possibility of some colored blood, Mills had to show a pattern of deception and connivance if he hoped to prevail. Raising questions about Alice's morality was one way to accomplish this goal. Although Leonard's recounting of the events was characterized as "expressionless and broken," what he had to say caused quite a stir. From the start he proved a troublesome witness even for his own seasoned advocate. Instead of painting Mills's portrait with the fine strokes of corroborating detail, he confessed, "I asked her if I might accompany her there." He further implicated himself in the events that followed when he admitted that he registered them as "Mr. and Mrs. James Smith from Rye, N.Y." "Did you sign the register yourself?" the old judge inquired. "I did," came the reply. The pair went out briefly, the young Rhinelander told the court, and returned to the well-appointed room with its own bath that evening. Unable to tear themselves away from this new privacy and freedom, the love-struck couple spent a week together at the hotel, excluding Leonard's brief absence to attend an annual Rhinelander Christmas party.[31]

Here, finally, was true scandal. Premarital sex was certainly not unknown in the 1920s. But the open admission and publication of details was nothing short of sensationalism. Accordingly, interest in the trial grew overnight, fueled by unparalleled media coverage. The next day the doors of the court opened three-quarters of an hour ahead of schedule to satisfy the growing swell of court watchers. The gathering crowd had grown restless during the wait and tried to force its way into the court. These efforts were stymied, but a decision was reached to let the interracial and intergenerational assemblage into the room early to avoid further trouble.

· · · ·

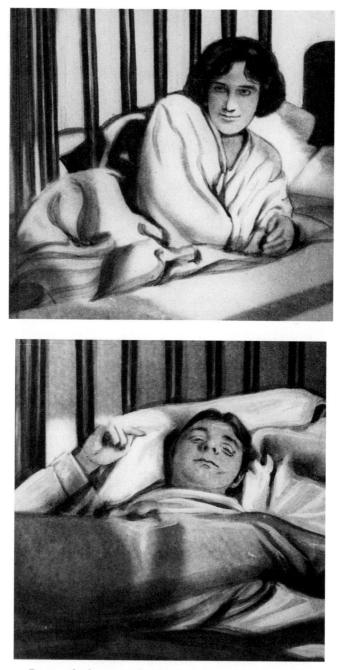

*Personal photographs taken by Leonard and Alice
at Marie Antoinette Hotel, c. 1921.
(Note the heavy shading and outlining added by newspapers.)*

ATTITUDES ABOUT SEXUALITY underwent a marked transformation between 1900 and 1920. Throughout the late nineteenth century, reformers and nationalists vilified the many millions of working-class immigrants for their supposedly lax sexual behavior, even attacking familial patterns of taking in boarders and lodgers. Some warned that such behavior encouraged promiscuity and other vices. By the 1920s, however, many middle-class families had relaxed their expressed attitudes about sexuality. Foundations such as the Milbank Fund began to study the sexual habits of Americans. Early surveys showed that women who came of age in the first decades of the twentieth century were two to three times as likely to have engaged in premarital intercourse as those who came of age in the Victorian period. In fact between 1900 and 1920 more Americans approved of divorce, birth control, and premarital sex than had previously. At the same time many Americans held firm to a Victorian sensibility about sexuality and propriety; birth control was still illegal in many states.[32] Nonetheless the Rhinelander Case occurred in a period of measurable societal change.

This shift was exemplified not only in the generation gap between opposing counsels but in public perceptions of the early courtship between Leonard and Alice: Patterns of dating and intergender socializing had changed. It was not an unusual event in 1921 for young men and women to meet and hang out in public areas. The historian Kathy Peiss has documented this movement in the focus and location of working-class leisure activities. Organized in the nineteenth century around male-only or family-dominated functions, by the 1920s young people's social activities centered around heterosexual groups and pairings. Many working-class American-born daughters of European immigrants were unable to earn a living wage despite working full-time, and most lived with their families or relatives before marrying, as did the Jones sisters. Even then, working-class single women had to scrimp and economize to afford recreation, using such strategies as skipping meals or relying on single men for financial assistance and gifts. Women's wages never compared to men's wages. The custom of "treating," then, developed as an early form of modern dating. Single men and women might spend time together without necessarily being interested in marriage, and men were expected to treat, or pay for the ticket and any accompanying expenses of the women. Men might also pay for or contribute to the cost of clothing, accessories, or other personal items.[33]

In this changing social milieu many reformers fretted that it was becoming difficult to tell prostitutes from respectable women. Public streets, theaters, and parks played a new role in urban areas as settings for these new patterns of socializing.[34] Where clothing and behavior had once been clear markers between the classes, these divisions were fading too. Working-class women were dressing with greater freedom than they had before, mimicking both upper-class ladies' and prostitutes' fashion. They were also moving into public spaces—streets, theaters, dance halls, and youth clubs—spaces previously reserved for male-only or family-oriented activities. The accompanying concerns over the sexual dangers posed to single young women were heightened by the changes in their behavior and attitudes, reflecting modern challenges to Victorian culture. Shorter hair, higher hems, smoking, dancing—middle- and working-class gender roles were shifting. It would not be surprising, then, that Mills would interpret the presence of Grace and Alice Jones on a public sidewalk and their subsequent meeting with Leonard and Carl as suspect behavior. Nor was it unusual for the young people and many onlookers to consider their behavior quite normal and innocent fun.

Once Leonard's testimony regarding their hotel stay emerged, however, the young couple's behavior was less easily seen as innocent. And even in such a relatively fluid, open time, it was still a humiliation for Leonard to be forced to discuss explicit sexual matters, and for Alice to be forced to listen to her sexual behavior exposed before the world. With Alice's eyes fixed on his every movement, Leonard struggled to explain the most intimate of details about their relationship. Alice's erect bearing gave way during some of the testimony, as she fought an internal fight to maintain her dignity. Observers noted tears in her eyes as she bowed her head during Kip's accounting of that first evening at the hotel. Yet even the most casual observer would have understood what had transpired on the two stays at the hotel. Shielded by the excitement of assumed identities and protected by the security of Rhinelander wealth, they stole away from the social taboos of race, class, and sexual behavior. And although this opportunity for physical and emotional intimacy would be short-lived, it would continue to represent not only their sexual fulfillment but the deepening of their love and commitment to each other.

Only the arrival of a Rhinelander retainer ended their stays at the

Antoinette. Leonard's father eventually learned of his son's dalliances with Alice and sent his longtime friend and attorney from the firm of Bowers and Gerard to retrieve the lad. Mr. Bowers did as instructed, taking the young man to the Belmont Hotel in New York City for three days. Thereafter an associate of Bowers took him to Atlantic City for several days. The senior Rhinelander clearly wanted his son to end his untoward romance. Whether Philip had been fully apprised of Alice's background is not clear. However, his disapproval of his son's behavior was clear. Leonard recalled that the chain of events ended his stay at the Orchard School, and for the next few years his father repeatedly sent him away from New Rochelle, to Cuba, California, Arizona.

Yet the forced separation from Alice did not end his attachment to her. After a couple of weeks in New Jersey, for example, he learned Alice was sick and visited her in New Rochelle. He told the court, "I returned to New York because of a letter from Alice stating she was very ill. I had been there, at the Traymore in Atlantic City, ten days when I received her telegram. Mr. Bowers came back to New York with me." Leonard then made it clear that he "went to see Alice."[35] After their stay at the hotel, their letters became more explicit as they tried to maintain their emotional and physical connection over distance and, eventually, time apart.

The next day began with another set of Alice's love letters read into the record, after initial anxiety that some had been stolen. Lawyers on both sides had wondered what had happened to nearly fifty-five letters written by Alice to Leonard. Just before the session adjourned the previous day Davis told Mills to check his associate's office for the missing letters. After leaving the court he did just that. Co-counsel Jacobs found the letters intermixed with other papers. Their whereabouts determined, the court returned to the business at hand: Leonard's charge of fraud.

Typical was another letter read into the court record that second day of testimony:

Thursday 29, 1922 9:15 p. m.

I would do any think you asked me dearest for you, whatever you ask me.

I just love to have you. I just adore that. As I feel this way. Your there. And I cant do nothing else, but do it for you. Len do you remember in old Marie Antoinette the good times we have had and now look how we after suffer for it. Do you remember how you loved to chase me around.

Well dearie. I still keep my diary, and I write in it every day I destroyed the sheets in my book, what happened in Dec. and January. I will never forget that. That is when I was happy. But I shall never be happy again until I can be with you again. A many a night, I feel as though I want you badly but what can I do. but never mind dearie I shall wait, there is always a time for every thing.[36]

Alice's letter highlighted what social analysts and psychoanalysts were just coming to terms with—namely, the existence of female sexuality. Alice's choice references to caresses once given revealed her as a sexual being. At the same time, however, Alice's letters demonstrated, in plain, unschooled language, her profound attachment to the man she called Len. Though she and many of her contemporaries may have dated and engaged in premarital sexual relations, Victorian conventions had not completely disappeared. Moreover, the late nineteenth and early twentieth centuries still traded on notions of respectability and delicate female behavior. Alice's blunt, sensual language stood in sharp contrast to much that was printed, save for some of D. H. Lawrence's novels. Most likely in a bid for readership, even some of the most respected dailies did little to hide the erotic nature of some of the letters. Others did try to avoid the sexual references and severely chastised their less restrained colleagues. Even the tabloids sometimes drew the line at printing certain passages. But it was not until much later in the trial that letters would surface that courted obscenity charges because of their sexually explicit content.

Although the cumulative effect of the letters was mounting sympathy for Alice in some quarters, her lawyer understood that her reputation and character were under attack. Davis objected strenuously to further notes that revealed his client's most private and intimate thoughts. He understood all too well the implications for the jury and the throngs who gathered outside the White Plains building, clamoring for admission to the courtroom.

Leonard himself began to look distressed as more and more of Alice's private words and thoughts became public. He gave every appearance of a man who hated his role in exposing the woman he had loved to such humiliation. Viewers sensed that he ached inside, and had he had the power, would have announced that he hated to do this. Contrition alone would not be enough. Mills sought to use Alice's own words to indict her and her motives for loving Leonard. Letters revealed an affair of the heart that grew and deepened relatively quickly. One reporter editorialized, "As the afternoon wore on . . . the consistency and heart-longing of the writer became apparent. . . . [A]s the narration progressed one felt more inclined to pity the simple girl who put them on paper than to censure her."[37]

On his second day on the stand other details of their romance came to light. At one moment in the trial Mills asked his client, "Did you intend to marry her?" Leonard answered this question with a firm "I did." "Did you love her?" his lawyer continued. Again answering in the past tense, he professed his love. The exchange confounded those court watchers hoping to gain a glimpse of Leonard's current affections toward his wife. After nearly a day on the stand it was clear he had little taste for the public spotlight. And he refused to look Alice's way, perhaps out of deference, or sadness, about their shared humiliation. Perhaps his affections had grown distant and his love had moved into the past over the intervening year.

Just prior to quizzing the young Rhinelander about his bride's racial background, Mills had to have sensed a change in mood in the courtroom. Many had snickered at the reading of Alice's first letters. Her closings sounded trite and a little too gushing; her words of endearment a little too rehearsed and pleading. But as the letters mounted and details of the couple's determination to stay together increased, snickers gave way to tears. Even those who had sneered, remarked one reporter, no longer questioned the sincerity of their mutual love. The simple girl's charms made her likable, and the whole affair a tragic tale of love lost.

On one critical point, however, Leonard neither wavered nor altered his gaze. He continued to maintain, as he had since filing suit, that he had thought Alice white. Mills provided the opening for Leonard to discuss race. "Was there any talk at any time before your marriage of the question of color?" The young Rhinelander answered, "There was."

Leonard then elaborated. "Between May and December, 1924, in the presence of Alice and Mr. and Mrs. Jones, Mrs. Jones told me that they had done everything in their power to prevent Emily from marrying Brooks, but seeing it was of no avail they denied Emily and Brooks the house for two years, telling me they were not colored, they were English." Could the Joneses have elevated the importance of their nation of birth over the imprecision of race in 1920s America? Certainly. Was it possible to have some nonwhite ancestry and not think oneself colored? Of course. Leonard in fact suggested this as a possible explanation. He continued, "They were born in England. They said, '[T]he first we ever saw a colored person was on our arrival in America, walking on Sixth Avenue.' "[38]

IT BECAME MILLS'S job to remind all in the courtroom that Leonard had been duped—made to believe Alice was white and not colored. After establishing that the parents had been a party to the alleged deception, he returned to his questioning of his client.

MILLS: "Was anything said to you at any time by Alice in regard to their being of Spanish extraction in any way?"
LEONARD: "In one of her letters she told me that she had become acquainted with a Harvard man in the Adirondacks, and he asked Alice, 'What are you[?]' and Alice replied, 'I am of Spanish extraction.' "
MILLS: "And do you remember that that was expressed in one of her letters to you as well?"
LEONARD: "I do."

With Alice in the background dabbing at her eyes, Mills moved to demonstrate pattern of deceit. He next asked Leonard what Alice had to say to reporters who quizzed the pair about her race once the marriage gained national prominence.

MILLS: "Was anything said at that time by her as to whether she was of colored blood or white?"
LEONARD: "Yes."
MILLS: "What did she say on that subject?"
LEONARD: "I told Alice what the newspapers said. She said, 'This is terrible, it is not true.' "

MILLS: "She said that?"

LEONARD: "Yes."

MILLS: "Did she say anything more on that subject?"

LEONARD: "Afterward when we returned to the Jones house there were many reporters around and after they asked her about it, she said, "It is not true. I am white and I shall sue the newspapers through my attorney, Judge Swinburne.""

MILLS: "Through Judge Swinburne?"

LEONARD: "Yes."

MILLS: "Did you believe that statement when you heard it made?"

LEONARD: "Absolutely."

MILLS: "If you had known what is now conceded to be true before you married Alice, that she is of colored blood, would you have married her?"

LEONARD: "Absolutely not, no."

MILLS: "When you married her did you believe her statement that she was white?"

LEONARD: "I did. I always believed her."

MILLS: "You trusted her implicitly?"

LEONARD: "Always."

With that "always," often described as "emphatic," Leonard essentially ended his first two days of testimony. This was, for many, the "peak of pathos and tragedy . . . the despairing ring in Leonard's voice when he told of his trust in Alice and his absolute conviction that she must be white if she said she was."[39] His words hung in the air.

Love, trust, deception, betrayal, anguish—a full array of images, emotions, and feelings encapsulated a love affair that had now become a national scandal. Neither Alice nor Leonard had intended so much exposure. Certainly neither wanted to be the subject of so much public inspection. Theirs was an ancient story: Two people meet, exchange secrets and gifts of affection, fall in love, but because of status, religion, age, or circumstance the sanctity of their love is called into question. It was a tragic tale, to be sure. What had started as a commonplace love affair metamorphosed into a trial about the vagaries of love, race, class, and sexuality. Most who watched the proceedings or read updates in their newspapers realized this. Yet even the most clairvoyant could not have anticipated what was to come.

7

⤳

ON THE FACE OF IT

HIS TURN ON the witness stand brought a stir and a grand sense of excitement. Born Asa Yoelson in the 1880s in Russian Lithuania, by 1925 Al Jolson had become the perfect symbol of racial ambiguity and cross-cultural exchange. It was a remarkable irony that he found himself in the middle of this trial as a powerful representative of the Jazz Age and of the issues of racial identity and cultural transformations raised by the Rhinelander Case. On this day Isaac Mills had a much simpler task for the talented singer and actor. Mills simply wanted to continue to build his case by proving that Alice had deceitfully entrapped poor Leonard into a relationship and subsequent marriage. In Jolson he imagined a powerful example of the extent of her guile. Nevertheless, Jolson's appearance reverberated with some of the deepest issues raised by the Rhinelander Case. What was race? If blackness and whiteness were such strongly divided categories, why did so many people exist between or outside of or across the social lines they drew? And what about all the new immigrants from Asia and Eastern and Southern Europe, whose physical appearances, cultural practices, and ethnic heritages did not clearly fit into American racial categories?

Jolson's involvement in the Rhinelander Case stemmed from one of

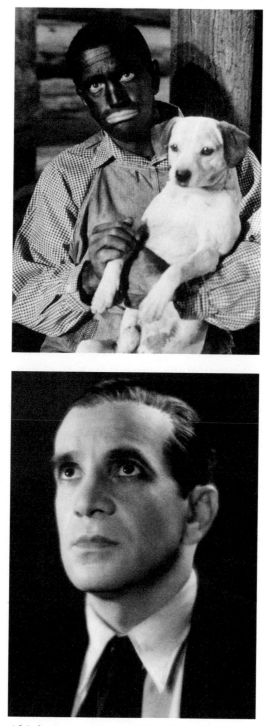

Al Jolson in and out of blackface character.

Alice's letters, which contained an explicit reference to the celebrated vaudevillian. Writing from her 1922 summer job at Paul Smith's, a well-known Adirondack resort, Alice told her love, "I was talking to Al Jolson today, he was in swimming but he is some flirt with the girls . . . his cottage was next to ours."[1] Alice had been working at the upstate New York retreat and was describing for Leonard her socializing with other camp workers. In this letter she also claimed, or perhaps erroneously believed, that in addition to Jolson, Irving Berlin was among the artists hired there.

Her casual reference had forced Jolson to appear that morning without his familiar makeup to testify before the court. But Jolson was better known for his performances in the stylistic manner known as "blackface," not only blackening his face, but speaking, singing, and acting in ways that mimicked black behavior and culture.

Jolson's anxiety was etched all over his face. Since Alice's letter had been read into the transcript, his name had been all over the newspapers, paired with that of Alice Jones. His involvement in the Rhinelander Case, however tangential, was clearly an embarrassment to the prominent man, although he managed to use his skills as a performer to take control of the questioning and play to the audience. Reintroduced to readers all over the nation in subsequent accounts of his testimony as the "blackface entertainer," Jolson wanted all to know that he had never met or even seen the raven-haired defendant before that day's court proceedings.

Jolson's appearance provided comic relief in the middle of a brutal day of questioning for Leonard. To start with, Mills seemed completely unaware of the identity of his own celebrity witness. He interrupted Davis's cross-examination of Leonard to announce that he had a witness who needed to leave for an afternoon public engagement. "Al Johnson or Jolson, I believe he is." The court audience roared with laughter and Jolson took his oath with an "excellent comedy flourish."[2] Trying to muzzle the impulse that made him a noted comedian and entertainer, he earnestly and energetically answered Mills's questions. "Did you ever have any talk with the defendant?" Leonard's lead attorney asked. As he asked the question he turned and pointed at the well-dressed defendant. Jolson immediately exclaimed, "Never in my life." Mills followed, "Did you ever see her?" Louder and more curt than before came Jolson's "No!"

Desperate to take control of the examination and hasten its conclusion, he pleaded to "talk in my own way." Mills conceded, and Jolson offered his version of events. "I never saw the defendant, never spoke with her, don't know her—" Mills interrupted, "Well, Mr. Jolson don't get excited. We don't claim you know her." With a vibrato in his voice audiences identified as his signature note, Jolson sighed, "Thank God for that." He admitted that the headlines regarding his supposed flirtation with Alice had upset him. Although he explained that "everybody in the theatrical business was a flirt," he denied ever having spoken with the defendant. "I never been to Paul Smith[']s in my life," he told the rapt courtroom. Until then Lee Davis had sat attentively, declining to interject. But when Jolson proclaimed, "I got hotel bills from Atlantic City, proving where I was," Davis soothingly reassured the singer, "That's all right." Visibly relieved, Jolson rushed back to his narrative.[3]

The entertainer's presence now engrossed the White Plains courtroom. "That's fine," he continued, ever the performer, "I can go home and make up with my wife." This was his first of many hints that his wife, Ethel, had not appreciated the attention or suggestions of possible infidelity. Did it incense her that Al had flirted with other women while he conveniently ignored her in his consuming search for an audience and affection? Even if she was not concerned about her husband's loyalty, the connection of his name with the now-notorious Alice could not have been comfortable for her. Of course, Jolson may also have been exaggerating or even creating the image of an angry wife waiting at home in order to entertain and gain sympathy for his situation. It certainly got the attention of the papers. The *Daily Mirror* ran a photograph of the Jolsons kissing, with the caption: "Ha! Ha! The Jolsons are at peace once more. Mrs. Al's mind is now at ease. Al went up to White Plains yesterday and denied he had ever, ever even met the dusky Alice. . . . On the comedian's return Al and the Missus kissed and made up."[4] The *Daily News*, on the other hand, preferred to stay with the image of the Jolsons' marriage on the rocks. They illustrated their coverage of his testimony with a small cartoon of Ethel chasing Al with a rolling pin and raised fist.[5]

In the briefest of cross-examinations, Davis remarked to Jolson that this appearance might actually be good publicity, then turned to the question of why Alice had claimed to flirt with the famous man.

DAVIS: "You are a prominent chap, aren't you? Don't be modest about it, now. This is a good headline for you?"

JOLSON: "I know, but the other wasn't. Make this different, will you?"

DAVIS: "You understand, don't you, that sometimes people are given the nicknames of prominent theatrical persons?"

JOLSON: "Yes."

DAVIS: "Now, let me relieve your mind. Did you know up at Paul Smith's there was a chap that was nicknamed after you because he was witty and funny?"

JOLSON: "No, I did not."

DAVIS: "Are you relieved?"

JOLSON: "Yes—a lot."[6]

Davis then excused the reluctant witness, having made his point that Alice had mistaken the nicknamed Al Jolson for the renowned original.[7]

But Jolson was not finished yet. Relieved of the taint of involvement with the case, he could now leave the courtroom with some choice lines for the newspapers. Jolson confided to the captive audience, "Every time I go to my dressing room the orchestra plays 'Alice Where Art Thou Going.' I tell you I've suffered."[8] Everyone laughed at that one, except for Alice and Leonard.[9] His parting shot as he prepared to leave the witness stand played with his claim that his wife had stopped speaking to him over the controversy: "I hope I'll eat breakfast at home tomorrow!"[10]

Writers for the *Daily News* thought that Jolson's remarks had "some of the earmarks of a press agent stunt."[11] They were certainly amusing and distracting enough that Judge Morschauser had to call a brief recess after his departure to return order to the court. Indeed, the legal significance of Jolson's testimony is hard to see; he was only one of a handful of men Alice mentioned in her letters as she tried to test Leonard's commitment to and interest in her across the divides of time and space. Except for his fame, Jolson's part in the case was insignificant. After all, Alice had told Leonard that she had received a ring and an offer of engagement from firefighter Eddie Holland. (Holland also appeared in court to deny this.) And she confessed that she had had a previous sexual relationship with Robert Rose, a white man who was now married and who showed up at the trial but was never called to testify. In fact, Jolson was not even the only prominent name to emerge that day. Alice's reference to meeting "the music fellow," Irving Berlin, brought him to the attention of trial watchers, too. But most newspapers completely ignored Berlin's role, or gave it only the briefest of mentions.[12] Of all these alleged male acquaintances of Alice's, only Jolson made headlines across the country. Clearly he was the most celebrated, and perhaps the most evocative as well.[13]

THE BLACKFACE ENTERTAINER had made his cameo appearance in the trial and had only confirmed what most had probably already assumed: that he and Alice had not actually flirted together as she had implied in her letter. His presence, however, did serve to underscore the complexities of race in the modern United States. The image of Al Jolson next to Alice and George Jones drew into sharper focus the impossibly thin line separating blacks and whites in America, and the anxiety that closeness produced. This was a reality that many contemporaries observed and a few had the acumen to analyze.

Many papers seemed to have an intuitive grasp of the deeper connections between the person and persona of Al Jolson and the issues raised by the Rhinelander Case. Some papers printed photos of Jolson and Alice next to each other, and almost all of them made sure to remind readers that Jolson's primary claim to fame was his blackface act. The coupling of their faces reminded readers that Alice was on trial for allegedly trying to pass as white. The juxtaposition of their category-defying faces raised in the open the perplexing question: What is race, anyway? Was it possible for a woman with some African or Indian heritage to be white? Was it feasible for a man of Eastern European ancestry to play black? Why would others believe his playacting?

Both in literary imaginations and in historical analyses, commentators presented either-or options for people such as Al Jolson and Alice Jones and her family. They were to be either black or white, never both and never neither.

The phenomenon of racial "passing" was at its height in the 1920s, if not in actual numbers then certainly in the level of awareness and concern on the part of Americans. "Are you Positively Sure that You are Not Part Negro?" read the provocative blurb for a 1929 publication, *From Negro to Caucasian, or How the Ethiopian is Changing His*

Skin. The author warned white Americans that there were "thousands
. . . in this country who are accepted as white and know they are
Negroes. . . . [and] still more thousands who are Negroes and believe
themselves to be white."[14] Anthropologists, census takers, and students
of race tended to agree. One popular journal article reporting on the
findings of racial anthropometrist Charles Davenport, estimated that
"nearly 10,000 persons of fractional Negro ancestry each year 'cross the
color line' from Negro to white society." Another editorial remarked
that "[m]any pass for white in whose genealogy research would discov-
er a few drops of negro blood" and cited an example of "ancient
records" uncovering a single "colored ancestor" of one white family.
"Now with no fault of their own, and no change in themselves, they
were thrust, with all their whiteness, into outer blackness."[15]

In a 1926 *Crisis* editorial on the Rhinelander Case, W. E. B. Du Bois
suggested that it was actually white Americans' uncertainty about their
own racial identity that underlay their obsession with identifying race.
He charged that concern over white "racial purity," or the lack thereof,
explained white America's treatment and portrayal of Alice Jones
Rhinelander: "Why could the press persecute, ridicule and strip
naked, soul and body, this defenseless girl? Because so many white
Americans have black blood which might come to light, they pounce
and worry like wolves to prove their spotless family."[16]

In truth an unknown number of Americans lived not just in a limi-
nal state between black and white but in a world that forced them to
make choices they found neither easy nor comfortable. Sometimes
they defied the socially acceptable and expected. While performing,
Al Jolson became what he never was—black. Perhaps during her daily
dealings, Alice lived as if she were white because she did not see herself as black. Or perhaps she simply allowed others to think what they
wanted to think.

Was Alice passing? This term was a convenient shorthand assigned
to people who seemingly belonged exclusively to one racial group but
somehow found themselves living as a member of another. Passing
had been used throughout the twentieth century to refer to a racial
role-playing or identity shift. Most often it suggested light-skinned
black people who were able to "pass" as white either by specifically
denying their black ancestry or by permitting others to assume that
they are something other than black. This definition and usage sup-

ported the social construction of racial categories of whiteness and blackness: The person of mixed ancestry "really" was black but only pretended to be white, whether on a temporary basis for employment, or more permanently in order to avoid the limitations of discrimination and racism.

But by succumbing to the elegant simplicity of this understanding of passing, writers for more than a century have actually made it harder to understand people like Alice and her family. Although Alice admitted to having some colored blood just before the trial commenced, that in and of itself is not conclusive evidence of her self-identity. How she thought of herself is not known.[17] In terms of how she described herself up to the trial, Alice was most certainly other than black. Her sister Emily may have married a black man, but Alice did not live in New Rochelle's black community; she did not attend churches, social clubs, or other organizations with a predominantly black membership; nor was she remembered by older black residents as a community member.[18] Alice had black blood but was probably not socially black, although her own lawyer worked to convince the jury that Leonard had to have known he married a black woman. Nor was she exactly white either, however. As reporters discovered when searching for clues to her racial identity, many teachers, coworkers, church members, and neighbors had known that George Jones and his daughters were not white.

In effect Alice Jones confounded the conventions of racial membership so heatedly debated in 1920s America, the decade by which most segregation laws had been passed and rigidly enforced. Racially ambiguous Americans complicated and potentially threatened the logic of Jim Crow and the definition of race that underlay it. To speak of Alice as passing for white reassured Americans that there were two distinct categories that, when properly policed, could be separated. In how she actually lived her life, however, Alice posed a threat to this ideological and social system.

In his own way so too did Al Jolson. Al Jolson had known no African Americans before moving to the United States. However he had come to embody them onstage for thousands. What did this mean for American racialism? For the better part of this century a coterie of African American intellectuals have written that race is the fiction by which we identify one another. This is how W. E. B. Du Bois could wryly note in "The Souls of White Folks": "The discovery of personal whiteness among the world's peoples is a very modern thing—a nineteenth and twentieth-century matter, indeed. The ancient world would have laughed at such a distinction."[19] Yet one of the remarkable features of the late nineteenth and early twentieth centuries was the degree to which various European immigrants, often representing distinct racial groups, became considered white in the United States.

In his blackface routine Jolson showed not only that the differences between black and white were subtle variations on themes of the human condition, but that a man new to the United States could learn to be what he had not been before and do so convincingly—if at times stereotypically. Race, Jolson seemed to signal, was entirely malleable if the individual had the requisite physical features, and thus difficult to regulate. As a black-faced figure Al Jolson symbolized the messiness of racial order and hierarchy. Think of it: If he found it so easy to play black, how many blacks found it as easy to play white? This question made the Rhinelander Case more than a social curiosity, it made it a singular moment in the nation's struggle to maintain a Jim Crow ethos. Whether in the North, South, or West, many had settled on the need to separate blacks and whites. Jolson's presence served as an indirect reminder of the larger contradictions within.

Like the Jones family, Jolson had negotiated national, cultural, and racial lines, attempting to remake himself into an American. The difference was that Jolson became an assimilated American in part by mimicking blackness. George Jones and his children found their efforts at assimilation limited by their apparent blackness. In other words African Americans were excluded from full citizenship at the same time that they were incorporated into mainstream American identity through social practices like minstrelsy, which mimicked white Americans' ideas about, or versions of, black culture.

That Jolson was Jewish both complicates and illuminates his racial position in the issues raised by the Rhinelander Case. As a Jewish immigrant, Jolson and his family also embodied the American experience of cultural assimilation. Like George and Elizabeth Jones, Al Jolson and his family had emigrated from Europe in the 1890s. Like all immigrants, they had to struggle to adjust and acclimate to their new country and to American culture. This process of assimilation or acculturation was, for many, also a process of personal reinvention and one in which racialization could play a key role. As a dark-skinned man from England, George Jones found himself forced to contend with American categories of race that defined him as a "negro" and attempted to control the course of his life accordingly. As an Eastern European Jew and a child, Jolson had perhaps greater freedom to determine who and what he would become. At the same time, however, his very fame and prominence set him apart from the common experience of Lithuanian immigration in several important ways.

Jolson's underlying significance for the Rhinelander Case, then, involved the specter of racial passing and the tensions over immigration and the assimilation of new immigrants into the dominant Anglo-American culture. Both of these issues revolved around defining Americanness. In the quarter century after the end of the Civil War a consensus emerged among historians, for example, as to the evolutionary inferiority of blacks on all grounds. At the same time many historians championed the superiority of Anglo-Saxons by contrasting them with Europeans from other areas. These discussions were considered crucial in the determination of U.S. national identity. If ethnic ancestry determined character and behavior, then the ethnic makeup of the nation's citizens would determine the future success or decline of the country.[20] As an article in the *Birmingham Age-Herald* reminded readers: "Mongrelization is Fatal" and the United States was in danger of becoming the next in a line of Caucasian civilizations that had been absorbed and destroyed by the "colored races."[21]

In a famous 1893 address before the American Historical Association, the historian Frederick Jackson Turner discussed "The Significance of the Frontier in American History" and questioned the link between the hereditary argument and U.S. prominence. According to Turner the American national character derived in large part from the ability of Americans to conquer the frontier, to lay claim to the wilderness, rather than through a tally of the accomplishments of certain Europeans and their descendants. "American social development has been continually beginning over again on the frontier. This perennial rebirth, this fluidity of American life, this expansion westward with its new opportunities . . . furnish the forces dominating [the] American character."[22] His conclusion touched off an enduring storm: "And now, four centuries from the discovery of America, at the end of a hundred years of life under the [C]onstitution, the frontier has gone, and with its going has closed the first period of American history."[23] American identity, then, was constantly changing, reinventing itself at its borders. Although Turner meant to refer only to physical borders, we can also see the ramifications of his thesis at the level of social, ideological, and cultural borders: race. Physical and racial frontiers came together explicitly in the immigration crises of the late nineteenth and early twentieth centuries.

In pronouncing the close of the frontier, Turner acknowledged a need to account for the millions who immigrated to the United States and contributed to its greatness. In the years immediately following Turner's address, Americans of elite background worried mightily about the nation's ability to absorb and integrate the scores of Europeans who still migrated to the United States in large numbers despite a closed frontier. Social scientists and commentators made formal distinctions between what we think of today as nationalities and races. Europeans, for example, were subdivided into several different racial types, depending on language, culture, phenotype (skin color, hair texture, and other physical traits), religion, and other characteristics. Jews were viewed as a race apart, but so too were Asian Indians, Middle Easterners, and Eastern Europeans. Once in the United States, buttressed by the nation's legacy from the days of slavery, many of these questionably white groups became whiter with time. In effect, the black-white dynamic in the United States enabled former European "races" to become white. Some did so by drawing a sharp distinction between themselves and African Americans.[24]

WITHOUT A DOUBT Al Jolson used the black-white dichotomy to make himself a white American. Jolson's biography is the story of a boy reinventing himself, even to the point of creating a new birth date. His father, a cantor, fled pogrom-ridden Lithuania, eventually settling in Washington, D.C. Once established in a synagogue, he sent for his family. Tragically, Jolson's mother died soon after arriving in the United States, leaving her two sons without the maternal guidance upon which they had heretofore depended. Between 1900 and 1904 Asa and his brother, Hirsch, left their father and his new bride to find employment in theater, vaudeville, and finally minstrelsy. During that period they made the transformation from Asa and Hirsch Yoelson to Al and Harry Jolson.[25]

Al Jolson's first big break came in the premiere American production of Israel Zangwill's *Children of the Ghetto*. Jolson's biographer Michael Freedland states that this production infected Jolson with the "show business virus" and he never fully recovered. The young Al was a clumsy and awkward performer until he found a vehicle for making himself over. At the suggestion of another member of a burlesque troupe, he put burnt cork on his face for the first time. Immediately he felt more at ease. There, in October 1904, Al Jolson was born. The blackface served as his "passport to a completely different world."[26] By 1908 Al had met producer Lew Dockstader and signed on as one of the Lew Dockstader Minstrels. Within a year he got his first notice in *Variety*. And after his stint with Dockstader ended, before 1910, he got his first shot at a Broadway production. In *La Belle Paree* (1911) he brought his blackface persona to the legitimate stage.

The interplay between performer and audience made blackface entertainment a powerfully supple vehicle for whitening America in the nineteenth and early twentieth centuries, as the nation struggled to absorb millions of immigrants from Eastern and Southern Europe—questionable Anglos at best, reasoned such social guardians as Madison Grant and Theodore Roosevelt. In adopting blackface, Jolson, as one of those new immigrants, not only traded on a form that had grown in popularity during the nineteenth century, he also found the perfect means of becoming white.

SINCE THE FIRST casting of Shakespeare's *Othello*, white actors had darkened their faces to become other than themselves, aspiring to become the Moor who enthralled and outraged audiences on both sides of the Atlantic.[27] Minstrelsy, however, emerged as an expression of popular culture in the 1830s and was performed well into the late twentieth century. During its heyday hundreds of whites painted themselves dark and imagined themselves as blacks. Certainly the blackened faces, exaggerated and whitened lips and eyes, and overstated dress, speech, and mannerisms exposed racial and often racist underpinnings. White caricatures of the black man and woman operated to rob them of dignity and self-respect, presenting flattened, stereotyped images for white audiences to enjoy and laugh at. But to dwell solely on the racist aspects of minstrelsy is to distort its historical and cultural meaning. For in being blacklike, no matter how extremely so, whites signaled that blacks had cultures, folkways, personas, and a basic humanity that war-ranted recognition. Minstrelsy was not just about lampooning black life, it was also about highlighting the contours of a compelling cultur-al world. Or, as the scholar Eric Lott observed: "Minstrelsy brought to public form racialized elements of thought and feeling, tone and impulse, residing at the very edge of semantic availability, which Americans only dimly realized they felt, let alone understood."[28]

The process of understanding occurred in the most public of places. Sometimes the minstrels were lodge brothers, union members, or joined by another fraternal allegiance. They spent isolated moments on the other side of the racial fault line, acting on their imaginings about blacks and black life. Some traded the amateurish for the profes-sional, performing in famous traveling troupes such as the Georgia Minstrels, and became known throughout Europe and the Americas. That some of these early minstrels were actually black is not that inex-plicable, given the public demand for the "authentic" reproduction of a false black life. That some African Americans blackened their own faces—as if to prove that they too were masking their real selves in the job of social transference—became one of the intriguing features of race in modernizing the United States. Black blackface actors herald-ed the public ability to assimilate incongruous elements long before Continental scholars such as Gunnar Myrdal armed Americans with a vocabulary to explain what scores had seen and experienced.

Even as minstrelsy aimed to expose the peccadilloes of blacks, it revealed the degree to which the modern world could not escape the fact that the United States was a mongrel society, to borrow from the work of the historian Ann Douglas. The commodification of enter-tainment meant that Americans were free to export their art forms and thereby reveal to the world something of the genius of the peo-ple that went beyond the elaborate systems of categorization, segre-gation, and disenfranchisement that characterized American racial policies and practices.[29] In other words, minstrelsy depended on and even evidenced the value of black culture even as it mocked and dis-enfranchised it.

And by the 1920s blackface had become so popular a vehicle for entertainment that critics, audiences, and performers alike were remarking on the "darkening" of Broadway. In the 1922 *Ziegfeld Follies*, the white singer Gilda Gray sang that on Broadway "Real darktown entertainers hold the stage, / You must black up to be the latest rage," referring to both the emergence of African American performers in mainstream venues and the increasing popularity of "blacked up" white performers. Furthermore, the height of blackface popularity coincided with the more deeply entrenched cultural synthesis of such musical forms as minstrelsy, ragtime, and jazz.[30]

While some Jolson biographers go out of their way to describe his raceless adoption of blackface, it was impossible to become a successful blackface minstrel in twentieth-century America and remain oblivious to the insidious and pernicious features of race. Starting from concerns about the white man's burden, colonialism, segregation, race riots, and restrictive immigration, the matter of race snaked its way into conversations, social practices, and social understandings. In even the short time between Jolson's arrival in the United States and his adoption of the darkening paint, racial matters appeared again and again as a factor in American politics. It was certainly there when the nation entered into the Spanish-American War and subsequently assumed oversight and possession of Cuba, Puerto Rico, and the Philippines. More than one American leader asked about caring for the "little brown people" who populated these new extensions of America's imperial world.[31] Questions of race surfaced in the assault on black political power in the South at the close of the nineteenth century, and again repeatedly during the first two decades of the twentieth.

Yet, somewhat ironically, minstrelsy also showed that complete racial separation was an impossible ideal. By the turn of the century both white and black Americans had spent too much time in the other's company to affect a complete separation. They shared foods, customs, religious views, languages, music, and a nation, no matter how imperfectly. They also learned about each other from common cultural cues. Power differences, after all, could not negate the fact that to be an American, especially a modern American, meant to be black, white, and other.

Music became the means that smoothed the way for questions of racial inclusion and exclusion to reach a mass public. And ragtime became the form. The typical ragtime tune had a "regular straightforward bass and a lightly syncopated melody"— a ragged rhythm. With the emphasis on syncopation, songwriters whose origins were in writing songs for minstrels began to experiment, producing what became known as "coon songs," most of which had little to do with ragtime. This changed in 1896, when Ernest Hogan penned the instant hit "All Coons Look Alike to Me." The song won immediate favor with an overwhelmingly white listening audience, while to many black musicians and listeners the title conjured up the worst stereotypes possible.

But the tune's popularity sent many songwriters to Tin Pan Alley, the New York commercial strip that turned lyrics and keystrokes into published sheet music. For the black musicians who grew in stature during this time but who often lacked formal training, access to Tin Pan Alley validated them as major players in American culture. In nightclubs, churches, and whorehouses, would-be entertainers perfected their craft and exposed white Americans to another cultural form. Ragtime made the little-known Scott Joplin into a famous man, earning him the sobriquet "King of Ragtime." In turn Joplin's "Maple Leaf Rag" focused the United States and the world on a genuinely American contribution to the modern age. To master this and similar tunes, a player had to demonstrate showmanship, instrumental virtuosity, and the ability to harness the technicalities of syncopation.

Like minstrelsy, ragtime generated immense opportunities for non-black musicians, too. One of them was Al Jolson's fellow Rhinelander trial referent, Irving Berlin. While Berlin never donned blackface, and thus never so clearly indicated the ambiguities of race, he too lived in a world between black and white. His status as a ragtime master hinged on his ability to borrow openly from black culture and repackage it as American. At times Berlin, a merchant of hybridness, epitomized the sense that the whole never cohered as neatly advertised, that ragtime was about the melding of musical and cultural traditions rather than the mere appropriation of one cultural form by someone ostensibly outside the boundaries of that culture.[32]

The cultural borrowing, sharing, and altering gave salience and significance to ragtime. Yet the politics of race made it possible for Jewish immigrants such as Berlin and Jolson to gain greater access to Tin Pan Alley and the world of Broadway than did many black actors and artists. Berlin frequently minimized any substantial debt to the black artists who originated the form, insisting at times that "our popular songwriters . . . are not Negroes."[33] In his attempt to capture aspects of black culture and life without surrendering his membership in a larger white world, Berlin registered the angst of an immigrant whose whiteness some found suspect. In effect ragtime allowed Berlin and others to become white and pass for American, by showing that the music, the symbol of modern America, was not exclusively black-derived after all. He seemed to say that he and others had created the sound, and they were "of pure white blood . . . many of Russian . . . ancestry." The careful excision of any mention of a Jewish cultural, social, or religious identity provided the veil so clearly sought.

Still, he undeniably belonged to that intersecting world of black, white, and other—the multicultural and racial world of New York in the first two decades of the twentieth century, which made it possible for him to take from black culture without recognizing the need to acknowledge a debt to it. The heterogeneity of the cultural world became its own mask, allowing individuals to masquerade long enough to render indecipherable their old and new selves. Was this passing? Or was this an apt metaphor for the Jazz Age, an era, like its music, predicated on structured improvisation? In that sense was Alice trying to dupe "poor" Leonard into believing she was other than what she professed to be, or had Leonard already decided that he liked his Jazz Age love well enough to enjoy as well as accept her embellishments and improvisations? The jury and those who filled the courthouse seats were drawn back to these questions as they fixed their gaze on Al Jolson—and no doubt on Alice, George, and other members of the Jones family.

8

A MAN OF STANDING

 AFTER THE COMIC relief of Jolson's testimony, the focus of the trial returned to the relationship between Leonard and Alice. During the first week of evidence, court attendees had heard salacious details about the couple's romance, and of the supposed physical, mental, and social weakness that would explain Leonard's choices. However, the Leonard revealed on the stand during the trial's second week was far from the stumbling victim of his lawyers' portrayal. Yet in bits and pieces he did emerge as someone decidedly different from the rugged, upstanding ideal of elite manhood so famously manufactured by the likes of former president Teddy Roosevelt. Buffeted by Davis's accelerated and wilting cross-examination, Leonard increasingly became at once laughable and incomprehensible to many who watched the trial. As Mills continued his attack on Alice and her character, Davis's attack on Leonard began to gain momentum. And as the trial continued the revelations of the testimony began to erode Leonard's standing as a representative of white upper-class manhood. Davis in effect attacked the very notion of elite society.

ON MONDAY, NOVEMBER 16, Davis introduced a crucial question: "Your mind is all right, isn't it?" Leonard said it was and explained that the only difficulty he had was an occasional stutter. Davis quickly moved on to his next concern, but onlookers took note that the young Rhinelander had just contradicted several hours of his own lawyers' arguments and witnesses' statements testifying to extensive mental defects. He would not support the portrait of himself as a stupid, naive dupe. He stammered, yes, but he had also earned very good grades at his Arizona prep school, edited the school newspaper, and established himself as a more than capable student.[1]

Davis, meanwhile, was just getting started. After listening to a morning filled with the reading of more of Alice's letters, the fortunate few who managed to bull their way into the courtroom witnessed a turn in the procedures. Davis's primary intention this day turned less on who Leonard thought he was and more on what Leonard had done. The seasoned counselor understood that Leonard's mindset held immense importance for the trial, and so too did his actions. By suggesting that Leonard had acted without regard for Alice, her family, or her reputation, Davis hoped that he could expose Leonard the man: not mentally deficient but overly determined to hold on to his privileged life and status.

The first line of attack was the question of how Mills had obtained Alice's letters to Leonard. They had obviously been in Leonard's possession, and he had promised Alice many times he would keep them safe. Were they not, Davis suggested, a sacred trust that Leonard had betrayed by allowing them to be publicized, thus dragging his wife, whom he claimed he had loved, through the gutter? Leonard defended himself by saying it was neither his idea nor his initial intention to use the letters. At one point he offered the rather weak explanation that he had not actually handed them over to his lawyers but only told them where they were hidden. But eventually he admitted that he had buckled under their pressure. He attributed his acquiescence to the protracted haranguing of his father's lawyers. Whether this justification was true or not, the young Rhinelander had finally given Leon Jacobs tacit permission for their use in this lawsuit.

DAVIS: "Were you willing to have these letters read as long as it was for your benefit—after you had promised this little girl that you'd keep them sacred?"

LEONARD [with some difficulty]: "I-I-did on the advice of my counsel."

DAVIS [somewhat contemptuously]: "You're a man, aren't you?"

LEONARD: "Yes."

DAVIS: "And a gentleman?"

LEONARD: "I-I-try to be."

DAVIS: "But you were willing to do this to that little girl, and still consider yourself a gentlemen?"

LEONARD: "I can't answer that."

DAVIS: "You made the promise many times to your wife that you'd keep those letters sacred—that meant secret?"

LEONARD: "Yes."

DAVIS: "You did break your promise didn't you?"

LEONARD [weakly]: "My attorney used them."

DAVIS: "You were willing to break your promise to this girl as long as it was for your benefit?"

LEONARD [with more spirit than at any other time in the exchange, shouted]: "No!"

DAVIS: "But, you did it?"

LEONARD: "On advice."

DAVIS: "Were you willing to accept that advice?"

LEONARD: "No—it was not in my power."

Alice broke into quiet sobs at this point, and Davis triumphantly revealed his true motivation in pursuing this line of questioning.

DAVIS [shouting as if to fill the room]: "It wasn't in your power to control your own lawsuit?"

Leonard shook his head as if confiding a secret.

DAVIS: "You were unwilling to have [the letters] used and powerless to prevent it?"

LEONARD: "Yes."

This final response was almost inaudible. Acutely aware of the damage inflicted, Leonard's lawyers struck postures of professional indifference, bowing their heads and looking out of windows.

Already Davis was beginning to set up what would become a prevalent theme in his case: Leonard had not behaved as a man should. In drawing this picture he chose his words carefully, repeatedly referring

Leonard Rhinelander, looking the role of a gentleman.

to Alice as a girl, despite her four years' seniority over Leonard. This choice of wording reflected in part the times and conventions of language in the United States in the 1920s: It was far from uncommon for a grown woman to be called a girl. At the same time the use of "girl" conjured other interpretations, implying that she was not quite a woman, or perhaps not a lady, because of her racial lineage, class status, or relative educational disadvantage. The word "girl" also emphasized her weaker status and her innocence. A girl would not vamp a man. A girl could not seduce a man. And a gentleman should not take advantage of a girl. Furthermore, by crying Alice supported Davis's construction of herself, suggesting a vulnerability to counter Mills's portrayal of a manipulative and calculating vixen. By combining Davis's words and her own emotions, Alice slipped into those places of recognition and understanding so critical to convincing the jury and the public of Leonard's power over her rather than the other way around.

More important, few could miss the disclosure that Leonard was not in control of his own legal affairs. And Alice's claims that Leonard had been forced to sign a complaint already drawn up by his father's lawyers may have been partially true. "Thus," one New York paper editorialized, "was the code of chivalry of the great Rhinelander family descended of Huguenots, torn into miserable little shreds [*sic*]. The ease with which Davis forced Rhinelander to [con]cede one of the most important points in the litigation was pitiable."[2] In another hint of the groundswell to come, this comment connected Leonard's admission with a failure of masculine honor, of chivalry.

The next day Leonard fared no better. Davis spent the morning playing a cat-and-mouse game with Leonard, getting him to confess to material falsehoods and then moving on to another line of questioning. The tension in the courtroom mounted. Through hours of merciless grilling, Leonard admitted that the bill of particulars attached to his annulment suit contained five statements that were not true, although the entire document was only four paragraphs long. This was a legal document whose purpose was to provide the defendant with an explanation of the basis for the suit, with particular details of events and conversations. Unlike the suit itself, this document had been drawn up with Leonard's participation, and he, of course, had signed it, attesting to its accuracy.

Of the five misstatements, some were hardly crucial; for example, one involved whether certain statements had been made orally or in writing. Several, however, revolved around Leonard's knowledge of Emily's marriage to a black man. The document claimed that upon discovery of that marriage in May 1924, Leonard had asked Alice whether she and her sisters were white and she had told him that she was. Thereafter she had assured him in repeated conversations on the topic that she was white. Davis easily got Leonard to confess that he had met Robert Brooks in 1921, not 1924; that he had known Brooks and his family well; and that he had never asked Alice whether she was white. Neither had she repeatedly told him she was white.[3]

Why had Leonard signed the complaint when he knew it wasn't accurate? The boy replied that he had followed orders. Had he pursued the annulment as a free agent? Yes. Davis leaned forward and stared intently, forcing Leonard's gaze to meet his own.

DAVIS: "Do you still want to proceed in this law suit?"
LEONARD: "Yes."

Perhaps at no other time was Leonard more free to walk away from this suit, but he did not. Nevertheless there were those who believed that he did not care if he lost, and some hoped it was because he still loved and wanted to be married to his wife.

Alma Sioux Scarberry, an occasional contributor to the *New York Daily Mirror*, seemed to have a special ability to gain access to private interviews with the major players of this case. She reported a conversation with Leon Jacobs that suggested that even Leonard's counsel believed he was trying to save his marriage somehow. Jacobs reportedly told Scarberry that there was no doubt his client was still in love with his wife "or he would not be balling up the testimony so." Scarberry then approached Alice in the courthouse restroom. Alice readily admitted that she still loved Leonard and would take him back. Her suffering in the courtroom, she confided, was all for his ordeal.[4]

Davis also forced Leonard to make other admissions that weakened both his case and his character. For example, Leonard had stated under oath that he wouldn't have knowingly married a black woman because he did not wish to be on intimate terms with blacks. Under Davis's guiding queries, however, he told the courtroom that he had played cards with Robert Brooks, Alice's colored brother-in-law, and that he maintained close relations with Brooks's family. Asked if knew he was writing to a colored man in a postcard addressed to "Bob and Em," Leonard answered that he did. Davis asked the young man if he would call that being on intimate terms? Rhinelander was forced to concede it was: He had pursued and continued a relationship with Alice with the full knowledge that her brother-in-law and niece, at least, were colored.

Shifting legal direction, Davis inquired of Leonard's feelings toward Alice, his innocence, and his intent. First he had to establish that Leonard consciously pursued and fell in love with Alice. The topic now was his eager role in the development of his physical relationship with Alice. The outline of their progression from the relatively innocent kisses and caresses and tender, hesitant endearments of the first few months to the full blown sexual relationship had been laid out the

Emily and Robert Brooks, Alice's sister and brother-in-law.

previous week. Davis's questions sought to determine who initiated these evolving romantic and sexual steps.

DAVIS: "How soon after you met her did you fall in love with Alice?"
LEONARD: "A few weeks."
DAVIS: "And of your own volition?"
LEONARD: "Yes."
DAVIS: "That wasn't a long time for her to pursue you, was it?"
LEONARD: "No."
DAVIS: "You pursued her, as a matter of fact, didn't you?"
LEONARD: "Yes."
DAVIS: "You were mad about her, weren't you?"
LEONARD: "Yes."
DAVIS: "You weren't seeking this girl's love without honest marriage in view, were you?"
LEONARD: "No."
DAVIS: "When did Alice return this love?"

LEONARD: "About the same time."
DAVIS: "You imposed your love to her and she hers to you?"
LEONARD: "Yes."[5]

In a few words Leonard told the world what Mills had had him readily deny: He had openly and knowingly pursued Alice. He had fallen in love with her long before she started writing about their caresses and stays at the hotel. If there had been aggressors, they shared equal responsibility. Both delighted in the company of the other. Moreover, Leonard characterized his attraction and feelings as love.

Seeming confident of the answers to come, Davis asked the young man directly about his innocence and naïveté. Leonard admitted he had played cards and drunk alcohol before meeting Alice, and he did have some experience with women. "What?" Davis asked, "You knew how to make love before you met Alice?" To which the serious-looking young man mustered a strong yes. The courtroom listeners understood that this did not necessarily mean he had previously been in a sexual relationship. The phrase "making love" was not then a synonym for sex, as it is today. Instead it referred to verbal and physical seduction or courtship. Leonard was confessing that he knew how to hold a girl's hand and how to kiss her even before resting his eyes on the alluring Alice. Throughout this questioning Leonard did hedge a bit, making Davis and the court wait before offering each piece of information. But when asked, "[T]hen you weren't innocent about love when you met Alice?" Leonard still claimed, "I was."

Davis was too shrewd a lawyer to be knocked off stride by this last remark. He asked the young man to describe his approach to romancing Alice. Before long the bright red in Leonard's face gave away his embarrassment. With great difficulty he told the opposing lawyer that he first put his arms around her, then kissed her. Davis asked if this was his first thrill with Alice. Leonard replied that it was, and Davis rejoined, "You didn't know when you put your arm around Alice that you were going to get a thrill? What prompted you?" Without embellishment Leonard answered simply, "[H]uman nature."

At this point Davis circled back to Leonard's standing as a man and gentleman. By arguing that Leonard had jump-started an intimate relationship with Alice, he shifted the focus from Alice's intentions to those of Leonard.

DAVIS: "When were your acts toward Alice not those of a gentle-
    man?"
LEONARD: "My acts were gentlemanly until the Marie Antoinette."
DAVIS: "Before you went to the hotel you had done nothing but hold
    her hand and kiss her?"

Leonard nodded yes.

DAVIS: "Had you ever been intimate with Alice Rhinelander before
    going to the Marie Antoinette?"
LEONARD: "No."
DAVIS: "What had you done looking toward that end before going to
    the hotel?"
LEONARD: "I had been fairly intimate with her."

Leonard now became even more tongue-tied and reticent. Inching
closer and wagging his finger, Davis tried to draw the young man out.
But the beleaguered plaintiff folded his arms and closed in on himself;
he was wilting under this grilling and seemed loath to divulge more
details.

Apologizing to Leonard—and presumably Alice—for invading their
private lives, Davis repeatedly reminded the court that he did so only
because Mills had made such an issue of Alice's morality and integrity.
Lunging ahead, he demanded to know more about Leonard's desires
and fantasies, returning to his earlier courtship.

DAVIS: "Didn't you have the idea in your head that you could prevail
    on her to have intimate relations with you?"
LEONARD: "Yes."
DAVIS: "At this juncture did you have marriage in mind?"
LEONARD: "I did not."
DAVIS: "Your object then was complete intimacy?"

Leonard never answered that question, and Davis did not press him.
The answer seemed obvious. Although he claimed to be in love,
Leonard had wanted to have sex with Alice, with no intention of mar-
rying her to make an honest woman out of her, as the saying went.
Besides, Davis had elicited a great deal from the witness by this point.

He appeared satisfied that the supposed dupe had lost considerable standing in the eyes of the jury and in the court of public opinion.[6]

Nor was Davis finished. When the questioning resumed he turned to an event that took place only a few months before Alice and Leonard's marriage. In August 1924, the couple had traveled for several days to Massachusetts and upstate New York. Leonard had left his Arizona school but had not yet made good his long engagement to marry Alice on reaching his majority. To give himself privacy with his bride-to-be, he told Elizabeth and George they were traveling with a married couple as chaperones. Davis read from a letter Leonard had sent the Joneses from Worcester, Massachusetts, which referred to the fictitious Mr. and Mrs. Matthews. Leonard told his fiancée's parents that the women were out at a movie while he and Mr. Matthews rested at the hotel. Building on that image of same-sex socializing, he assured them that they need not worry about their daughter as he was "taking the best of care of her as I usually do."

Now Davis could claim that George and Elizabeth Jones had been manipulated and victimized by Leonard. He charged that the elderly couple would never have permitted their daughter to travel alone with Leonard before they were married. Even if the Joneses were aware of the young people's physical involvement, they would have understood the importance of appearances and reputation. Grace Robinson of the *Daily News* declared that Leonard was "obviously . . . on the point of collapse," but that the supposed dupe had revealed himself as "a master in the manipulation of affectionate words. Far from being a stupid, backward boy, . . . [he was a] master at 'kidding the old folks' and in the ancient art of winning at [sic] woman's love." Calling most of Leonard's description of his courtship "unprintable," Robinson agreed with Davis that the day's testimony had clearly shown that the then eighteen-year-old man already had an "amazing technique in the art of persuasion."[7]

In a particularly clever move, Davis constructed this scenario in class terms, intimating that Leonard would never have pulled such a stunt with the daughter of his father's peers.

DAVIS: "Would you have used the same deception to the mother of a girl of your own class under the circumstances?"
LEONARD: "If the girl was willing, yes."
DAVIS: "Is that your idea of morals?'

LEONARD: "Well, not my idea of morals, no."

With the witness gulping glass after glass of water, Davis paused for a moment and then continued his offensive.

DAVIS [shouting]: "Do you know you have dragged her in the gutter to help your cause, and because of the prominence of your case have dragged her in the gutter before the whole world?"
LEONARD [feebly]: "She deceived me."
DAVIS [barely controlling himself]: "So, if a woman deceived you, you would drag her in the gutter? Is that your idea of manhood?"
LEONARD: "No, it isn't."
DAVIS: "But you have done it haven't you?"
LEONARD: "I followed advice."

When asked why he allowed the intimate details of his sexual affair with Alice to become known, Leonard's lips moved without words coming forth. He finally answered.

LEONARD: "Any man would."
DAVIS [agitated]: "What, you believe any man would reveal it and besmirch a woman?"

This time Leonard had exhausted all reply.

DAVIS: "You wouldn't lie like a gentleman to protect a woman, would you?"
LEONARD: "Not when she had deceived me."[8]

But Davis had him. Before the glare of the media's watch Leonard had acknowledged that despite wealth and privilege he could not rise above the particulars of the moment to claim the manly deportment befitting a gentleman.

THE NEWSPAPERS SEEMED to support Davis's perspective. Leonard Kip Rhinelander became a sometimes bewildering example of how 1920s racial and class ideologies complicated the history of

American gender roles, especially manhood. If the heir of old aristocratic blue blood and hard-earned millions could not be a gentleman,
who could? If betraying the trust of a working-class mixed-race woman
and refusing to claim responsibility for her was ungentlemanly or
unmanly, what did that mean for the direction of white America's public policy and discriminatory legislation? In this post-Victorian era, in
which flappers and fundamentalism vied for the attention of America's
youth, the demands on men were often unclear and sometimes contradictory. This case struck a nerve because it exposed and forced
watchers to wrestle with larger questions of national purpose, inclusion, and exclusion, and how to police the boundaries of something as
well known and yet difficult always to pinpoint as race. And a few
managed in the process to inspect and ridicule wealthy men such as
Rhinelander and their assertions of manly superiority.

INDEED, LEONARD'S FORCED confessions about his treatment of
Alice brought swift and decisive condemnation from many parts. The
white-published *New York World* wrote that Leonard had been com-
pelled to acknowledge that he was not the innocent youth described
by his lawyers. "[H]e was a sophisticated young man who had known
how to go about breaking down her resistance and bending her to his
will."[9] More important, the *World* also observed that these disclosures
had impaired his standing as a man. The "protective armor of imper-
turbability [Leonard] had built around himself was still holding him
up at adjournment, but there were unmistakable evidences that the
man inside was weak and fainting."[10] A "protective armor" was a hall-
mark of twentieth-century American manhood. Displays of sentiment
were taboo, and a "weak and fainting" inner self was exactly the wrong
core to have.

How was an upstanding man expected to behave in 1924? That all
depended on who you were. From the late nineteenth century to
World War I, there was an important distinction between the understandings of the terms "masculinity" and "manliness."[11] Of the two,
"masculinity" was the more general term, dealing with characteristics
all men were expected to share, regardless of race, class, or culture.
"Masculinity" described distinctions between men and women.
"Manliness," however, was a more specific and more limited category,

denoting an ideal of moral achievement, civilized and honorable behavior, and political and social power. Growing political movements among white middle-class women and working-class men threatened the functional definition of white manliness. One of the effects of these attempts was that, by the early twentieth century, working-class codes of manhood had begun to affect upper- and middle-class men's expectations of their own behavior. Growing interest in physical prowess brought assertiveness and even violence as well as open expressions of male sexuality into the equation. Behaviors once thought manly, such as reading and public lecturing, began to earn pejorative epithets such as "sissy," "pussy foot," "cold feet," and "stuffed shirt." Clearly contradictory, these demands for men to be at once aggressive and gentlemanly, civilized and savage, culminated in such wildly popular icons as Rudolph Valentino's classic role in the 1921 silent film *The Sheik.*[12]

The Edith Hull novel on which the movie is based presented a white man, descended from British aristocracy, who comes of age in an Arab world, raised by people more primitive and primordial than he. In the fictional account the sheik acquires a palpable sexuality, little constrained by his noble British ancestry. When a white woman happens into his world, herself a captive, he cannot contain his attraction to and lust for her. Virile, assertive, forceful, and brutal, he forces himself on her—at least in the novel, censors not permitting the display of such scenes in 1920s films. Thus the alluring, dark, handsome Latin lover became a rapist caught in the vortex of civilization lost (raised in the Arab world) and claimed (of noble British heritage), and of pure aggression. If popular culture was one barometer, what was permissible, even expected, of a man was changing—and confusing.

Where did this leave the educated, pampered bluebloods of Leonard's class? If reaction to that week's testimony was any indication, they were falling outside the new cultural ideal of manliness. *The New Yorker* would brag, "Four hundred years of civilization has at least taught him to mask his emotions." But this tongue-in-cheek salute did him little good elsewhere. Several articles and cartoons printed around the same times suggested that this was a broader condemnation of elite white men in general. The *New York Evening Journal* cartoon by T. E. Powers depicted young women turning their backs on society men, called "kippered wall flowers." With the obvious reference to Leonard, Powers suggested that Leonard Kip and his peers were no longer considered "real men" by female Americans.[13]

In the Victorian United States manliness was supposed to be reserved for white upper- and middle-class men. Sharp contrasts therefore emerged in popular images of black and white men. White men were seen as civilized and manly, sexually contained, rational, refined. Portrayals of nonwhite men drew them as savage and beastly, sexually aggressive, emotional, and physically violent. For members of the black community, therefore, the continued racial exclusivity of American definitions of manhood required urgent redefinition. Since the end of the nineteenth century black women and men had signaled an alarm at the efficacy of lynch law and its implications for white manliness. Journalist and social crusader Ida B. Wells Barnett, a prominent African American activist, charged that whites created images of black male beastly behavior in order to hide the beastly behavior of white men.

The presumption that white men were the bastions of manly virtue while black men were categorically denied true manhood was so strong in the late nineteenth century that lynching was commonly described as an example of the triumph of white civilization over rampant violent black savages.[14] Many white newspapers portrayed these horrific murders—scenes of white mobs rejecting legal avenues to hunt down, torture, burn, mutilate, and finally kill their black victims—as imposing control and containment on a race too uncivilized to control itself. Unreflectively, in many instances, the same papers revealed the violence and savagery of the white men who lynched. Along with others who kept records of lynchings, Wells observed that lynchings routinely targeted successful black entrepreneurs and professionals and often were a response to incidents of black resistance or refusal to submit to whites. On those occasions when a charge of rape was involved, circumstances suggested that the lynching and accompanying myth of the black rapist and white victim served to erase evidence of clear attractions across the racial divide. Since black and white men and women had found favor in one another's company since before the formation of the United States, it stood to reason that despite the social taboo, some would find mutual attraction, both physical and emotional. Instead of considering the obvious, many all too quickly concluded that the relationship had to have been one of force—a black man raping a white woman. Many a white lynch mob took its direction from the crowd's cry that the virtue of a white woman had to be upheld. This in turn justified the lynching of the black perpetrator.[15]

In the bloodcurdling screams of lynch mobs, black Americans saw the soft underbelly of whites' claims to perfection and superiority. What but a society of savages would turn the twisting body of a dying man into an occasion for a picnic and souvenir gathering? What kind of man would delight in seeing another hanged, burned, and then mutilated? Why would any man take pleasure in bringing his children and wives to such a spectacle? Were white male lynchers insecure about their own sexuality and manliness? Had they listened fully to the demagogic chants of New South Redeemers, who predicated southern pride and rebirth on black submission?[16]

Black newspapers, then, became the first and the loudest to reject the image of Leonard as a superior man on account of his wealth and whiteness. They were far more likely than their white counterparts to pick up explicitly on Davis's charge of unmanliness. As the front page of the *Philadelphia Tribune* announced, Leonard had been "Unable to Say He Is a Man,"[17] and editors across the country hastened to agree. Months before the trial's start, in fact, the *Baltimore Afro-American* was proclaiming that Leonard was certainly no gentleman, and really not even a man. In January 1925, as Alice continued to resist pressure to accept an annulment in exchange for large sums of money, an editorial summarized the paper's assessment of the couple. The fact that Alice had refused to be bought off revealed her to be "of good character," raising the question, of course, of why she would want such a poor specimen for a husband. Rhinelander, on the other hand, had "let himself be kidnapped" by his family. The paper's editor then continued, "If I were an American girl of any color whatsoever, I would not accept him off a Christmas Tree with a million dollars wrapped up with him. For such a creature is not a man; he is a Millionaire's Cub."[18] To label a Rhinelander a "creature" and a "cub" depicted Leonard in words more often used to characterize and dehumanize blacks, who were expected to be most animalistic and primitive according to turn-of-the-century social science and popular ideologies.[19]

Choosing a "cub" as the animal that best represented the young scion was both dismissive and a warning. Leonard Rhinelander might be a baby, nonthreatening, playful, and not to be taken seriously, but one day he would have power. Right now the danger in playing with him lay in the threat of the adult bears or lions lurking protectively in the woods. As a "Millionaire's Cub" he could certainly count on the protection of his father, who had shown his power in removing his wayward son from the "danger" of his marriage to Alice and protecting the mindless creature by slapping a lawsuit against his wife and sending lawyers to push a settlement.

In fact the black press had a field day with Leonard as a questionable representative of supposed white superiority. In effect black papers sought to use this case to challenge racism itself. And by the second week of testimony, this seemed to be a successful endeavor. As the *Houston Inquirer* proclaimed, the Rhinelander case had hit the doctrine of white supremacy with "a solar plexus blow."[20] The *Baltimore Afro-American*, highly critical of Leonard's decision to allow her letters to be read, charged, "Virtue means nothing to this scion. . . . Blood means everything."[21] The Rhinelanders, in other words, valued their family name and ancestry over honor and virtue—a harsh charge in a world in which wealth and station were supposed to reflect moral superiority. "Alice had a little Kip/His brain was LIGHT as snow,—/And everywhere that Alice went,/For years he tried to go," chanted an editorial in the *New York Amsterdam News*. The author, William Pickens, went on to suggest that Alice only married Kip to get rid of him, knowing that no American white millionaire worthy of the position would remain married to a "colored girl." Pickens's commentary was reprinted in black papers across the country.

In this light Alice's decision to marry Leonard did require some explanation. "What this poor girl wanted of this specimen of a man is more than we can fathom," remarked W. E. B. Du Bois, continuing that "if Rhinelander had used this girl as concubine or prostitute, white America would have raised no word of protest. . . . It is when he legally and decently marries the girl that all Hell breaks loose and literally tears the pair apart."[22] The *Chicago Defender* scoffed at the "poor little rich white boy with the vacant cranium," adding that "Mrs. Rhinelander should be given a medal for her bravery in marrying Kip and her sacrifice in the interest of redeeming some of the worn-out Huguenot blue blood." The *Chicago Broad Ax* was characteristically more reserved, blaming Kip's father for Kip and Alice's troubles, remarking that "if [Kip had] possessed a stiff backbone" none of this would have happened.

Although black papers remained the most critical of Leonard and his pretense, white editors also started to question Leonard's standing as a gentleman. And in many cases their criticism extended to the upper crust of society as well: Leonard became the negative symbol of the idle rich who inherited money and gave little to society. The *Hartford Times* suggested that he would have been better off if he had never had a fortune. Ironically, all his money, which had led to his moral downfall, was now being squandered to pay trial costs. Similarly, another paper noted that his wealth had tempted him into "riotous living."[23] "Hereafter when you want to accuse a man of fibbing," sneered the *Philadelphia Inquirer*, "you may call him a rhinelander [*sic*]."[24] The *Des Moines Register* quipped: "Kip Rhinelander's dad sent him out to Arizona for the benefit of his health, but the climate didn't seem to help his mentality any."[25] "The glory that was Rhinelander," intoned the *New York Evening Journal*, "has fallen."[26]

White southern papers were equally harsh, for very different reasons. For them the fatal flaw in the young man continued to lie in his willingness to marry below his class and across color lines.[27] Southern editorials continued to focus their criticism on the lack of anti-intermarriage laws in the North. By this point, however, Leonard could no longer be seen as the hapless victim of fraud. The *Richmond Times-Dispatch*, for example, published an editorial on November 12 that harshly criticized the violation of "racial integrity" evidenced in the Rhinelander Case. Reporting on the New York obsession with this scandal, the editor clung to the comfort that the "one redeeming feature of the whole distasteful affair" was that Leonard had brought suit for annulment as soon as he realized Alice was black. The fault, then, clearly lay in New York State's "laxity" in regulating and opposing interracial marriage. Presumably, if there had been such a law, Alice's identity would have been discovered sooner, or Leonard would have had no need to go through an annulment suit to end his marriage. After two weeks of testimony, however, the paper had dropped its support of Leonard: "Since this weak and fatuous Rhinelander went into marriage with his eyes apparently open, there is no cause for anxious solicitude as to him." Of course the *Times-Dispatch* maintained its stance on interracial marriages and the need for northern states to provide legislative barriers to further racial mixing.[28]

But what was Leonard expected to do? How should a 1920s man

worthy of that designation behave? Know better than to pick up a girl on the street? Restrain himself from sleeping with her? Stand up to his father? Run away with her? Refuse to pursue an annulment? Follow the complaint he had signed? Repent his betrayal of his station and beg the jury to release him from his shameful marriage? Repent his betrayal of his love and beg Alice to forgive him and take him back? Show no emotion or concern about the outcome of the case?

With each passing moment, members of the jury, court watchers, and those who quickly purchased the next installment of their daily or weekly newspapers came away with a greater understanding of the choices Leonard made. By his own admissions he acted in a manner that protected his narrow self-interests but not in a manner that endeared him to a larger world. Less of an enigma than in the trial's early days, the Leonard that had become known proved other than appealing. Fewer watchers were asking why he had deigned to dishonor his race and family by marrying below his station. Rather, some were starting to ask why all his money and privilege could not prevent his moral downfall . . . or whether they had caused it. Leonard may have come from the elite, but he could not claim superiority. After all, he had confirmed himself less than a gentleman in his dealings with Alice—and in the eyes of many commentators hardly a man.

9

THE FALLEN PRINCE

 EARLY IN THE trial Lee Parsons Davis denounced Isaac Mills for introducing filth and injuring Alice's reputation and promised to injure Leonard's in return during cross-examination. He kept his pledge. Leonard had simply wilted under the precision of Davis's exacting grilling, and the public took notice. In a few short days Leonard had shown himself to be a liar, more worldly than at first professed, and a male of questionable manliness. Davis turned the tables on Mills's questioning of Alice's behavior and made Leonard's manhood and gentleman's code the issue. Despite his racial and class status, Leonard began to lose ground in the media and public responses to the case. How, they wondered, with Davis's deft direction, could this blue-blooded symbol of elite society call himself a man or gentleman and so disgrace the woman he professed to love? Perhaps he, not she, was the one who was morally and behaviorally inferior. After all, it was one thing to hail from the working class, it was another to be a déclassé man of standing. And just as Leonard's image had been losing ground in the popular press, Alice's was gaining respect, especially in the New York tabloids. For some she became representative of the average working-class Americans' dreams of improving their economic position, and the promise the American capitalist ideal held out that they might do so. Their sexual behavior, however, threatened the images of both Leonard and Alice. For some the simple fact that they had engaged in premarital sex degraded their characters. For others, the fact that both had playfully and longingly referred to their physical relationship in letters put them beyond the pale. However, it was in this complicated intersection of class, race, and sex that the two found their positions turning in the public eye.

On the afternoon of Thursday, November 19, however, the trial came to a halt. New evidence had emerged that might reveal Leonard's true nature or end the trial altogether. After a grueling day of examination, Davis pulled out an ace he had apparently been hold-ing for some time. Having spent the last few days circling around the linked themes of Leonard's manhood, his behavior toward Alice, and their sexual relationship, Davis introduced a new line of questioning:

DAVIS: "There was nothing . . . unnatural about your love?"
LEONARD: "No."
DAVIS: "You understand my question?"
LEONARD: "Yes."
DAVIS: "Nothing could change it? Well, read this letter."[1]

Davis then produced a letter but did not read it into the record. Instead, he gave it to Leonard, still on the witness stand, and asked him to identify it as his own and read it to himself.

There was a long pause while the exhausted young man read his words. He flushed, and those whose job it was to try to discern emo-tions on his immobile face inferred chagrin. Davis then asked for a ten-minute recess and conferred with Mills and Morschauser in the judge's chambers. Ten minutes grew to twenty. Morschauser emerged and adjourned court for the day, an hour earlier than usual. Mills and Davis remained in the chambers for a while longer, then refused to answer the reporter's questions regarding the content of the letters. Leonard was hustled out the front door, through a phalanx of onlook-ers. The *New Rochelle Standard Star* described the moment:

Two detectives guarded Rhinelander from the curious crowd as he walked from the courthouse to a curtained limousine. As Rhine-lander descended the steps a thousand spectators waiting for him in

the street set up a cry of "[T]here he is!" His guards closed in on him
and the trio ran to the automobile. With a guard on each side of
him on the back seat, Rhinelander was driven rapidly away.[2]

Was this the last time these curiosity seekers would see Leonard Kip
Rhinelander? The mystery of this letter threw observers into a frenzy
of conjecture and suspense. The predominant speculation was that
they would bring about the end of the trial, the concession of the case
for Leonard.

The next morning the court reconvened, only to have Mills request
and receive a further stay, until Monday morning. Mills explained that
on Thursday an emergency had arisen of which he had previously
been unaware. He needed additional time, he argued, to research the
matter on behalf of his young client. The lawyers left, again refusing to
discuss the contents of the letter, and the newspapers were left with little to tell their readers. The lawyers weren't talking. Alice was locked
up in her home. Elizabeth answered the door but refused to speak to
reporters, admonishing them that it was no use waiting for her daughter to come out. And of course the trial itself, with its endless revelations and details, had come to a halt, probably permanently.

In fact, many were surprised that another stay had been granted,
expecting the trial to end on Friday morning with Mills withdrawing
his client's case. Despite the continued denials of lawyers on both
sides, newspapers across the country were sure a settlement would be
reached in order to avoid publication of the mysterious letters— there
were rumored to be more than one. It also appeared that Mills had
been completely caught off guard by this turn of events. Maybe he was
on the verge of detaching himself from Leonard's legal team. Perhaps
there was even a breach among the attorneys caused by this new revelation.[3]

Morschauser reminded the jurors not to read the papers over the
weekend. But all the papers could do for the next few days was to follow rumors, recap prior events, and report on the activities of every
major player in the case. The middle days of autumn had taken hold
outside the White Plains courtroom. Autumn in New York can alter-
nate between the brink of frost and the remains of summer. On Friday,
the day of adjournment, the air had turned cooler, chilled by a northwest wind. Mills worked on Saturday and went for a drive on Sunday.

Davis spent the weekend hunting rabbits and then turkeys. Another lawyer played squash. Alice stayed at home with her family. Leonard was back in hiding.

THE CONTENT OF the letters, of course, could provide matter for speculation. What had Davis meant in suggesting that Leonard and Alice's love was unnatural? Though most thought it doubtful they would ever be put into evidence, there were really only two possibilities suggested. The first was that they had contained clear evidence that Leonard knew Alice was not white prior to marrying her. After all, interracial relationships themselves were seen by many as "unnatural." In that case, however, why had Davis not simply read them into the record and rested his case? The second possibility seemed more likely: The letters' contents would be so degrading or embarrassing to Leonard and his family that Davis was offering them a chance to withdraw and avoid publication.[4]

When the trial resumed on Monday, November 23, the chill on the outside did little to freeze the spirited enthusiasm of would-be observers. They gathered in knots and bunched by the door, all hoping to claim one of the prized chairs in the chamber. Extra guards were posted to deal with the even bigger crowd now hoping to hear these mysterious letters.[5] It is inconceivable that the weather mattered much to Leonard. His attire varied little: suit, spats, and topcoat. He remained in the proverbial hot seat and each day the temperature of his emotions, thoughts, and actions inched up by degrees. His face, moreover, began to betray his feelings as his skin gleamed with perspiration. A long weekend of speculation was now over; the trial was apparently continuing. Leonard looked stricken by the proposed disclosure. In a case that already revealed love across the color line, premarital sex, and class transgression, what more could he fear?

The day's session opened anything but quietly. Within moments the letters became the focus of the proceedings. Mills demanded to address the court and to set the record straight, which drew a quick retort from Davis. Judge Morschauser cleared the elder attorney to speak. Mills reread Davis's last words before the trial adjourned the previous week. Then he complained, "That, your honor, was a deliberate threat that unless the plaintiff discontinued this trial this letter besmirching him would be spread upon the record." Davis could contain himself no more. He jumped to his feet and thundered, "This is the most improper statement I have ever heard from a lawyer. It was made for one purpose, to bring about a mistrial in this case. A younger lawyer would not dare to make such a statement. Are we trying this case on the evidence, or an attempt to poison and prejudice—" Mills cut Davis off in midsentence. After a few more histrionics from both sides, it was concluded that the trial would continue. In utter exasperation Mills shouted: "Now, I defy this man to do his worst. Let this trial proceed."[6]

When it became clear that Davis did intend to read Kip's letters, Judge Morschauser interrupted the proceedings to address the listeners. "If I were a woman, I would not stay," he admonished the mostly female crowd. "I give you ladies an opportunity to go while there is a lull." Several dozen did so, but fifty or more refused to budge. Alice, her parents, and sisters were among those who left the room. Alice certainly knew the letters' contents; like Leonard she had turned over her lover's private correspondence to her lawyers. But she didn't wish to hear them read in court and have more of her affair with Leonard mocked, criticized, and analyzed. In a subtle reminder of the distinction between money and class, Alice made much of her father's decision to flee the courtroom at this juncture. Grace, Alice's sister, lost sight of her father in the mayhem as the crowd left the room but clustered near the door. "Oh, he's out here, all right," Alice assured her sister. "He'd never stay in the courtroom while those terrible, vile letters were being read. Father is too much of a gentleman." The elder Jones approached his daughters and agreed: "I ain't going to listen to that stuff. When I was courtin' I never wrote that kind of stuff. I never wrote anything, for that matter. That stuff should never go down on paper."[7] The Jones women also demonstrated with their actions that they were not the type of women who cared to hear a public reading of an indelicate letter.

Morschauser noted that he was pleased that "many decent women" responded to his hint. He then asked Davis to show him the first letter. A silent tension filled the room. Some of the remaining women shifted uneasily in their chairs as Morschauser skimmed the contents. The judge lifted his head and looked pointedly at these women. "Everybody in the shape of a woman, who has no business here, will now leave the room," he ordered. He repeated this command three times before getting the desired response. Still some sat rigidly in their chairs, almost petulantly defying the judge's orders. He then urged "younger persons to go." With a slow shuffling of feet, most of the stragglers walked out, leaving only a few to be physically escorted from the room. The court took a ten-minute recess to complete its last removals. Only three women were allowed to remain, all reporters.[8]

Davis began as he had ended the proceeding Friday. Leaning in to Leonard, he commanded, "Did you tell the jury that your relations with Alice Rhinelander were natural?" The stolid Leonard mustered a weak yes. "Did you love this girl when you wrote that stuff?" Davis asked in a voice much softer and lower than had been his practice. Leonard maintained that he had. "Did you intend to make this girl your wife when you wrote this stuff on June 6, 1922?" In reply Leonard answered, "I had visions of it, yes." Back in command of his emotions after his earlier run-in with Mills, Davis continued, "Were you writing that letter to give pleasure to yourself?" "In a way I was," came the timid reply. He finished his statement with the claim he simply sought to make his letter to Alice "interesting."

Davis then read the first letter, including several passages that were considered obscene. "[A]s revolting and perverse as the most sensational prophets had predicted," it was the "filthiest dirt ever read in any courtroom," commentators sermonized. Many newspapers published the text of the letters, but all that did so omitted several sections considered unsuitable for publication.[9]

(Clift Hotel,
San Francisco, California.
Tuesday Night, July 31, 1922.)
(Last Letter until
I get to Honolulu.)

My own dearest girl.
    All day long I have been dreading this very moment and thinking how can I ever write Alice tonight, because dear, do you realize this will be the last letter you will get from me for probably two weeks that's the reason, darling. I hate to sit down at this desk tonight, because it will be long, long time before I can mail you another one and dear, it will be a longer time still. I am sorry to say, before that letter reaches you. . . .

Last night, sweetheart, after writing three full pages to you. I undressed and scrambled into bed, but not to go to sleep. No baby, do you know what I did? something that you do when my letters arrive at night. Yes, loved one I took everyone of your notes which I received at General delivery and read them while laying on the bed. Oh! blessed sweetheart of mine, some of the things you told me brought tears to my blue eyes. Others made my heart seem as though it would burst with joy and when you mentioned the time we were in bed together at the Marie Antoinette. . . . Oh, Sweetheart, many, many nights when I lay in bed and think about my darling girl. . . . God! Alice can you imagine me reading your tempting notes in bed last night and. . . .

Baby love, do you remember. . . . Sweetheart, am I tempting you and doesn't it bring back memories of past days?

Oh! Alice, love, be good, dear child, because I want you in the days to come and remember to keep our SECRET locked safely in your heart. You asked me if I met any other girl, didn't you, dear sweetheart, what a foolish question to put before me because you KNOW perfectly well that I havent bothered with anybody since I left you and NEVER will, old scout, for you, are my ONLY ONE, NOW and ALWAYS. . . .

Good night, love, and have patience, for I will write as soon as I reach Honolulu. Do those two things two things for your boy and pray for my safe voyage over and back.

Your ever true, loving Len.

(I LOVE YOU ALICE.)

On the witness stand while this was read, Leonard Rhinelander lowered his head but otherwise did a remarkable job of hiding his feelings.

Readers in 1925 were left to speculate about what followed the ellipses. The trial transcript has been lost, which puts modern-day readers at a similar disadvantage. Moreover, by today's standards the letters' contents may have been quite tame. Piecing together texts printed in different newspapers makes it clear that some refused to include passages referring to "caresses" and physical proximity, or to Leonard reading Alice's letters while "in bed." Davis's twice-mentioned reference to unnatural acts raises the possibility of other activity here. The first ellipses offer a tantalizing hint. Leonard was in bed, thinking about Alice. Whatever he thought led him to exclaim, "God!" Then she is told to imagine him in his bed with her letters and remember . . . what? The memory of those times rekindled the excitement for Leonard; perhaps he told Alice he had masturbated while reading her letters and thinking about her. Masturbation was certainly considered an unnatural act in 1925.

But there was more there. General descriptions of this letter, as well as others we have discussed, suggest that Leonard made explicit references to things that he and Alice had done together while staying at the hotel. Grace Robinson, writing for the *Daily News*, observed that the first of the two letters "proved to be a narration of abnormal practices in the love tryst at the Marie Antoinette."[10] As a sidebar to the lead story, the *Daily News* staff left an important clue for their readers who couldn't stand leaving the mystery unsolved. The paper reported that behavior described by Leonard was not only unnatural but criminal. The penalty for these offenses could be as much as a twenty-year jail term. Boldly and forthrightly the paper told readers which section of the New York Penal Code outlawed the acts described by Leonard. This article described various aspects of sodomy, defined as a crime against nature in which both the person committing the action and a person who willingly submitted were considered guilty of these crimes and any amount of sexual penetration, however slight, was sufficient to qualify. As defined in 1925, sodomy included sexual activity with any animal or bird, or intercourse with a dead body. But it also included both anal and oral sex, and it was probably one or both of these that Leonard described. In practice the laws against both of these types of sodomy were most often enforced against same-sex activities. Then, as now, heterosexual couples could engage in these behaviors privately with little fear of discovery, let alone arrest.[11]

Back in the courtroom, where everyone remaining in the room knew exactly what the letters said, the grilling began:

"Did you love this girl, Len?" asked Davis in a low voice after reading this letter.

"I did," Leonard offered.

"Why did you write that?" shouted Davis, reading a passage of the letter. Then followed a series of questions more brutally frank than any previously asked.

Rereading the most vivid passages, Davis kept demanding to know the purpose behind Leonard's words.

DAVIS: "Didn't you do this to excite her?"
LEONARD [offering his longest answer yet]: "I had no way of relieving my emotions except in my letters, in which I put my whole heart and soul."
DAVIS: "How did you relieve your emotions before you met Alice?"
LEONARD [firmer and less flustered than ever before]: "I didn't."
DAVIS: "You realize this was just smut?"
LEONARD [feebly]: "Yes, I was trying to keep my word of honor."
DAVIS: "In order to keep your word of honor, it was necessary to write this smut?"

Leonard managed a controlled "Yes," and the questioning continued with Mills voicing objection after objection, intending to mute the damage done by Davis and to try and throw his opponent off stride.

After another set of interruptions Davis asked Leonard again about the phrase "Am I tempting you?" in his letter.

DAVIS [jabbing]: "Did you mean what you wrote?"
LEONARD: "Yes."
DAVIS: "Then you admit you were tempting this girl?"
LEONARD: "No[,] I was merely asking a question."
DAVIS: "Did you want an answer?"
LEONARD [curtly]: "No."

Incredulous, Davis demanded to know, "Why did you ask a question to which you didn't expect an answer?" Leonard had no reply.

Davis then read the second "mystery" letter, which had been written almost two months earlier from the same San Francisco hotel.

(Clift Hotel,
San Francisco, California.
Tuesday, June 6th, 1922.

My own darling girl.
This morning after I had gotten back from my walk through

Golden Gate Park. I found two more of your cheery letters, dated June 1st. waiting for me under the door. Do you know dear that I have received five of your sweet notes in the last two days. It is hard to believe and almost seems to good to be true, but I have them all before me on the desk and looking them over while I am writing to you. It makes me feel so happy, darling, when I hear from you and especially when you write about how you used to caress me and make me feel as though I were in heaven. . . . Do you ever long for my lips? yes love. my warm, lips and . . . You said you liked my ways, didn't you dear? Do you remember, honeybunch, how . . .

Well, Alice, darling, maybe when you have read these things you will feel blue or maybe they will make you feel happy. I don't know which. But loved one you asked me to write an interesting letter like you sent me, so I have tried my best. Have I tempted you sweetheart and have I made you imagine that I am right next to you? . . .

Listen Alice when you get this letter dont write to me at the Hotel Clift any more because my pal and I will be starting in a day or two to the Yosemite Valley. I hate to ask you not write here any more because Lord only knows when I am going to get another of your letters. However, dear, I got along for three weeks without hearing from you and I will get along this time because I have faith in you, dear, and will always trust you.

Your loving boy.
LEN.

Davis recommenced his cross-examination:

DAVIS: "Did you love this girl when you wrote this stuff?"
LEONARD: "Yes."
DAVIS: "Did you intend to marry her?"
LEONARD: "I had visions of it."
DAVIS: "Did you mean to tempt this girl when you wrote this?"
LEONARD: "I wrote to make it interesting."
DAVIS: "Were you attempting to tempt her."
LEONARD: "I believe I was."
DAVIS: "So you were trying to tempt her in June but not in July?"

Leonard struggled unsuccessfully to answer this last question.

DAVIS: "Did you ever get a letter like this from Alice?"

LEONARD: "No, I think not."

DAVIS: "You knew it was the vilest kind of smut?"

LEONARD: "Yes."

DAVIS: "And you were trying to excite her?"

LEONARD: "At her request I was."

DAVIS [somewhat shrilly]: "Let me have one letter showing a request from Alice for this sort of letter."

Stressed from the strain of the cross-examination, Leonard started to twitch and stammer. He proclaimed he wrote the letters to "keep his word of honor." Yet he and his lawyers admitted they had no written request from Alice for such letters from Leonard.

"Did you mean the things you wrote in the last letter?" Mr. Davis continued. "Yes," responded the visibly shaken Leonard. "Did you do the things?" Alice's attorney demanded to know. Leonard mustered a cautious "Yes." "You know that what was mentioned in the letter was unnatural?" Davis continued. "No, I didn't," Leonard answered in his own defense.

An incredulous Davis snapped, "Never occurred to you?"

"No," Leonard admitted.

Pushing the witness, "You've discussed sex matters in your life?" Davis asked.

"A little bit," the shamefaced young man acknowledged.

"You discussed it in boarding school?" Davis continued to probe.

Leonard answered simply, if a little evasively, "Yes, a little bit."

"Did you discuss these things?" Davis asked with a slight hint of irritation.

"No," Leonard told Davis.

Refusing to let Leonard evade the heart of his questioning, Davis demanded, "You didn't realize that . . . was unnatural?"

"No," the witness replied.

"You don't realize it now?"

"No."[12]

BUT DAVIS PERSISTED: "You talked with Judge Mills about these letters?" Leonard replied, "Yes." Altering his line of questions ever so slightly, Davis continued, "Sitting on the stand, reading the letter, you thought what you did was natural?" Affirming his position, Leonard offered a prompt "Yes."

The 1920s marked a period of transition in the nation's social confrontation with sexuality. In academic treatises, psychiatric sessions, popular books, birth control clinics, and newspaper and magazine advice columns, Americans addressed all aspects of the confrontation. Some clung to traditional modes, wanting nothing to do with more open discussions of sexuality and love. They frowned on the work of Margaret Sanger and others who campaigned too forthrightly for widespread use of birth control devices and techniques. They took little notice of Sanger's own biases and the exclusion of immigrant and African American women from her purview.[13] Opponents argued that birth control interfered with the divine purpose of human sexuality: reproduction. Modern romances that elevated women to the same status as men violated other religious precepts, especially ones that placed men in control. The guardians of the status quo favored chaste relationships with clear gender delineation.

Others, however, found solace in a modern world that enabled them to discuss love and romance in both oblique and transparent ways. They sought out romantic love, love that led them to surrender a part of themselves for the sake of a lasting and fulfilling relationship. They had probably heard of, even if they didn't fully understand, the work of Austrian psychiatrist Sigmund Freud. In this more modern world, sexuality lay at the center of both male and female psychological development. For women, love legitimized or at the very least naturalized female sexuality.[14] Moreover, medical experts now told them it was okay to have sexual feelings, which were often discussed as synonymous with love. With increasing regularity many turned to advice columnists for validation of their feelings, yearnings, and faith in the correctness of love. Across urban America more and more love-struck individuals asked informed outsiders for advice. Instead of a priest or minister, friend or parent, these socially approved advisers dispensed advice, counsel, and guidance. Doris Blake, who wrote for the *New York Daily News*, became one of the better-known social advisers in metropolitan New York.

As much as anything, however, the talk was of sex and not just love. Commentators and social analysts still held that only unrespectable girls expressed themselves sexually outside the bounds of marriage. Love led to marriage, which provided the reason for sex. Women who had sex outside of marriage were perceived as somehow delinquent and the victims of their own desires. Men who wrote Doris Blake said as much. Only a woman with unchecked sex appeal who wanted to be kissed needed to fear "improper" advances, some wrote. Women who subordinated their sexuality could be sexual beings without attracting the boorish actions of men. A true man, reasoned the authors of the letters to Blake, would never force himself on a woman without a clear invitation. In such constructions men controlled their sexual selves if women submerged theirs. Thus, in a powerful reminder of the social flux that characterized the United States in the 1920s, scores believed in male and female sexuality in the modern age, championed the importance of romantic love, and still held on to Victorian notions about "good" and "bad" behavior, "good" and "bad" women and men. The Rhinelander Case both underscored the changes wrought by these modern perspectives on sexuality and love and highlighted strongly held views about propriety.

Since the 1870s the fearless few who sought to write about sexual matters and to have their views distributed had butted heads with high-placed guardians of public morals. The battle was most fiercely drawn out between Anthony Comstock and Free Lovers such as Ezra and Angela Heywood. The Heywoods, and others like them, believed in the free expression of sexuality. They encouraged others to embrace their sexual selves, to experiment, and to talk candidly about sexual matters. Angela Heywood actually enlivened public discourse with explicit terminology for sexual practices, organs, and procedures. Such behavior riled moral protectors such as Comstock, a one-time Connecticut dry goods salesman who founded the New York Society for the Suppression of Vice in 1872. Through that group he persuaded Congress to amend the Postal Act a year later. The new law, known as the Comstock Act, prohibited the distribution of lewd, obscene, lascivious, and indecent articles, advertisements, or writing materials. Under particular attack were newspapers, which Comstock believed aided in the corruption of American youth. He once railed that newspapers "open the way for [the] grossest evils." So successful was Comstock's crusade that soon even the most daring of papers shied away from a direct confrontation with the postal inspectors.[15] Rather than risk violating some unclear definition of obscenity, most papers offered their readers carefully edited versions of what was read in court on this day of the Rhinelander trial.

Not everyone agreed that women particularly needed, or wanted, to be protected from sexually explicit materials. Morschauser's decision to remove nonjournalist women from the courtroom prompted several different responses. The most common was to chide or laugh at the reluctance of many women to give up their seats just when things were getting really juicy. A cartoon in the *New York Evening Journal* showed a quiet audience of matronly white women attending the hearing, carrying little dogs. (Alice was distinguished by a black dress.) When the judge suggests that the ladies leave, a mad rush of dozens of frenzied women pours through the windows and the doors, knocking the judge off his feet. Another editorial comment hissed that no doubt the same women who had to be ordered to leave the courtroom that day also demanded respect as ladies in their communities. But most coverage of the incident was humorous, and accepted as a given that women were openly interested in hearing the sexual details of Alice and Leonard's affair.[16]

One F. D. Calderwood of San Francisco, however, wrote a letter to his or her editor complaining about a "recent case" in which the judge had removed women from a courtroom where "objectionable evidence" was to be heard. What authority, the writer asked, did the judge have for "arbitrarily discriminating between the sexes?" If the material was contaminating, would it not be so for men as well? "Adult women," Calderwood concluded, "are as competent as men to decide what they may safely hear, and what is unfit for one sex is unfit for the other. This kind of babying of women is hypocritical and absurd."[17] Interestingly, this letter never mentioned the Rhinelander trial by name, although its details and the timing of its publication leave little doubt this was the provocation. Furthermore, the letter suggests that as far away as California, people were following and discussing the implications of the Rhinelander case. As a final commentary on the flux of American perceptions of sexual openness versus careful censorship of behavior and obscene writing, Leonard's letters were literally sold on the streets as pornography within a few days of the trial.

DAVIS SENSED THAT Leonard had regained his equilibrium a bit, so he altered his legal assault again. "When did Alice tell you she'd been with another man?" Davis's intent was obvious: Alice risked demeaning herself in Leonard's eyes; while revealing the most private dimensions, surely she wouldn't lie about or hide her race.

LEONARD: "I don't recollect. It was in her letters."
DAVIS: "See if you can't recall. Didn't you make this inquiry?"
LEONARD: "No."
DAVIS: "She volunteered it?"
LEONARD: "I believe she did."

After a couple of additional exchanges, Davis made his final point about deception, race, and sexuality. He appreciated the delicate balance between sexual activity and the hint of promiscuity. Craftily he wanted the jury to question Leonard's words and the logic behind them. A working-class girl risked much by divulging a sexual history, especially in relations with a man of means. Telling Leonard about her sexual past marked her as available and "easy." To tell him meant either that she had the utmost faith in his integrity or that she was not concerned with her reputation. Davis hoped to convince the jury that Alice hid nothing from Leonard because she loved him; she trusted him and she gave him every reason to trust her.

DAVIS: "This girl, who has been pictured as chasing you, did freely confess to you she had been with another man?"
LEONARD: "Yes."
DAVIS: "After this confession she deceived you about her color?"
LEONARD: "Yes."
DAVIS: "Have you any letters, except those introduced in evidence, in which she told you she hadn't been pure?"
LEONARD: "I don't know."
DAVIS: "When you were going through this performance did you love her?"
LEONARD: "I might have."
DAVIS: "Did you intend making her your wife?"
LEONARD: "No, I did not."
DAVIS: "You were willing to marry a girl who did these things, who confessed she was unchaste, but you were unwilling to marry her if she had the least taint of colored blood?"
LEONARD: "As to the color, I draw the line."[18]

At this point Davis asked for a break in the cross-examination of Leonard, which the court honored.

When the trial resumed Davis quickly asked a number of concluding questions and then ceded the floor to Mills for redirect examination. Mills stuck to his theme: Alice was both the aggressor and conniver in the relationship. He opened with an excerpt from a letter Alice wrote Leonard that hinted at a possible amorous dalliance between her sister Grace and Kreitler, the Orchard's maintenance man. Establishing that Grace may have had sexual interests, he then turned to Alice's parents and their ostensibly lax attitude about sex and propriety. Mills asked simply, "When you spent the weekends at the Jones house, did Alice sleep with you sometimes?" Leonard answered affirmatively that she had. A series of other questions from Mills allowed Leonard to try to salvage his reputation. He had kept his promise to Alice about gifts and marriage. She had cooperated with him to deceive her parents about their trips and his father about their marriage. Mills concluded his redirect with a series of questions about Alice's habits. With Leonard's aid he painted a portrait of a modern young woman who had sexual partners, drank alcohol, and smoked. For the entire world Mills put the modern working woman with independent means and twentieth century sensibilities on trial.

Leonard's almost cavalier attitude toward Alice and her parents incensed many court watchers. In his words as long as the woman was willing the man had no larger obligations. But most surmised that her class and/or racial status had made it easier for him to ignore any responsibility or honor. By his own admission Leonard first sought Alice for sex. He used the words of love but they lacked currency for him. They were merely tools for him to achieve his satisfaction. As significant, by revealing his own intentions, he robbed himself of the cover of being in love. While many Americans frowned on premarital sex in 1920s America, a couple could claim some grace if they maintained they were in love, particularly if they eventually married, as of course Alice and Leonard had.

Did Leonard's admission of more sexual than romantic interest at the beginning also cast doubt on the sincerity of Alice's love? It's hard to say. Certainly without such protection working-class women like Alice too quickly fell into the category social writers such as Robert Dickinson, author of *The Single Woman* (1931), bemoaned. In his account working-class women could not control their sexual impulses and thus freely gave away the thing they should most highly have prized: their virginity, and with it their virtue. However, Leonard's equivocations on the question of when he began to truly love Alice may also have served to highlight her emotional and social vulnerability. Perhaps it was she who was seduced by his declarations of love precisely because his words mirrored her feelings.

In either case Leonard's refusal to protect Alice and her reputation enraged many.[19] Margery Rex of the *New York Evening Journal* suggested that the reason Leonard had not carefully examined Alice's family was that initially he was not looking for love. But, she argued, if it had been Alice's idea for them to marry, she was only fulfilling her proper role and doing what any woman would: "When Kip met Alice he was the enemy of her purpose, the purpose of a woman, her birthright, be she white or black . . . but [when] she got him to marry her she ensnared him, but that is what all women try to do—get men to do the honorable thing and marry them."[20] Writing from a complicated perspective, Rex here suggested that both lawyers might be partially right: Alice might have manipulated Leonard into marriage, but if he sought to exploit her sexually and then move on, she was within her rights to do whatever it took to protect herself.

The *Detroit Free Press* saw the situation only in terms of class, however, noting:

> A section of an ancient family's code of honor—that a liaison with a housemaid is the privilege of a gentleman—was written into the record today in supreme court here when Leonard "Kip" [*sic*] Rhinelander admitted [to] the sordid affair of a rich man and a servant. It developed into love later, he said.[21]

Clearly, from a working-class perspective, this kind of "code of honor" held no virtue at all.

By the 1920s few had not heard of Horatio Alger, the nineteenth-century author in whose novels, such as *Ragged Dick*, everyday protagonists exemplified tremendous economic mobility by dint of hard work and moral behavior. His stories came to encapsulate the masculine version of the rags-to-riches tale, but there was also a feminine version: "Cinderella." Like Cinderella, Alice achieved her economic rise through love and sexual allure. Like Cinderella, she may even have schemed to get her prince. But Cinderella is a heroine, and as some scholars have pointed out, a particularly American one. In her brief analysis of the history of "Cinderella" in the United States, Jan Yolen argues that the tale has become popular in part because of its similarity to a general myth about rags-to-riches. There is, she notes, an "American creed . . . that even a poor boy can grow up to become president [with an] unliberated corollary . . . that even a poor girl can grow up and become the president's wife."[22] As the *Reno Evening Gazette* acknowledged, Alice's dreams of future wealth were neither criminal nor unusual. The realities of the class system in the United States prompted many to "wish to lift themselves into what they think is a broader sphere." This white editor did not even blame her for concealing her race in this pursuit.[23]

Perhaps it is not so surprising, then, that Alice came to symbolize a "modern Cinderella." The male and female versions of the rags-to-riches tales functioned as parables of the virtues of strong character and high morals. Hard work, diligence, and right action resulted in material success and happiness, went the story line. Writing nearly a quarter of a century after the trial in *Ebony*, writer Ralph Matthews observed, "The reason the story of Cinderella is universally and perennially popular is because it is constantly being re-enacted in real life by lucky lassies of all races in each generation." Matthews clearly saw Alice as one of those Cinderellas; she was the most famous of the cases he cited of black women who married white millionaires. For Matthews what differentiated these women from their fictitious counterparts was that they "made their own slippers" without the help of fairy godmothers and "crashed [the] color line to fame and fortune."[24]

Several contemporary observers saw Alice as a Cinderella figure as well. The *Philadelphia Inquirer* noted that: "from the start of their strange romance Rhinelander had played to the mind and emotion of Alice Jones as a prince charming to a dark Cinderella, who worked as an 'upstairs girl.' Rhinelander had a hard time saying whether his intentions were 'honorable' or not."[25] Likewise the *Herald-Tribune* described her as "a sort of dusky and commonplace Cinderella."[26]

Many, after all, questioned the rigidity of existing social boundaries, and American mythology sanctioned such questioning by offering examples of men who overcame the limits of their birth status to achieve considerable financial gain. So in broad outline the narrative of Alice and Leonard flaunting certain conventions fit what others came to know and believe about the promise of American mobility. Like the Prince Charming in folklore, Leonard had inherited considerable wealth and power. His father had the means of assembling scores of faithful attendants to look after the young man's welfare. Yet Leonard was not a fantasy character; he was a man with advantages and limits. Leonard had a pronounced speech impediment that his lawyer tried to depict as a mental weakness. He was neither classically handsome nor particularly accomplished. Worse, he betrayed himself as a liar and a lout who buckled under the pressure of a stern and dictatorial father. In the press accounts Leonard appeared a feeble example of what wealth and privilege produced: inarticulate, self-centered, powerful, frivolous, and carnal.

Alice, meanwhile, became a Cinderella ill at ease with her class ascent. Her letters revealed the limits of her education. In effect her prince had not been able to produce a Pygmalion effect: Her words retained the cadences and syntax of her working-class background. She dressed well, but with the rise of a consumer culture and independent means achieved through gainful employment, many working women had begun to mimic the style of the upper middle class, if not the aristocratic class. The abundant evidence of sexuality further distanced Alice from the role of the classic Cinderella. Alice not only had a sexual relationship with Leonard, she talked openly about it in the letters they exchanged.

Furthermore, this story was about more than social mobility across the class line. At the same time that Alice represented the aspirations of scores who wished to climb above their social position, she was always described as a dusky or dark Cinderella. Rarely did race disappear from the image of her social climb. Not only had she tried to exchange her life of domestic servitude for one of idle comfort, but she had apparently tried to hide her black ancestry, if not from her husband then at least from his friends and family. Despite the class sympathies Alice received from many white news reporters and apparently onlookers and readers as well, her racial status was never long forgotten. And within a few hours of the reading of the mystery letters, both her racial identity and the limits of her status as a representative of the working woman were to be tested in a highly shocking and public manner.

10

THE LAST VEIL LIFTED

 LEONARD'S MYSTERY LETTERS provided sensation and scandal enough for the evening papers. By the next morning, however, American readers discovered that Leonard's sexually explicit writings had been merely the opening act in a dramatic day, with plenty more to come. In the afternoon, Davis followed the presentation of Leonard's unprintable descriptions of sexual activity with another depiction of human sexuality: a woman's body exposed. In what was arguably the most memorable and troubling point in a trial already filled with drama and emotion, Alice Rhinelander partially disrobed, baring her breasts, back, and legs before the court.

This excruciating image both demands and defies explanation. It reverberates through a violent racial history and flickers with the remembrances of a multitude of atrocious vignettes: enslaved men and women standing on auction blocks, stripped before the examination of potential purchasers; the icon of a half-dressed woman in chains on her knees pleading to her white abolitionist "sister" for help; the "Hottentot Venus," a southern African woman named Sara Baartman, brought to England and put on display, usually nude, for scientific and curiosity-seeking audiences; Sojourner Truth baring her breasts to prove to a hostile audience at the Akron, Ohio, Women's Rights

Convention that she was a woman, reminding them that white men had seen her breasts before when she wet-nursed them as a slave—that the shame of her nudity was theirs, not hers. As well, slave narratives detailed depictions of brutal beatings, rapes, and tortures inflicted on African Americans by slave owners. And then there were Dahomey female warriors brought to the 1893 Chicago World's Fair to represent, with their "masculine" role and bared breasts, the lowest level of human cultural and racial evolution: the savage African matriarchy. Even in the 1920s eugenic and anthropological studies produced endless photographs, measurements, and assessments of the bone structure, skin color, facial features, hair texture, and sexual organs of Africans and African Americans.[1]

That moment of her partial disrobing, then, thrust Alice into a long history of race and color. Even if she had no ancestry that tied her to an African past, she was black in the eyes of most who read or heard about the deliberations in the Westchester County court. In 1925, after all, men and women still lived who had inspected others for profit on auction blocks, or who had themselves been so inspected. The common thread: black bodies, no matter how fair, could be identified on review, which marked those people as different, and white treatment of them as appropriate. That was, at least, the logic that governed American race relations for centuries and made Alice Beatrice Jones Rhinelander forever colored. Alice was neither the first nor the last African American woman asked or forced to bare her body to satisfy the needs and curiosities of white men. In an insidious fashion, the viewing of Alice's body, the fact she didn't speak, the extent to which others redramatized the moment, truly objectified Alice and made her an item to be viewed and desired. In effect the display of Alice became pornographic.

But her ordeal was intended to help her win her case. What did Davis think the jurors would see? Clearly he believed that the physical appearance of Alice's body would convince them that Leonard must have known she was not white. Despite his repeated references to George's dark skin, and the "dusky" hues of Alice and her sisters' faces and hands, he needed strong evidence that Leonard's claims to have been deceived were unfounded. Did he have other expectations of how the jurors would react to this scene? Could he have hoped that, as fathers and upstanding citizens, they would take pity on the unfortu-

nate girl on display before them—see her as a victim in need of protection? Could he have been unaware of the risks of reinforcing an
image of Alice as oversexualized. Seeing her body might, therefore,
inspire less-than-paternal responses from the jury. Or was he hoping
that precisely that image of a sexually available, exotic woman would
itself reinforce the blackness he was trying to emphasize?

   And what about Alice? Her situation was not completely involun-
tary, but how much choice had she been given in this matter? She had
come to court prepared to do this—wearing a long coat which she
kept buttoned to cover whatever clothing was most conducive to this
task. Had she protested? Was she convinced that this was the best way
to win her case? Could she have been unaware of the emotional toll
on herself and public response to this moment? Was she hoping to
elicit a response from Leonard, to remind him of what he had lost? To
prove herself willing to suffer anything to defend her marriage and her
honor? Or had she been browbeaten into agreeing to the performance? Of course, no one knows the answers to any of these questions.
But in the events that transpired, and the responses to them, lie a few
clues and possibilities.

   Speaking in a courtroom that had already been cleared of all women
for the reading of the mystery letters, Lee Parsons Davis began the afternoon session by asking Judge Morschauser to remove the remaining
spectators—all men who had no business there. Davis wanted his
client, he said, to show the jury her legs and torso to prove that her race
was obvious in her physical appearance. When Mills objected that he
did not want a "demonstration of a naked body at this trial," Davis
rejoined: "[I]t will not be entirely naked." Morschauser agreed that seeing Alice's body was important because, "It must be shown in this sort
of case." For all three men Alice had quickly ceased to be an individual
person in their language and had become a body—an "it," not a
"she"—another step in the process of objectification. Davis suggested
they use the judge's chambers, and he and Morschauser discussed who
should be present. Mills objected again to this "indecent procedure."
Davis explained again that he would only ask the jury to look at his
client from the waist up, and at her lower limbs.[2]

   Alice and her mother were summoned from the corridor, where
they had retreated during the reading of the letters. With her mother
beside her, the young woman went into the jury room, crying quietly.

They remained behind closed doors for a few minutes with the judge, lawyers, and Leonard. When the doors opened, she reemerged, supported by her mother and weeping bitterly. What that experience had entailed for her we can only imagine. Once she had let herself be vulnerable and showed her body to Leonard with love and desire. What, if anything, passed between the estranged lovers in that room? What thoughts and memories went through their minds as she methodically displayed her body for the jury? She was on the verge of total collapse as she left the courtroom. Her father had to carry her out of the building, where guards barely restrained the "morbid and sensation-baited crowd." None of the Joneses reappeared in court that day.[3]

Alice was now entered as an exhibit, still silent except for her weeping. Leonard returned to the witness stand, still showing no emotion. Mills offered one final objection, to no avail, and at last Davis could ask the questions that lay behind the entire proceeding:

DAVIS: "You have just viewed portions of your wife's body?"
LEONARD: "Yes."
DAVIS: "Is it the same shade it was when you saw her in the Marie Antoinette?"
LEONARD: "Yes."
DAVIS: "That's all."[4]

And that was all. Davis simply sought to show that Leonard, having seen Alice's body almost three years before their marriage, must have known that she was not white. The legal purpose of this "most trying of all ordeals" for Alice, then, was to prove that Leonard must have known his wife was colored before he married her.

Throughout the trial Davis had sought to establish that Alice's "colored blood" was manifest in her physical appearance, and anyone who suggested otherwise risked the ridicule of Davis, the always-packed courtroom, and the media. Leonard's lawyers had the difficult task of maintaining that Alice's "colored blood" was invisible—a more unsettling stance for most white Americans. But they simultaneously maintained that any "taint" of colored blood, however unapparent, was enough to make Alice a "Negro." Alice's lawyers resorted to the comforting belief that race was easy to determine and differentiate. Alice, they repeated, was clearly black, for anyone with reasonable intelligence to see. Even if she had hidden her hair and powdered her face, her lover/husband and now the jury could easily see from her body that she was not white.

On the other hand, it was clear that not all who saw Alice saw a black woman. Although the question of her racial status had been settled with her own signed admission that she "had some colored blood," observers still disagreed about her racial appearance. The specific problem for the trial was determining what *Leonard* had seen when he looked at Alice and her family. A week before the disrobing, Davis and Leonard had an exchange that reached the core of this question:

DAVIS: "What is the color of your wife's body?"
LEONARD: "Dark."
DAVIS: "How dark?"
LEONARD: "Fairly dark."
DAVIS [shouting]: "How dark?"
LEONARD: "It isn't any darker than the arms of some women I saw in Havana."
DAVIS: "Well[,] after seeing your wife's body and seeing Mr. Jones, did any suspicions crop into your mind?"
LEONARD: "No."
DAVIS: "You are telling the jury that from 1921 until 1924, after seeing your wife and her family that you had no suspicion your wife had colored blood."
LEONARD: "Yes."
DAVIS: "Was your brain working?"
LEONARD: "I think it was."
DAVIS: "Eye-sight good?"

Leonard did not answer this question.

DAVIS: "How is your eye-sight—are you color-blind? Can you tell black from white—brown from white?"
LEONARD [feebly]: "Yes."[5]

This, in a nutshell, was the problem evoked by the Rhinelander Case that resonated with current white American anxieties: Was it possible to tell black from white or brown from white? The courtroom enjoyed quite a few laughs at the expense of the stammering Leonard and his inability or unwillingness to admit that Alice or her sisters, or even her "dark-skinned" father, "looked colored." Again and again Davis harangued Leonard, each time provoking laughter from the mixed audience in the courtroom. Couldn't he tell that George Jones was black? That Alice was black? That Grace and Emily and Emily's husband, Robert, were all black? Hadn't they looked the same three years earlier as they did now? Everyone could now see who was black; if Leonard couldn't, he must really be stupid or lying.

Leonard Rhinelander's inability to tell black from white represented white America's inability to tell black from white. Davis's incredulous scoffing at his "color-blindness" served to further Alice's case in part by offering white Americans (including the jury) a way out of their dilemma: If they decided that Leonard was lying when he said he couldn't see that Alice and her father were black, they could reassure themselves that race was real, was obvious.

NOT SURPRISINGLY THE scene, or at least the imagined scene, of Alice partially disrobing, quickly emerged as a defining moment of the trial. As far away as England, newspapers called it the climax of the scandalous American trial.[6] Although no reporters were actually in the judge's chambers, many journalistic "descriptions" of the incident immediately appeared in dailies and weeklies, ranging from sedate reconstructions to dramatic imaginings.[7] In stark contrast, white southern newspapers studiously avoided mention of Alice's disrobing.[8] Overall, the "eyewitness" reports provided detailed, sometimes voyeuristic, often quite sympathetic, and conflicting reports as to what happened, who was there, and which parts and how much of her body they saw. Generally, however, the papers agreed that the purpose had been to "test" or "determine her color," and that her body was darker than her face.

Physical appearance was not the only method Davis relied on to demonstrate his claim that Alice was obviously not white. Just as the reporters seeking confirmation of the race of Leonard's unknown bride had relied on multiple forms of evidence, so too did Davis seek multilayered criteria for racial identity. At one point during the second week of the trial, he pulled out a letter from Leonard that referred to a "strut-ting party" Alice attended. What, Davis asked the plaintiff, was a strut-ting party? Leonard explained it was slang for a dance. But Davis suggested it was a "typical negro expression," which should have clued Leonard in to Alice's linguistic and perhaps social participation in this form of black culture.[9]

Davis also tried to get Leonard to remember exactly when he began to suspect that Alice was not white.

DAVIS: "When did you say you first had suspicions as to your wife's color?"
LEONARD: "When I read the newspapers."
DAVIS: "No doubt ever came into your mind before then?"
LEONARD: "I had a suspicion."

Davis had Alice stand up and remove her hat, exposing "crinkly" black hair.

DAVIS: "Did she look the same at the time of your marriage as she does now?"
LEONARD: "Yes."

Nor was Leonard the only witness forced to bear the illogical weight of American racialism in that Westchester County courtroom. A few hours after the partial disrobing, a social acquaintance of the couple, Joseph Rich, testified that he had also thought Alice was white prior to reading the newspaper headlines. With hindsight, he suggested, she had been trying to hide her dark skin by wearing long sleeves and explaining that she was Spanish. But, no, he had never suspected that she was not white. Looking at her now, however, he allowed that she "appeared darker to him . . . than she had then." How could that be? Perhaps, he suggested, it was because she was nervous. The crowd snickered.

"Oh!" said Davis, jumping on this nonsensical explanation. "You think nervousness is turning her face black?"

"It could," said Rich, muttering that he still thought she looked Spanish.[10]

Nonetheless, Leonard's plight was not unique. And Davis's question reexposed several cavernous fault lines in white Americans' definitions of racial categories and their understandings of how to determine and measure blackness. Was race dependent on heredity, cultural behavior, or physical appearance? What defined the difference between white and Negro? How could one tell? In the context of these anxieties, then, Alice's disrobing served to reduce her racial ambiguity by establishing that she had discernible "colored blood" that was marked on her physical body. In asking the judge to order Alice to show her body to the court, Davis was challenging the jurors to test their own racial eyesight, their own ability to tell black from white. On the afternoon of November 23, the jurors in the Rhinelander Case were given the opportunity to test their ability to "see" the black ancestry of a person sometimes perceived as white or Latin.

Accordingly, most recountings emphasized physical descriptions of Alice's body betraying clear evidence of her blackness. The *Detroit Free Press*, for example, assured their readers that "the Alice that the jurors saw was dark—so dark that even the most unscientific observer must have concluded that she was undoubtedly of Negro blood. Her back, especially, was a near-ebony."[11] The article also pointed out that Alice's face, when rouged and powdered, looked Latin. The *Detroit Free Press*, however, had anticipated the disrobing and predicted that it would prove her too dark skinned to be white: "The shapely back of Mrs. Leonard Kip Rhinelander . . . will be bared here when the trial is resumed. . . . It is said that although Mrs. Rhinelander's face is virtually pure white, her back is very much more dusky."[12] The *Daily Mirror* reported that "it was said that Mrs. Rhinelander's body was so black as her father's face. Jones is a dark chocolate color."[13] And the *Philadelphia Inquirer* reported that her body was "perceptibly darker than her face."[14] In fact, the only person to claim otherwise was Mills himself.

Nor was skin color the only presumed physical evidence of racial ancestry. Scientific racism, and its popular counterparts, posited several such markers by which one could always separate a "white Negro" from a "pure white." Physical anthropologists and eugenicists published numerous studies that cataloged physical measurements of skin, bone structure, facial features, hair texture, jaw angles, and other gauges believed to divide humanity into biological categories. A pursuit now invalidated by most scholars, these studies sought to deter-

mine exact criteria by which remote ancestry in mixed-race individuals could be "found" and proved. Outside academia, white Americans
had their own theories of how one could distinguish between a white-
appearing black person and a "true" white person. For example, one
anonymous "white Negro" recounted a conversation with a white
southern man who claimed he could tell a "white Negro" from a
white " 'by their hair, their eyes, their skin. . . . But the surest way is by
their finger-nails.' He leaned forward and took my hand in his. He
pointed to the base of one of my nails. 'If you had a single drop of nig-
ger blood in you, you'd have a dark-blue circle right there.' "[15]

Although such tests were never explicitly used during the trial, they
were discussed in those terms by the media. When the *Chicago Broad
Ax* reported the findings of one Dr. L. H. Snyder that "chemical reactions of the blood in certain combinations" could be used to determine racial purity and ancestry, the writer dryly noted that "much aid
will thus be available to the courts and other analysts who may be
called into duty . . . amid such cases as that of the Rhinelanders."[16]

A 1948 *Ebony* magazine cover article entitled "Five Million White
Negroes" recalled that "One highlight of this nonsense [the
Rhinelander trial] was the prosecuting attorney's contention that Alice
had 'passed' as a white person. To prove that she was a Negro, she was
forced to stand naked from the waist up, so the jurors could examine
her breasts—these, they believed, would be the dead giveaway!"[17]
Although *Ebony* mistook the purpose of the episode, their misunder-
standing was a common one. The express purpose was to demonstrate
the obviousness of Alice's black ancestry, not to prove that she had
black ancestry. But both endeavors relied on the supposed physical
markers described by the magazine as presumed "dead giveaways."

It was an understandable misperception. Had Alice not admitted to
having "colored blood," she would likely have been examined for such
a purpose. In fact, some newspaper editors had anticipated that possibility as soon as the suit was filed—recall the *Chicago Defender* article
that emphasized the impossibility of determining the "exact propor-
tion of the different bloods," particularly given the ambiguity of her
father's ancestry. They had predicted that, to settle the question, "scientific ethnologists" would be brought before the court, adding that
since all races were one, the scientists would be likely to fail to reach a
"definite conclusion."[18]

The ethnologists predicted by the *Chicago Defender* and others never appeared as expert witnesses to ascertain the presence and amount of "African blood" in Alice. Their presence was rendered moot by her initial admission that she had nonwhite ancestry. In their absence this episode of her undressing served as, or at least was widely understood to serve as, an unofficial test of the presence and visibility of her black ancestry, presided over not by scientists with anthropometric devices, but by the twelve Westchester County jurymen.

Some commentators went further, suggesting that such "dead giveaways" were undependable, even ludicrous, challenging the premises behind such methods and theories of determining racial identity. Soon after the verdict a cartoon appeared on the editorial page of the *Chicago Defender,* under the title "The Purity of the White Race Must Be Preserved." In the sketch, an apparently white man asks his apparently white sweetheart several questions to ensure that her racial ancestry is not tainted with black blood. The second question this prospective suitor asks his sweetheart directly evokes the scene of Alice exposing her back: "Do you know whether or not your grandmother's back was the same color as her face and arms?"[19] The cartoonist then went on to list, tongue firmly in cheek, other spoofs on "screens" for black ancestry: owning black shoes, playing with black children, and so on. In fact, a variety of popular, political, and educational sources in the early twentieth century *did* strongly urge middle-class white men and women—particularly women—to investigate the racial, as well as medical and moral, backgrounds of potential spouses. The cartoon parodied these concerns, and the lengths to which white Americans went to avoid racial mixing with African Americans—in particular, the methods of detection that, however unfounded, allowed many whites to maintain their firm belief in races as discrete, physically marked categories of inferiority and superiority.

Regardless of region, the black press generally paid a great deal of attention to the implication of Alice's disrobing, although a few, like the black-published *St. Louis Argus,* paid little attention to it, or at least sought to downplay it in favor of extended attention to Leonard's mystery letters. In a subheadline the *Argus* revealed that Alice broke down "under [the] trying ordeal," and in the text referred in passing to "the baring of Mrs. Rhinelander's skin."[20] More commonly, however, black papers gave the episode front-page headlines, provided detailed descriptions of the event, commented heatedly on its significance, and continued to refer to it in the weeks and even years that followed. The *Cleveland Gazette* emphasized that this color examination had subjected her to "an ordeal such as no other woman has been called upon to undergo in a court in this country."[21] In a pointed recap of events, the *Dallas Express* deemed the day the climax of the trial:

> The disrobing of Mrs. Rhinelander before the jury set a disgraceful though spectacular precedent in New York court practice. The embarrassed wife was required to remove all her clothing, save a small band around her waist, while the curious eyes of ignorant jurors were allowed to satisfy themselves as to her racial identity.[22]

Again, note the discrepancies over what Alice wore, what parts of her body were uncovered. More important, here the wording suggested that the jurors may have been satisfying themselves in other ways, gazing at Alice's seminude body. The *Houston Informer* also invoked the voyeuristic aspect of this episode, commenting dryly that reports of the event "failed to state how many jurors have had to call in eye specialists."[23] These descriptions acknowledge both the underlying assumptions about race behind Alice's ordeal and the sexualized dynamics of a woman, especially a black woman, undressing before a room full of men, particularly white men.

This depiction of Alice fell squarely into a white tradition of depicting mulatto women as sexually available, sexually victimized, and/or sexually predatory. By the 1920s many white Americans, particularly northern whites, joined African Americans in blaming southern white men for the existence of the substantial mulatto population that now (supposedly) threatened the racial purity of white America both by its very presence and by the behavior—particularly the sexual behavior—of its members. Indeed, northern writers continued to be fascinated with the supposed rituals of white-male-controlled interracial sex in the South, particularly exclusive "octoroon balls" at which light-skinned African American women competed to be the mistresses of socially elite white men who would support them financially in return for sex and companionship, all in the name of romance. Such depictions, however, painted the women as desperately competing for their shared goal: a rich white lover. By the 1920s images of mulatto women focused even more directly on their supposed obsession with "landing," either as a wife or mistress, a rich white benefactor—and on using that liaison to appropriate white money, property, and even power.[24]

One of the most powerful depictions of popular stereotypes of people of mixed ancestry was found in D. W. Griffith's 1915 film, *The Birth of a Nation*. In this historical drama of Reconstruction in the South, the real enemies of the birth of the new nation were the mulatto characters: Lydia Brown, the housekeeper and mistress of Northern senator Stoneham, and Silas Lynch, an aide to Stoneham. Within the narrative of the film, these two mulattoes manipulated the senator's misguided liberal doctrines of racial equality into black Southern rule at the expense of white Southerners. Like many white-created fictional mulattoes, Lydia Brown and Silas Lynch were mentally and emotionally unbalanced, devious, manipulative, treacherous. In one of her more memorable scenes, Lydia, outraged that a white man has refused to take her hand, tears at her clothes, pulling her collar partly off her shoulders, and throws herself into a frenzy. Both desired white mates—Lydia's relationship with Stoneham presumably allowing her some access to the power he represented, while Lynch's violent attempts to "marry" Stoneham's daughter woke Stoneham up to the dangers of social equality—and, in the real world, inspired white racists to resurrect the Klan.

Images of the sexually wild, seminude light-skinned black woman abounded in American popular culture in the 1920s. Onstage, Josephine Baker had just left her Broadway career as a dancer and was in France, dancing what would become her signature performance. Opening in September 1925, this new *Danse Sauvage* featured a scantily clad Baker gyrating to "African" rhythms, dressed only in feathers and nude from the waist up.[25] Her sexualized movements soon became the show's primary draw, attracting a devoted audience made up primarily of white men. By 1926 Baker was an international star, wearing her trademark banana skirt, "a perfect symbol of both sexuality and primitivism."[26]

By offering her body as evidence, then, Alice's lawyers placed her within this iconography, which pictured black women as highly sexualized bodies available for the entertainment of white men. In doing so they risked playing directly into the opposition's portrayal of Alice as a promiscuous seductress who manipulated the young, naive, and rather

Josephine Baker performing in her famous banana costume.

stupid Leonard into bed, into love, into marriage, and into giving her his money. They reinserted her into a racial iconography that operated largely to serve white male desire, and they reduced her role in the trial to an objectified, sexualized presentation of a dark-skinned body.

BUT THIS WAS not the dominant response at the time, either in the black or in the northern white press. Aside from the shock value, and the implications for Alice's racial identity, the primary response to her disrobing was outrage and pity. In part this was because the New York commentary included another group of journalists who had their own interests in this scene, albeit with a slightly different emphasis than that of the black papers. Since the turn of the century, white female reporters had been gradually moving from the society pages to the front pages. Margery Rex of the *Evening Journal* and Grace Robinson of the *Daily Mirror*, for example, were seasoned veterans of other prominent trials and socially oriented stories of the type that might now be called "human interest."[27] They sat with other reporters at the trial and wrote both dry accounts of each day's events as well as opinion pieces commenting on the social, moral, or gender implications of some aspect of the situation. They often wrote editorial or highly analytical articles on the case, sometimes on a daily basis, and their commentary was picked up by papers outside New York City. In fact the prominence of women's responses to Alice's experience was noted in the media's continued coverage not only of the trial itself but of editorials and coverage in their own and other papers.

By the 1920s it was not unusual for newspaper editors to use female reporters to cover stories they determined had a particular appeal to women readers. "Sob sisters" was a common term for one resulting style of journalism, which specialized in "tear-jerking accounts of flamboyant events" from a woman's perspective. But not everyone appreciated the genre.[28]

The *Los Angeles Times* published a disdainful editorial called "Sob Stuff," which ridiculed an unnamed female reporter's melodramatic description of Alice leaving the jury room. The unnamed woman's portrayal was detailed and emotionally empathetic:

> Unseeing, unhearing, the girl reeled through the congestion with her weeping mother's arm around her waist and from her bloodless lips came a crooning moan. Through it ran a note of fear, of terror, and it rose to a stifled scream, then fell to a hoarse muttering; then rose and fell again. The quavering, long-drawn, rolling moan, sounded a woman's helpless protest against fate itself. Although she staggered from the room like a stricken animal seeking a place to die, she went through the ordeal as one might walk through Gethsemane.[29]

From the late-twentieth-century stylistic viewpoint, this sounds overly sentimentalized, if not maudlin. It is tempting to join the California editor in rolling his eyes at the response of this "sob sister."

The acerbic writer then closed with the strangely striking comment that it was a good thing that that reporter had not been asked to write up the raid of the Sabine women.[30] This "raid," more often and familiarly called a "rape," was a classical scene from Roman legend, often depicted by artists through the centuries. The implied connection between Alice's experience and a rape was probably unintended here. But the parallels between her disrobing and a rape may have been what resonated so strongly for this and other female reporters who had been the only women to hear Leonard's letters and witness Alice's entry and exit from the jury room. While Alice does not seem to have been touched physically during this procedure, the women may have been more likely to interpret her experience as one of sexual humiliation and violation.

Writing for the *Daily News*, Grace Robinson expressed great empathy for Alice. In an editorial masquerading as an article, Robinson waxed poetic in a similar, although somewhat less effusive, tone: "It was a pitiable spectacle, this unwilling girl baring her body before a battery of male eyes. No heroine of persecution ever walked to the stake with more reluctant feet than [did] Mrs. Leonard Kip Rhinelander."[31] For the moment at least, Robinson was fully in Alice's corner. In vivid phrasing reproduced by other papers, Robinson presented Alice as a heroine, even a martyr. In addition she gave Alice the full traditional name of her husband, while other papers continued to refer to her as just "Alice Jones."

However, it was not only the female journalists who played up Alice's emotional response to her horrifying experience. Frank J. Dolan, also writing for the *Daily News*, described Alice as "shrinking like a frightened animal before the cold appraising stare of twelve good men and true." Dolan emphasized that Alice had willingly chosen tribulation in a "desperate attempt to hold as her own the husband of her dreams," had willingly humiliated herself to "keep her man." In fact, the headline for this article said it all, announcing: "Alice Tears Her Pride to Shreds To Hold Her Man."[32] Several hundred miles south the *Norfolk Journal and Guide,* in reporting the day's events, wrote that the disrobing was "as excruciating to a woman's modesty as [a] woman ever was called on to bear."[33]

Of the day's events Margery Rex noted that "Kip has bared his soul. Alice her body." "Both," she observed, "have done these unpleasant deeds bravely. You pity both of them." The main thrust of Rex's article, however, was Leonard's attitude toward Alice, which she compared with a notorious Rudyard Kipling poem:

I've taken my fun where I've found it. . . .
The things that you learn from the yellow and brown

Will help you a lot with the white. . . .
She knifed me one night
When I wished she was white,
But I learned about women from her.

As Kipling wrote it, Rex intoned, so Kip lived it; one white man had celebrated the excitement and danger of pursuing "yellow and brown" women for sexual experience, the other was living it. Of course Kip hadn't moved on to use his knowledge with white women yet. Nevertheless, Rex's analysis assumed that Alice's color had not only been obvious to Leonard but had been part of her appeal for him.

Rhinelander learned about women from the tawny girl he loved— still loves, no doubt? It is not impossible that the frankness with which Alice Jones admitted a previous love affair, and her remorse because her husband was not "the first" awakened the boy to a grown man's sense of tenderness toward all women, to this woman in particular.

The purpose of the disrobing, Rex believed, was "to show that her color is no secret and that he who runs, as it were, may read." Yet, it was unnecessary, she thought, as the skin on her arms and hands, apparent without disrobing "could scarcely be considered as characteristic of even a well-tanned Caucasian."[34] Rex did not try to explain why the disrobing would have been deemed necessary by Davis and Morschauser if her hands and arms were dark enough to be evidence of blackness.

For Rex and for Dolan, and for other onlookers as well, the disrobing scene demonstrated Alice's willingness to use her body—although perhaps reluctantly—to win her case. Did Alice have enough knowledge of how race functioned in America to realize the possible effects of her disrobing? In the minds of many white Americans, black women were defined by their physicality, their sexualized body, their capacity for menial labor. White men were defined by their supposed intellectual ability and higher level of civilization, education, and refinement. Leonard possessed the power of privilege, education, class, and race. Alice, in turn, possessed the power of using race and the presumption of blackness to undermine Leonard's hold on credulity. If she was obviously nonwhite, and willing to turn herself into an exhibit to prove such, then Leonard had to be either lying or severely incapacitated. The latter seemed unlikely, given his testimony to date, leaving only the former as a possible answer. Through this ordeal Alice became a more sympathetic and more fully drawn human character, despite her possible racial heritage.

EXCEPT FOR THE details of her entrance and exit, the numerous newspaper descriptions of Alice's partial disrobing focused on the unseen, the implied, or the imagined. Without fanfare or even public note, the display of Alice's body crossed the line between iconography—which recalled a long tradition of displaying black bodies for very public purposes—and pornography, which made the selling of suggestively nude images a commercial endeavor. Although no photographers were in the jury room when Alice disrobed, thousands of Americans saw recreations of that disrobing. Newspapers manufactured these recreations to sell copies. Others drew sketches, revealing in their hint of flesh.

Taken together, the sketches reveal some important shared assumptions and contrary speculations. The depictions of Alice disrobing uniformly showed Alice with her back turned or demurely folding her arms over her bare breasts. One leg slightly bent out with her ankle turned, knees together, head bowed, eyes downcast, she was always the picture of modesty and shyness, sometimes shame. She was never portrayed as boldly staring down the eyes of the men in the room.

The biggest divergence was in the darkness of her skin. Most showed her as light or white-skinned—no shading on exposed skin, or light shading that might be interpreted as shadow. But it is important to remember that these were only ink sketches, more detailed than cartoons but not necessarily meant to indicate an exact rendering. For example, the *Daily Mirror*'s version showed an apparently white woman wearing only a sheet tied around her waist standing in front of the judge's bench with the lawyers pointing to her body. But the headline noted the anguish of the "Ebony Bride." This sketch, without the accompanying headline, was reprinted in several papers, including the *Baltimore Afro-American*, which cut out only the figure of Alice and enlarged it. Both papers also ran a clothed sketch of a defeated Alice leaving the courtroom, supported by two women identified as her mother and a friend. With the exception of her heavy fur-lined jacket and hat, Alice's body is depicted very similarly here, bent over herself protectively, eyes almost closed, head hanging down.[35]

Toward the end of the trial the *Mirror* published another cartoon version of this event. This time, however, their portrayal of Alice was markedly different. Now she was sketched much darker than the lawyers or her mother, who surround her. She wore a ruffled slip that hung loosely to her mid-thighs and covered her breasts. Her arms were still crossed over her chest, and her eyes and chin were still downcast. Her legs were covered by black stockings, which ended a few inches below her slip's hemline.

The *Evening Graphic* beat all the competition, however, and made photojournalistic history, when it managed to publish a photograph of the scene. Denied access to the actual event, they hired a light-skinned, dark-haired model to pose as Alice and took a photo of her wearing only a slip. Then they literally cut and pasted it together with photographs of the judge and lawyers in the courtroom to create the imagined exhibition. The resulting "composograph" was an instant hit, skyrocketing the paper's circulation from sixty thousand to several

The Evening Graphic's *composite portrayal,
using an actress, of Alice disrobing.*

hundred thousand.[36] The image it presented, although exciting in its manufactured realism, looked very much like the sketches offered by less enterprising New York tabloids. "Alice" was posed with her back to the camera, topless, arms appearing to be crossed over her breasts, one leg bent in at the knee, head slightly bowed. There was nothing about the model to indicate she was anything but white.[37]

How did this moment of humiliation and vulnerability get recast for some as Alice's triumph? Again and again white newspapers articulated their respect for Alice's willingness to debase herself in order to save her marriage. Her act was seen as an example of the highest calling: loyalty to love and marriage. For some it didn't seem to matter what she did, it only proved her steadfastness and made her more deserving of being a Rhinelander—although being a Rhinelander was seeming less and less like a desirable goal.

11

~≥~

REVELATIONS

 AFTER LEONARD'S LETTERS and Alice's disrobing, there seemed few untold secrets in the annulment trial of Alice and Leonard Rhinelander. For more than three weeks the relationship of the socially mismatched pair had garnered attention in newspapers worldwide. After a day of exclusion, women reclaimed their places as ardent court watchers anticipating Alice's testimony. Scores speculated audibly about what Alice would say and how Mills would treat her. Would she break down again? Would Mills wrest a confession from her, an affirmation that she had duped poor Leonard? Would others come to her rescue, confirming definitively that Leonard had to have known her color before they married? What would her mother and sisters reveal? And, appealing to certain base instincts that kept the curious pouring into the court chambers day after day, what new revelations would emerge? This trial was many things, but perhaps most profoundly it was a sanctioned voyeuristic journey into the lives of the rich and idle. Through the experiences of a working-class girl such as Alice, more and more Americans could insert themselves—for a few moments at least—into the story line; wondering out loud, What if this had been me?

· · · ·

IT HAD BEEN Lee Parsons Davis's intention to call Alice as the defense's first witness on November 24. Alice, however, had wilted after the reading of Leonard's revealing letters and the baring of her body. A model of style and grace throughout the painfully public trial, she seemed to have reached her limit. Shoulders drooping, head bowed, and tears continuing to fall, Alice took her place at her counsel's table on the twenty-fourth. All could see her emotional strain. In contrast to Leonard, who now seemed more at ease, Alice struggled. A day after disrobing and wondering out loud if she could continue, only her mother's tender gesture of dabbing away her tears brought comfort. Characterized in the press as too weak to testify, emotionally distraught, and having suffered a breakdown, Alice became an even more sympathetic character in this drama of images and social standing.

Before Davis could call his first witness, Isaac Mills attempted to amend the complaint against Alice. In a technically significant move, Mills sought to shift the legal issue from a case of affirmative fraud to a case of negative fraud. Until this point Mills had alleged that Alice had

Newspapers emphasized the physical and emotional
strain on Alice late in the trial.

presented herself as white, which was the basis for his complaint of affirmative fraud. He now only wanted to show that Alice had failed to say she was colored, proof of negative fraud.

No one knew how Judge Morschauser would respond. Under the law an amendment of this nature required the removal of one juror, a special session of the court, and the declaration of a mistrial. Most observers felt that the judge certainly wanted an end to this trial. Moreover, in proposing the amendment, Mills tipped his hand, showing he thought his case weaker than first projected. Davis by this time certainly wanted to proceed. He had attempted to end the trial on two previous occasions; now he sensed he could win the case. He chided his adversary: "First they say she said too much and now they say she said nothing. I won't quarrel over the technicalities involved, but I feel that in asking an amendment at this late date they are guilty of laxity."[1] Morschauser allowed the proceedings to continue while he considered Mills's request.

Before Davis started his defense of Alice, Mills decided to call one more witness: Miriam Rich. The wife of the furniture storeowner who befriended the newlyweds when they set out to furnish their New Rochelle apartment proved a perky witness. In a way Miriam Rich returned the trial to the realm of banal human motivations. By her own account, she first became a witness at the behest of Alice's mother, who sought a character witness. Convinced of Alice's good character, Rich initially intended to testify that "Alice was a white girl . . . a charming white girl."[2] She became a witness for the plaintiff because she later realized that Alice had deceived her about her race, she told the court.

Miriam Rich's harsh antipathy toward Alice was matched by her loud voice. At one moment during his cross-examination Davis asked, "Do you like Alice?" "I did very much," Rich replied. "Do you now?" the lawyer continued. "No," came the terse answer. "Do you hate her?" Davis asked simply. "No, I never hate anybody," Rich explained. "Dislike her?" the counsel followed. "Yes." "Since when?" Davis inquired. "Since about four weeks ago," she answered. Rich acknowledged that her feelings had further hardened since that morning. And five minutes before she took the witness stand, she said, Alice's sister Emily had "sneered at her as a Jew." Rich then let it be known that she disliked Alice because she had deceived her.

Rich emerged as a bespectacled, somewhat matronly middle-class woman who desired the company of the rich and powerful. Hobnobbing with the couple enabled her to have it. This interest perhaps led her to accept without hesitation Alice's explanation that her skin appeared darker due to Spanish blood. As Rich testified, "She had sweet manners and I thought she was a beautiful Spanish girl." When asked if she had ever seen a Spanish woman, Rich answered, "Yes, on the stage. I thought Alice was even more beautiful than they were. I felt sorry for her because she said she was so dark the millionaires would not have her."[3] At this point many in the court smiled, reminded again that love was really on trial in this case.

But Rich had soured on Alice because her associations with Leonard and Alice had injured her standing in New Rochelle social circles. Rich explained how she often socialized with the couple, even visiting the Jones family for meals and social events. She was taken with the twenty or so "refined white people" who dined at the Jones house, and accepted Alice's explanation that "she was a poor girl of dark color of Spanish descent." In cross-examination Davis suggested and Rich acknowledged that now "[T]he whole of Mount Vernon had [had] a good laugh at me, and my husband, too."[4]

In a remarkable nod to the importance of language in the fixing of race, Rich mentioned that she accepted the Jones family's accounting of their racial heritage in part because Mr. Jones spoke with a British accent. There were other social markers, of course: twenty refined white people who shared the Jones dinner table, membership in the Episcopal church a block away, and of course residual ties to England. Yet, in a telling conflation of language and race, Rich remarked that Alice's father said "he was English and dropped his 'h's,' saying his 'appy 'ome had been broken up." Together these factors had led Miriam Rich to conclude that Alice had to have been white as suggested. Rich's testimony revealed one way that whites manufactured their own notions about race, and in so doing, created a place for Alice in their world.[5]

At the start of the afternoon session Leonard made one more appearance on the witness stand. Davis had one last set of questions for him, starting with, "You remember the day you applied for the marriage license, don't you?" To which Leonard replied, "Yes." "Did the man to whom you applied ask either of you if you were white or colored?"

Davis asked next. Leonard offered, "No." "He just put it down him-self?" "Yes." With that final exchange Davis ended his cross-examination, and Mills concluded the plaintiff's case. But just as he had with Rich, Davis got Leonard to admit that whites constructed notions of race: They fixed some as white and some as black. In certain settings whites made Alice white, too. In a futile move he asked the court to dismiss the suit since Leonard had failed to prove his case. Judge Morschauser said he preferred that the jury make that determination.

Davis understood what he had to do. He could not rely on whites simply understanding the complexity of Alice's racial standing. He had to show that Leonard was more complicit, that he had wanted to claim Alice as white despite other evidence to the contrary, that he had known and acknowledged her nonwhite ancestry. Delaying Alice's testimony, Davis turned to his first witness: Barbara Reynolds, the reporter for the *New Rochelle Standard Star* who wrote the first story about the union. "Do you know Mr. Rhinelander?" Davis started. "Yes, I met him November 13, 1924," the reporter answered. "Where did you meet him?" Davis demanded to know. "In the Jones residence," she said. "Under what circumstances?" "I was there to get an interview for the Standard News Association." Davis then asked, "What was said?" In almost a soliloquy Reynolds replied,

> I was waiting at the house and Mr. Rhinelander came along. The first question I fired at him was "Mr. Rhinelander?" and he said "yes." Then I knew he was my man. I asked him "[Is] it true that you are married to the daughter of a colored man?" and he said "yes." Then I asked him where he had been and he said he had been in New York. I asked him if his people were alive. He said his mother was dead. I asked him if it would make a difference if his father knew of the marriage. He replied, "Oh, yes, it means my wife's happiness and mine." He asked me to withhold the story.[6]

Reynolds offered a subtle confirmation of Davis's claim that Leonard had to have known. It is striking, however, that Reynolds did not ask Leonard if he knew his bride was colored; rather, she asked about the status of Alice's father. Leonard's reply affirmed his understanding of the question, and, more important, its social implications: If the father was colored so too was the daughter. He also implied that his concern was not with her ancestry, but with how his family would perceive her. Perhaps Leonard, knowing that she was not, wanted only that Alice appear white.

After a brief cross-examination of Barbara Reynolds by Mills, Davis called, in order, Leon Jacobs and Robert Brooks to the stand. Many expected a new round of fireworks when Jacobs took his seat in the witness box. Jacobs had emerged as a Rhinelander family lawyer and handler, and the object of Davis's scorn.

DAVIS: "How long have you been a practicing lawyer?"
JACOBS: "Since 1907."
DAVIS: "Whose office are you in?"
JACOBS: "I am all alone."
DAVIS: "Whom are you associated with?"
JACOBS: "Myself."
DAVIS: "Who else is in the office?"
JACOBS: "The estate of Philip Rhinelander, the estate of William Rhinelander, the estate of T. Oakley Rhinelander, the estate of Philip Rhinelander, 2d; the Atlantic Mortgage Company, the estate of Cornelia B. Kip and several other real estate companies."

Leonard (right) with family intimate and attorney Leon Jacobs,
who appeared as a witness in the trial.

DAVIS: "Don't the companies belong to the Rhinelanders?"
JACOBS: "They are interested in them all."

Jacobs minimized his involvement in writing up the annulment suit
that Leonard had acknowledged contained fabrications, instead fingering Philip Rhinelander and Mills.[7] To the surprise of most, after a
series of questions about when he first went to the Jones home, Davis
terminated his direct examination of the witness. For a change there
were no real revelations.

Next Robert Brooks took the stand. He had dozed openly during the
cross-examination of Miriam Rich and her husband. Now was his turn
to face the intense spotlight of public curiosity. The only member of
the Jones family whose African heritage was never questioned, Brooks
detailed a social intimacy shared by few blacks and whites, especially
ones from such radically different classes.

DAVIS: "When did you first meet Rhinelander?"
BROOKS: "September, 1921, at the Jones's [sic] house."
DAVIS: "In 1921, where was your baby, Roberta, living?"
BROOKS: "At the home of her grandmother, Mrs. Jones."
DAVIS: "How were you introduced to the plaintiff?"
BROOKS: "Mrs. Rhinelander, Alice, said: 'Mr. Rhinelander, this is
my brother-in-law Mr. Brooks.' "
DAVIS: "How often did you see Rhinelander between the early
autumn of 1921 and the spring of 1922?"
BROOKS: "Nearly every evening for quite a while."
DAVIS: "Did he ever object to your color?"
BROOKS: "No, he was very friendly."

Brooks, a butler, mentioned that Leonard seemed to take little notice
of his color or his working-class background. Grinning, he told the
court that he and Leonard "used to have tea together." In short order
the two called each other "Len" or "Leonard" and "Bob," respectively.
Robert and his wife, Emily, Alice's sister, often took Leonard to the
train station after he came to court Alice. And Brooks said he frequently helped Leonard work on his car.[8]

At this point the court took a noontime recess. Away from the scrutiny of the courtroom, Leonard seemed to relax. Not so Alice, who had

groaned audibly during the direct examination of Miriam Rich, clearly upset that Rich no longer liked her because she was, in the language of the day, a *negress*. The strain of the last couple of weeks showed; she seemed to have shrunk into herself. Maybe the intermission would help restore her equilibrium.

Both parties, in fact, seized the opportunity to leave the chambers. Just before the case was to resume, however, the elevator door opened, and Leonard stepped out onto the second floor of the White Plains courthouse. He bumped into a woman: Alice. For the first time in months the lovelorn couple made physical contact. Both paused. Leonard stared deeply into Alice's eyes, and then, yanked back into the reality of the moment, he removed his hat, said "Excuse me, please," and moved on. Alice, searching for any recognition of the love that had tied them, took the polite but distant exchange as a rebuff. She "leaned against the wall and broke into sobs." In a repetition of a scene much practiced over the last few days, her mother gathered her in her arms and offered comfort.[9]

Before recalling Brooks, Davis asked Miriam Rich to return to the stand. He asked her if she had been present when Bowers, of the firm Bowers & Sands, offered Alice money at the behest of Philip Rhinelander. Mrs. Rich maintained, "[H]e never offered her money." Davis thanked and excused her.

He called Brooks again. Davis established that Leonard moved easily in the Jones household. He freely played with Roberta, Brooks's daughter. He welcomed the opportunity to play cards with Brooks and his friends during his almost nightly visits to the Jones home in the months prior to his marriage to Alice. Modest in demeanor, Brooks added matter-of-factly, "All of my friends are colored,"[10] which served to say that Leonard had to have known that at the very least this was not a typical 1920s American white family.

Mills used his time to ask Brooks about his relationships with his in-laws, especially Elizabeth. He started by asking if there were periods when Brooks and Emily stayed away from her parents' home. "Emily never did, but I did," Brooks replied. Giving away his motive, Mills followed, "Was there any animosity shown you by the Jones because of your color?" Alice had reportedly told Leonard that Emily's marriage to Robert was not welcome news to her parents, prompting a period of estrangement. Brooks answered Mills: "I don't know whether they approved or not my marrying Emily, but they never showed that they minded."[11] Thus, in one reply, Brooks exposed the possibility of color prejudice and dodged its full impact on this trial. At this point Davis requested a recess for the day, and Morschauser agreed. At 2:50 P.M. the court and trial came to a rest.

THE NEXT MORNING Davis called members of Alice's immediate family, first her sisters, Emily and Grace, and then her mother, Elizabeth. Emily testified that her family had objected to her marriage to Robert because of her age and not his color. She and Robert had worked at the same hotel, and she knew without question that he was a Negro. Equally important, she identified herself as colored.

Then Grace, full of spunk and verve, approached the stand dressed in a vividly red toque hat, which Davis asked her to remove. Grace informed the room that she had married Albert Miller on April 25, 1922. Although her marriage certificate listed her as white, she too admitted that she considered herself colored. When asked why she had been listed as white, she offered the obvious explanation: Those officiating looked at her and Albert and made certain assumptions. She saw the mistake but saw no need to correct it. Who could have imagined the circumstances that brought her to the courtroom to authenticate her background? She essentially thought it was an innocent mistake that meant nothing. Unlike almost everyone else, Grace seemed to enjoy her time as a witness.

Throughout the year leading up to the trial Grace often appeared as the family spokesperson. Her words appear in many interviews, and she delighted in the public attention. Now, on the stand, she had her moment to revel in the spotlight one more time. She seized the opportunity to tell all in the room that she saw Kreitler forty times before ending their relationship; that Leonard had offered her a ring she was forced to return, which he then gave to Alice, an act that inflamed sibling rivalries. After a few banal questions and answers, Grace departed center stage with a big grin on her face. She had proved to be a loyal sister.[12]

The demure, white-haired Elizabeth took the stand next. Then in her sixties, she showed a fierce determination to support her daughter. Elizabeth Jones told the court that Leonard came to her soon after word of his marriage to Alice hit the national news. (The *New Rochelle Standard Star* headlines had dubbed Alice the daughter of a colored man.) Leonard's response to the publicity? He reassured his mother-in-law that he loved Alice and didn't care about the newspapers' coverage. Timid and clearly nervous, Elizabeth denied that she ever told young Rhinelander that her family was of Spanish descent.

DAVIS: "Did Rhinelander ever ask about color?"
ELIZABETH: "No."
DAVIS: "You remember the newspapers when they came out and called your husband a negro?"
ELIZABETH: "Yes."
DAVIS: "Were you surprised?"
ELIZABETH: "Yes. We didn't expect the headlines to read as they did. He expected to be called a colored man but not a negro."
DAVIS: "Did your husband ever tell Mr. Rhinelander he was of Spanish descent?"
ELIZABETH: "No, he never did."
DAVIS: "Did Mr. Rhinelander live at your house during the week beginning November 13, 1914, when the newspapers published those stories?"
ELIZABETH: "Yes. He said: 'Never mind. I married the girl I loved and I don't care.' "[13]

Respectable and dignified, Elizabeth, her modest attire topped by a black velvet hat, impressed all with her quiet presence on the stand. Furthermore, she supported several important pieces of her daughter's case. She emphasized that she and Leonard had never explicitly discussed race, or claimed to be Spanish. But she also reiterated their racial distinction between being "colored" and being "negro." As noted earlier, by some usages the latter term was reserved for those of full African ancestry, and the former could include other nonwhite as well as mixed-race individuals. Finally she testified that Leonard had continued to live with them, and therefore with his wife, after news reports that George was black.

But Isaac Mills wanted the world to see a more sinister character: devious, immoral, calculating, anything other than the matronly mother Elizabeth portrayed. He opened his cross-examination by going straight to the point. By this time it was widely known that Alice's parents hailed from England. Mills took her back to her land of birth, back to a time when she scrubbed kitchens and served an elite British family on a large estate, where she met George Jones.

Mills, however, wanted to unnerve her, expose her deepest secrets, and win his client his annulment. He began: "The shipping [manifest] shows you and Mr. Jones brought a child to this country named Ethel. She was listed as six years old. Was that child yours?" "Yes," Elizabeth acknowledged. "Was Mr. Jones the father of Ethel?" the senior lawyer pointedly asked.

Before Elizabeth could respond, Davis jumped up to object. In his most passionate defense yet, Davis boomed, "Are you really going into this?" Davis knew the answer to Mills's question, and what was at stake. As one newspaper observed, "Davis's face was red, his voice shook and his hand trembled. If his emotion was not genuine, then certainly it was the most effective acting seen in a courtroom in many a day." Mills finally answered him: "I am going into it. Here is a question of whether this woman guarded, as you contend, these young people." His voice rising, his contempt obvious, Davis exclaimed, "Thirty-six years ago! Seriously, you are not going into this and—" Mills cut him off, which prompted Davis to turn to Judge Morschauser and proclaim, "I object!"

Morschauser overruled Davis.

Mills repeated his question, "Was Mr. Jones the father of Ethel?" Her eyes searching the courtroom for what to do next, Elizabeth hesitated. Davis instructed, "You will have to answer the question." Turning her gaze on Mills, Elizabeth looked him squarely in the eye and said, "No, sir." Mills then asked, "Who was her father?" When Davis objected, Mills offered, "Why, it goes to her credibility as to whether she guarded these daughters or not."

JUDGE: "Mills is within his legal rights."
MILLS: "Who was the father of Ethel?"
ELIZABETH: "I do not wish to answer."
JUDGE: "Now she is within her legal rights."
MILLS: "Were you married before you were married to Jones?"
ELIZABETH: "I do not wish to answer that."
MILLS: "That I must insist upon, Your Honor."

The judge concurred.

DAVIS: "You will have to answer it. Go ahead and tell the truth."

Clearly pained by what she had to reveal, in an almost inaudible voice, Elizabeth told the court what most had probably guessed by now: "I was not." Those solemn words conveyed a secret she had kept from all save her husband. Her daughters—Emily, Grace, and Alice—did not know, and had she been able, they would never have known, that they had a half sister living elsewhere in the state of New York.[14] Describing this early out-of-wedlock birth transported Elizabeth to a place and time that bespoke volumes about her own vulnerability as a white woman of humble means in a rigidly class-oriented society.

Mills was not finished, however. He threw Elizabeth another question loaded with innuendo: "Did you ever have another child" he posed, "now living in England, named William, before you married Jones?" (Mills called George by his surname without adding the appellation "Mister." As in the South, a wall was drawn short of equal status, even in the northern court.) Elizabeth offered a determined "No." Next Elizabeth answered the question, "Is Ethel the only child you ever had before you married Jones?" She replied, "Yes."

By this time Davis had seen and heard enough. Livid over the tone and direction of Mills's questioning, he called for a recess. The court acquiesced. Judge Morschauser authorized a ten-minute break. Trembling and clearly shaken, Elizabeth stepped away from the witness stand. Alice met her halfway, embraced her mother, and both stumbled back to their chairs. All three daughters soon surrounded their mother, trying to comfort her, acknowledging throughout the extent of her ordeal. Photographers, meanwhile, snapped pictures as rapidly as possible, sending off tommygunlike sounds. Davis had seen enough. He asked the court to remove the photographers, which Morschauser approved.[15]

After a ten-minute break Elizabeth reassumed her seat in the witness stand, but not before Davis, in a grand gesture, walked past her, placing his hand on her back in a sign of solidarity and support. The act brought the first smile to Elizabeth's face seen that day.

Mills was not done by any means. He began anew by asking Elizabeth about her parents, their whereabouts, and her contact with them. He wrested admission that her daughter had lived with her parents for some period after her birth but before Elizabeth and George's departure for the United States. Elizabeth's parents, it seemed, still lived in England, but because they were illiterate, she only corresponded with them intermittently, mostly when one of her sisters would pen a letter.

Now Mills shifted his questioning to how well she tracked the comings and goings of her daughter Alice. Pointedly he sought to ascertain if Elizabeth had had any prior knowledge of Alice's stay at the Marie Antoinette Hotel. She said no, and that she only became worried after her daughter disappeared for several days. At that point she tried contacting friends in Manhattan but they hadn't seen Alice nor could they locate her. Elizabeth confessed that after this effort she simply gave up. The next time Alice went off with Leonard she merely thought she was working.[16]

AFTER A FURTHER break Mills doggedly pursued Elizabeth one last time. She again repeated her earlier testimony. No, she did not know Alice's destination. No, she had not asked Kreitler if he was married. And no, she had not inquired about other details of Alice's personal life. Seeing that he had exhausted Elizabeth and would get no more from her, Mills wrapped up his cross-examination.[17]

Over Mills's objections, Davis called Leonard to the stand once more. In an attempt to redirect the tenor of events, Davis returned to the amendment of the complaint that Mills had introduced the day before, which addressed the degree to which Alice had misled him about her race. "You know that your complaint has been amended?" Unaware of where Davis was headed, Leonard answered yes. "You say your wife deceived you by saying nothing?" Again Leonard answered yes. Davis's next question prompted an objection from Mills that Morschauser sustained. Davis rephrased his question: "Was the deception by her saying she was white?" Yet again Leonard answered yes. Davis's next question proved as innocuous as the last: "Now you say she kept quiet, too?" Baffled, Leonard maintained, "I don't know anything about that."

Rhinelander's surprise reentry into the day's drama electrified the courtroom. All sensed that Davis was building toward something. But what? With the witness a little unsteady, Davis sprang his trap. He asked, "You and Ross, the family chauffeur, were friendly, weren't you?" The unsuspecting Rhinelander answered, "I think so."[18] Davis asked Rhinelander if he had seen Ross Chidester recently. He answered no. Chidester had left the family employ almost two years earlier. Before dismissing Leonard, Davis requested that he identify a watch he had given Alice around Christmastime 1921, which he did.

With a grand gesture, to great theatrical effect, Davis pronounced, "Now bring in the witness from outside." Heads turned to get a look. In walked a slightly built man in khaki overalls. The look on Leonard's face betrayed his total surprise. Davis had found Ross Chidester, Leonard's erstwhile chauffeur. That he was prepared to testify for the defense signaled trouble.

After being sworn in Davis commenced his examination. The questions established that Chidester had worked for Philip Rhinelander for nearly three years, and then left his job to pursue other options. Chidester mentioned that he met Alice around Christmas 1921. He recalled seeing her first "in West Forty-eighth Street, on the day of the Miss (Adelaide) Rhinelander's wedding. She was with [C]arl Kreitler." Davis then picked up the pace of his questioning, asking the witness about the number of times he picked up Leonard in Stamford—Christmastime in 1921 in particular—and a gift Leonard proposed that Christmas season to give Alice. Davis produced the gift, the watch he had asked Rhinelander about only a few minutes earlier.

DAVIS: "What did you say to him about giving that to Alice?"
CHIDESTER: "I said, 'Don't you know her father is a colored man?'"
DAVIS: "What did he say?"
CHIDESTER: "He said he didn't give a damn."
DAVIS: "What did you say then?"

Chidester, aware of his surroundings, hesitated for a moment and then recalled the less than complimentary characterization of Alice he made for Leonard.[19]

Ross Chidester proved to be the everyday workingman who harbored intense feelings about race and place. He firmly believed that the relationship between Leonard and Alice was wrong. A veteran of World War I, Chidester observed and appreciated many of the conventions of his day. Ironically, the one he didn't allowed him to hurdle class differences, get close to Leonard, and try to protect him. To a degree the gesture was returned. Leonard treated Ross with great respect and narrowed the social divide by often riding in the front seat of the car. Thus Chidester became all the more infuriated when Leonard ignored his advice and continued to see Alice.

When Davis gave way to Mills the damage had been done. Leonard's chauffeur, former friend, and confidant testified that Leonard knew of Alice's mixed heritage and cared little. Mills tried to impeach the testimony of the thirty-three-year-old laborer, unsuccessfully. Chidester told the courthouse he became a witness for the defense because he read accounts of the trial in the papers and because Davis had sought him out. Repeated questions from Mills failed to find a flaw in Chidester's testimony. He was very credible.[20]

This last day of testimony before a break for Thanksgiving was indeed revelatory. Two events stood out, Elizabeth's confession and Chidester's confirmation. And, interestingly enough, most observers believed that Alice's case had been boosted by both witnesses. Chidester's contribution was most obvious. Although Mills tried to convince reporters that Chidester had been a "Godsend" to his client's case, he was dismayed at the overwhelming consensus of newspaper reports that the chauffeur's testimony had been extremely damaging. Even Mills's discovery that Chidester, too, had had a child out of wedlock, was largely ignored by the press. In a day of surprising disclosures the final outcome was that Leonard's driver had supported Alice's claim: Leonard knew in 1921 that her father was colored, and in the racial taxonomy of the United States that made her colored too.[21]

In his treatment of Elizabeth Jones, Mills had attempted to demonstrate that, as the *New York Evening Journal* put it, like mother, like daughter.[22] With broad strokes and fine details he painted a portrait of Elizabeth as a fallen woman who in turn instructed her daughters in the ways of seduction and manipulation, unconcerned with moral virtue or chastity. In effect Mills tried to portray the unquestionably white Elizabeth Jones as something less than the idealized image of white womanhood—perhaps something less than white. The effort boomeranged miserably.

Perhaps Mills should have been paying closer attention to the newspapers' depiction of Elizabeth prior to her turn on the stand.

Alice and Elizabeth remained close throughout the trial.

Elizabeth's appearance and mannerisms struck observers as charming, sweet, "homespun," and "old-fashioned." Her small stature and her status as a white woman and a mother combined with an odd tendency for writers to describe her as "aged" or "elderly"—she was in fact only sixty-three at the time of the trial.[23] Her quiet calm and steadfast support for her daughter's ordeal impressed many. Frank Dolan of the *Daily News* devoted an article to how "Her White Mother's Love Sustain[ed] Alice" during the most difficult days of the trial. He described in detail how the "crooning voice of a loving mother soothed the wounded spirit of Alice Jones Rhinelander, quieted her shattered nerves, cooled and comforted her shame seared soul and lent her the strength to carry on." Several times on the verge of physical collapse, he wrote, Alice turned to the loving arms of her mother, "her head pillowed on the breast she sought in childhood." That Dolan was far from alone in his admiration for Elizabeth's steadfast love and support was soon evident in the response to her experience at Mills's hands.[24]

Public opinion in this case seemed to mirror the newspapers' attitude. Although the *Daily News* published a regular column giving selected answers to various current interest questions posed to pedestrians in Manhattan, only once did they ask about the Rhinelander Case.

And the question they posed was, "Was it proper to force Mrs. Jones, Mrs. Kip Rhinelander's mother, to divulge her past?" Every one of the respondents included in the column answered no. Mary Dalton remarked, "It was a disgraceful proceeding. The sympathy of the public in general is with Mrs. Jones, and it has made itself felt through the public press." Edward A. Anderson, a Brooklyn accountant added, "What is past should be forgotten. This should not even apply in court procedure. . . . I think the evidence was irrelevant. None of us is too good and we should feel charitable toward her." Several commented on her advanced age and status as a mother. Margaret O'Shea deemed it a "disgrace to treat any woman like that." But it was particularly unjustified "when she is an old woman like Mrs. Jones, who is nearing the end of her life." Similarly Theodore Thompson pointed out that as "the mother of a large family" she should have been left alone.[25]

Perhaps the strongest support of Mills's tactics came from Margery Rex, but her recitation of the theory that Alice was following in the path laid by her mother followed its own twist. Like Mills, Rex believed that in marrying Leonard Rhinelander, Alice had fulfilled her mother's own "dead and buried wish, to marry a white aristocrat." Emphasizing that the father of Elizabeth's first child had been the son of the wealthy family on whose estate she worked, Rex told a sympathetic tale of the young Elizabeth: "Tiny, plump and pretty, like a sparrow. But—even the sparrow that falleth." An understandable fall, given an aristocracy that "believed in 'Divine right' and a humbler class who often feared to question such belief." Perhaps hoping for a less class-based society in America, Elizabeth instead found that her husband's color was more of a social barrier than they had expected. Rex suggested both that Alice's love for Leonard was somehow an expression of her mother's "suppressed desires" and that Leonard was now paying the debt of centuries of aristocratic men.[26]

LEONARD'S STANDING AS an elite white man had been steadily eroding from the first days of the trial. Whatever the expectations of white masculinity in 1925, he consistently fell short of the measure. At the same time, in contrast to his painful testimony and his absentee family, the Joneses emerged as ultimately more respectable despite— or perhaps because of—their relatively humble status. Now that most of the Jones family had withstood the hostile questions of Isaac Mills, while Alice offered her silent testimony, their stories and characters, however imperfect, were even more sympathetic to many observers. And, most agreed, the evidence was starting to weigh markedly in her direction. As the trial inched toward its conclusion, more and more observers became skeptical critics. Black and white, North and South, Americans came to believe the testimony of his own chauffeur: Leonard had known his wife had nonwhite ancestry, and he had still loved her and married her.

With the Thanksgiving holiday, the crowd that dutifully encircled the White Plains courthouse each day got a break from the high drama of scandalous love. As they left the trial that Wednesday, many must have wondered what Alice's turn on the witness stand would bring. Would her version of the story, her self-presentation, support the case her lawyers had built? Or would it prompt another shift in public perceptions of the case? Neither Alice nor her father had spoken at the trial. What new revelations would their testimony bring?

12

BEFORE GOD AND

MAN BE FAIR

IN THE LAST three days so much had been revealed that the four-day Thanksgiving recess came as an odd relief. It was not that the peering eyes of reporters shuttered during the break. Teams of journalists lined up outside the Jones's home on Pelham Road and Leonard Rhinelander's Gramatan Hotel retreat in Bronxville, New York. They recorded, as they had for more than a year, the idle moves and momentous actions of the couple that had brought infamy on themselves. Americans knew, as a result, what the Jones family ate that Thanksgiving at mid-decade—an American meal of turkey with all the trimmings. They knew as well of the more sedate and less festive Thanksgiving Leonard shared with his lawyers and bodyguards.[1]

The long moment of waiting ended when the trial reconvened on Monday, December 1, 1925. Of all the major players in this drama, only Alice had not yet testified. The raven-haired woman whose color became miraculously darker as the trial progressed had yet to testify in her own defense. She had endured Leonard's disclosures, the publication of her intimate letters of endearment, her mother's humiliating confirmation of giving birth to a daughter without benefit of a husband, and her own disrobing. But other than shrieks and cries, few had heard her voice and certainly they had not heard her explanations. Her body had until now served as her testimony.

Davis started the day by recalling Elizabeth Jones to the stand. He worked to remind all in the room of what she had endured and how she had been bruised by the previous Wednesday's testimony. Rather than go over the earlier events, he brought Elizabeth back, portraying her as a humble, loving mother who had been forced to tell more than she ever intended about her sexual history. Over the weekend, in fact, newspapers across the nation kept alive the image of the poor, elderly white woman wronged by an overreaching attorney and robbed of her privacy. In a winning strategy Davis simply asked Elizabeth about Alice's color. With brief exactness Elizabeth confirmed that Alice's color had not changed, nor had her portrayal of herself.

With Elizabeth's stay on the stand almost over, the drama began to build. Eyes fixed on Alice, seated at her counsel's table. A few in the court glanced at Leonard. Davis thanked Elizabeth. He then turned to Alice. And then, more quietly than he had uttered any words in three weeks, he declared, "[A]cting entirely upon my own discretion as an attorney and entirely upon my own responsibility as an individual, the defense rests its case."[2]

The words swirled around the room and many in the room gasped. The dramatic end shocked almost everyone. Leonard, who had spent much of his time in recent days looking at the table, cast an upward glance. Surprise framed his face, as it did many. Even Judge Morschauser found it difficult to disguise his bewilderment. Like the others in the courtroom, he had expected Alice to take her turn on the stand. Mills immediately jumped up, but his response to "this unexpected announcement" faded into the din, never gaining a hearing. With Davis's simple words the fall's most watched trial had come near to a conclusion. Only final summations remained before the jury would decide the couple's fate.

Davis knew that keeping Alice off the stand was risky. His co-counsels Samuel Swinburne and Richard Keogh had argued vigorously for Alice to testify. Davis, however, believed she had suffered enough. Moreover, after Chidester's appearance, Davis gave every hint that he thought he had won.

Meanwhile Judge Morschauser decided to trim Davis's sails a bit, forcing him to start closing arguments after the noontime recess.

Before the court took a break Mills recalled Leonard one last time. He asked the young man about Chidester's claim that the former chauffeur had confronted Rhinelander with affirmation of George Jones's color, which Leonard disavowed, calling the charge "perfectly preposterous."[3]

The summation began at 12:45 P.M. with Davis taking the offensive. Fearful that Mills's many years of experience in courtroom theatrics would sway the jury, Davis decided to make the case on two things: truth and race. For the next three hours, his voice alternating between trembling rants brimming with emotion and somber, barely audible reflections, he made his points. He asked the jury one thing: "fairness for this girl."

In the social language of the 1920s a plea for fairness amounted to a plea for racial neutrality. Rather than tiptoe around the subject Davis told the jurors that he feared racial hatred and prejudice. Now, facing the jury, shoulders slightly sloped, he preached:

> Gentlemen, I don't know whether you can know the feelings that are coursing through my body at this moment. I have a tremendous responsibility. I am the only one to stand between this young girl and absolute ruin. . . . They have torn from her ruthlessly every scrap of respectability that a woman loves most. There isn't another thing they can do to this girl except one, and that would be for you to add the last straw and say, "Alice Rhinelander, you must go out into the world as a fraud."[4]

Davis wanted all in the court that day to think of Alice as a woman. She was no Cinderella, no vamp, nothing more than a woman who had dared to love a man from a different background. How could it be, he wondered out loud, that Leonard's family and attorneys had not known about Alice's background, especially after they removed him from the Marie Antoinette Hotel? Without saying as much, he implied that Leonard and his lawyers had known all along. That was why they had resorted to the totally devastating tactics of exposing as much slime as possible.

Then without warning Davis whirled and addressed Mrs. Miriam Rich, the one witness he had a difficult time corralling. Demanding that she stand up, Davis chastised her for a fickle allegiance to a friend. Sneering, he charged, "She didn't want to hurt this girl. But she's sitting here in a court—what a place for a woman—as a vestige of the old gladiatorial days, wanted to be in at the death. Shame that she sits there smiling."

Davis moved next to Mills. He reminded the jurors that his seasoned opponent would try to beguile them with his charm and oratorical mastery, and asked them to be on their guard. The trial was about Alice and Leonard and the overwhelming evidence, and not about what Mills said and how well he said it. Davis cautioned the jury that Mills was as "cute as a fox."[5]

After recounting the strategy employed by Mills and Jacobs of dragging the Jones family through the mud, Davis returned to his critique of Mills. He asked what had been the intent of mentioning Leonard's mother's tragic death other than to elicit sympathy. Death by burning was tragic, he conceded, but, he maintained, "I doubt if death by burning is not preferable to the living death which Mills has inflicted upon this little old woman." Davis was prepared to arouse his own sympathy, this time for the treatment meted out to Mrs. Jones.

But Davis wanted to convey more than sympathy: He sought to convince the jury that the Jones family had integrity. After all, why would a mother have endured such public humiliation if she was not a woman of courage and principle? Why submit Alice to more pain if the only thing to prove was that she hadn't defrauded Leonard by telling him she was white? Davis circled back to Mrs. Jones. He continued, "[T]here is no use putting her [Alice] on the stand to deny that for it has already been denied by Mrs. Jones. There is not a man among you who can disbelieve that little woman."[6] Alice sobbed as Davis wound down his summation for the day. This last comment suggests another possible reason for keeping Alice from the stand: Perhaps Davis felt her mother made a more sympathetic and believable witness.

The next day Davis concluded his summation after four and half hours of additional commentary. Over and over he begged the jurors to follow their heads and not their hearts, to decide the case based on the evidence. He offered a portrait of a mixed-race woman with minimal education courted by the well-bred son of old New York wealth and influence. Leonard, not Alice, had been the pursuer, Davis reminded them. Alice fell for Leonard just as Leonard fell for Alice. And had it not been for the public inspection that put their love on trial, the two might well still be married and out of the public's view.

Speculation aside, Davis also took the time to summarize several critical facts in the case. First, Mills never called Philip Rhinelander or the attorney who found the couple in the Marie Antoinette Hotel, to the stand. "These men knew the truth," asserted Davis. They must have known about Alice's family's background as early as 1921. Second, Leonard had emerged as other than the brain-tied youth Mills suggested in his opening remarks. In fact Leonard admitted pursuing Alice, lying several times, and associating with her brother-in-law, someone unquestionably black. Third, despite earlier portrayals, Leonard was not innocent. "When he went to register at the Hotel Marie Antoinette . . . [h]e was a man of the world, wise even beyond his years." Soon thereafter Davis snarled, "[I]t is a wonder that they don't offer an additional amendment to their complaint to allege that Rhinelander is either color blind or totally blind. He knew her color. He knew the color of her whole family. He ate with them."

In the next breath Davis launched into a larger point, one on which many 1920s racial notions turned. Davis believed that the naked eye could detect and properly assign racial membership. In effect the foundations of racial separation depended on being able consistently and successfully to distinguish between black and white. His decision to have Alice bare her body rested in part on the belief that if jury members could see Alice as black then Leonard had to have done so as well. He returned to that argument in his closing. So, Davis told the jury, "[Y]ou know the color of her body and you know whether any man could possibly be deceived by it. He knew the truth and he liked it in spite of his family name."

In the final analysis only two questions really mattered, Davis informed the jury. "Did Alice Rhinelander voluntarily tell him she was pure white, and did he believe it?" Before answering those questions the jurors were reminded that regardless of their verdict, too much damage had occurred for Alice and Leonard to ever live together again as wife and husband. They were in essence being told that, in siding with Alice, they would not be supporting what they may have individually found objectionable—interracial marriage. Still, they had pledged to be fair, to look at the hard facts and render a decision. Based on the facts Davis offered they would decide in Alice's favor. After all, "[W]ould Alice Rhinelander admit her unchastity to the man she wanted to marry and yet voluntarily deceive him as to her color?"

Davis conceded that no matter what decision the jury reached Alice had been irreparably injured. "She is almost a total wreck," he offered. "[When s]he walks out of the courtroom she will be shunned by the colored race; she will be shunned by the white race." Voice lowering, he built to his final point: "I say to you that on the evidence you should bring in a verdict giving her a clearance on the charge of fraud. . . . May your verdict before God and man be fair."[7]

In the tradition of the court Davis got to sum up first. Now, having congratulated Davis on a job well done, the senior jurist—the man Davis had cast as a sly old fox—was to get his turn. Mills had to persuade the jury that Leonard could not have known the truth because Alice had made it clear that she was white.

First, however, he had to tackle the thorniest issue of all, the whereabouts of Leonard's father. To the average spectator Philip Rhinelander's absence smacked of elite indifference. Mills had done his best to stack the jury with fathers, men who were concerned about, and looked after the welfare of, their progeny. So Mills told the jury that the senior Rhinelander had abandoned his child, not only in this time of need but over a lifetime. He painted a picture of a man so concerned with profits and elite circles that he left his son to others, assuming that good money would buy very good attention. This was why he never ventured to visit Leonard in Stamford, why he had never visited the Jones family in New Rochelle, and why he never set foot in the courtroom. In Leonard he saw but failure and a Rhinelander. He could not accept the former, so he distanced himself from the latter— his son.

But if Philip Rhinelander was a culprit, the real tragedy and the thing to undo was the marriage of Leonard and Alice. As Davis had forewarned he would, Mills worked to make race, especially interracial marriage, the issue. Facing the jury, the seventy-five-year-old attorney proclaimed, "There is not a father among you . . . who would not rather see his son in a casket than wedded to this mulatto woman. There is a room in this fair county for blacks as well as whites, but decent blacks object to this marriage as do the decent whites." Thus, in the space of a few seconds, he forced each juror to ask and answer, Am I decent? Doing so enabled him to push aside Davis's charge that for the jurors to deal with race was to expose their prejudice.

During the hours of his first day of summation, Mills acknowledged that Leonard dearly loved Alice until he discovered her racial background. Returning to a theme developed in the first week of trial and reintroduced occasionally thereafter, Mills insisted that her mother taught Alice to seek a white man and that Alice conspired to entrap poor Leonard. Utilizing language as old as the republic, Mills charged that Alice had enslaved Leonard through a combination of sexual pleasure, calculated jealousy, and strenuous flirtation. In the end Leonard could not tell black from white, he just wanted Alice.

Still, Mills recognized a need to have the jury see Alice as white. His defense could not rest solely on the fact Leonard may have been blinded by love. Thus he turned to the few minutes during which Alice had bared her body. Striking a gentler posture, he said there was no doubt that her tears were genuine. Nor was there any doubt that she was colored. But she had raised enough questions to cause poor Leonard doubt. Mills went on, "Her appearance anywhere would convince that she was white. All men mentioned in her letters were white." After all, her father had the features of a white man, save for his dusky skin. Through this line of argument he wanted to raise once again the prospect that Leonard had mistaken the Joneses for West Indians or Spanish speakers, similar to those he had met in Cuba— "where white people grow darker by constant exposure to the sun." Furthermore, unlike all speculations about Alice's unclothed appearance, Mills insisted that her torso and legs were actually lighter than her arms and face.

To make his point time and time again, he appealed to racial ideas. While saying that Alice had every right to feel ashamed and to cry after disrobing, he concluded, "But with the buoyancy of her race she will regain her spirits. She will gain a husband of her own race and find happiness with him as did her sister Emily, who without vaulting ambition married her own color and kind." At another point that day he pronounced, "There is not a mother in this land who would not rather see her daughter with her white hands crossed above her shroud than locked in the embrace of a mulatto man." While denying that he sought to attack Mrs. Jones, it was clear that Mills was prepared to push forward with his central argument: that Alice's white mother had caused the need for this trial. She was the one who led Alice to seek a white husband, just as she herself had gone against the wishes of white mothers everywhere in marrying the mixed-race George Jones. In a way Mills put the Jones family's alien attitudes about race and place on trial that day. Fully American blacks and whites practiced restraint and did not flout the code of racial behavior; they married their own kind.

Even mentioning Alice's heretofore unknown half-sister, Ethel, stemmed from a need to demonstrate that Elizabeth was conniving. In his closing arguments Mills repeatedly tried to show that she had been twenty-four rather than seventeen or eighteen when she gave birth to Ethel. She had been a mature woman rather than a young girl, he informed the court. If a woman could lie about her age, have a child without a husband, marry a mixed-race man, and bear his children, then could she be trusted? Why believe her words that Leonard had to have known and that Alice had not tried to mislead her husband?

With the flair of an old pro, Mills stirred the emotions of the courtroom with his style and argument. He even managed to draw the ire of Mr. Jones, who had remained stoic in demeanor, save for the irritated expression on his face when his wife was forced to tell about her younger years. After sitting for weeks, George, who never testified, erupted when Mills demeaned his accomplishments by calling him a hack driver. This proved too much for George, who burst out in response, "I never was that!" Urged to hush by Davis, George Jones reluctantly took his seat.

Alice, meanwhile, cried at moments and stared back in others as Mills portrayed her as a black vampire who had preyed on his young client. Calling forth biblical references to Samson and Delilah, Mills recalled other instances of men entrapped by the beauty and sexuality of women. He asked the jury to free Leonard from his curse of love, a curse that had taken the lad to the gates of hell.

Finally Mills ended with a taunt and an instruction. He chided Davis for keeping Alice off the witness stand with the refrain, "Alice, where for art thou? [*sic*]" And then he concluded, "Now, gentlemen I'm at the end. God knows I've given the case of this young man the utmost that [is] in me. Your verdict shall answer once more the question of Holy Writ, 'Can the Ethiopian change his skin?' This mother entered upon that problem and found it couldn't be done. You can have no hesitation to give this young man a chance to live and to redeem the name that has been so bedeviled. From this horrible, unnatural absurd union I pray you grant him deliverance swift and true!"

With that the case that had captivated the nation ended, and all awaited the judgment of the jury.[8] No one knew if the appeal to ignore or embrace racial prejudice would prevail.

13

⤬

AWAITING THE VERDICT

Behind locked doors in the White Plains Supreme Court building, their windows shedding the only light to be seen, streaming out despite the steady sifting drizzle, the "twelve good men and true" who have for the last four weeks heard the testimony in the Rhinelander case deliberate.[1]

BY 11:30 A.M. on December 4, 1925, the closing statements ended, the judge's instructions had been given, and the jury withdrew down the hallway. While these twelve mature white married men sat isolated in deliberations, reporters, onlookers, and family members waited in the courthouse for the judgment, listening for any clues to the direction it was taking. Was that a fist banging on the table? Were those voices raised in dissent? Would they agree quickly or argue for days? The period of waiting for the jury to decide the Rhinelander Case provided a dramatic pause, a time for reflection on the trial and an anxious anticipation of its outcome. Throughout the afternoon of December 4, with the jury locked away behind a heavily guarded door in a scantily furnished room off the main corridor, people waited. Extra guards—150 according to the *Detroit Times*—protected the premises and the jurors from the violence threatened by the Klan and other similar groups.[2] Another hundred sundry onlookers loitered in and around the building. Lawyers for both sides lingered, showing signs of tension; Davis paced nervously and smoked. Alice and her family remained for several hours but finally left for dinner. Judge Morschauser also stayed—until six o'clock.

Meanwhile papers made the most of the tension and continued public interest. Editors of the major New York dailies continued to compete with one another for the photographs, private interviews, and interesting tidbits that had sold multiple editions of each day's paper throughout the trial. During these slow news days, as the trial wound down and the deliberations began, they sought to keep their readers' interest by running pictures and sidebar stories as well as interviews and opinion pieces. Among other things, they tried to predict the verdict and sum up the significance of the trial itself. What was the Rhinelander Case really about? Was it about the impossibility of interracial marriage? Was it about racism? Love betrayed? The New York Rhinelanders' family and class pride? Would the money, clout, and racial standing of Leonard swing the jury against what virtually all agreed was the heavy weight of the evidence against him?

As readers across the country awaited a verdict, the details of Morschauser's instructions regarding the issues before the jury also filled many columns of newsprint. Dozens of papers reproduced the full text of these questions, either in the text of an article or as a highlighted sidebar. There were seven:

1. At the time of the marriage of the parties, was the defendant colored and of colored blood?
2. Did the defendant, by silence, conceal from the plaintiff the fact that she was of colored blood?
3. Did the defendant, before marriage, represent to the plaintiff that she was not of colored blood?
4. Did the defendant practice such concealment or make such representations with the intent thereby to induce the plaintiff to marry her?
5. Was the plaintiff, by such concealment or by such representations, or by both, induced to marry the defendant?
6. If the plaintiff had known the defendant was of colored blood, would he have married her?
7. Did the plaintiff cohabit with the defendant after he had obtained full knowledge that the defendant was of colored blood?[3]

The first issue had been conceded by the defense at the trial's start, and Judge Morschauser ordered the jury to answer it in the affirmative because Alice's lawyers had admitted she "had colored blood in her veins for the purpose of the trial." The seventh question had not been conceded, but Morschauser told the jury that Leonard had answered it when he testified he had lived with her for a week after newspaper reports identified her as the daughter of a colored man.[4] The jury was then left with questions two through six to decide for themselves. The judge instructed them to discuss and vote on each one separately.

On these remaining five hinged the outcome of the trial.[5] Had Alice concealed her "colored blood" from Leonard? Had she told him she was white? Had she misrepresented her race in order to marry him? Would he have married her knowing she was not white? Morschauser cautioned the jurors to weigh the evidence and try to set aside racial prejudice in reaching their decision. He also advised them not to open any personal letters, since someone might be trying to influence the verdict. And, of course, he reminded them not to discuss the case with anyone, not even their wives.

Morschauser also summarized what he considered relevant testimony and cautioned the jurors to consider each witness's motives and position in weighing his or her words. The *Mirror* presented readers with four cartoon sketches illustrating Morschauser's summary of the case. First, predictably, was a downcast-eyed, dark-shaded Alice in a slip, captioned with the judge's words: "You saw her body. It is for you to decide whether the defendant concealed her negro blood." The second showed the "mental picture" the jury must have had of Leonard placing a ring on her finger: They had to determine if Alice had "by her silence induced the plaintiff to enter into marriage, [which] constitutes fraud." The third drawing showed Leonard and Alice obtaining a marriage license. Here the paper inserted a scene never directly mentioned by Morschauser, explaining that when he asked the jury to consider whether Alice had by silence or concealment claimed to be white, the *Mirror* assumed he referred to her marriage license, which listed her as white. Finally, the fourth sketch showed the young couple embracing, Alice in a sheer robe or nightgown. The last question asked whether they "had married relations . . . after a full knowledge of the facts" and noted that the judge had pointed out that they continued to live together after the newspaper announcements of her race.

These captions suggested that the newspaper saw the weight of evidence as falling against Leonard, and the pictures further emphasized the overall message that of course Alice was dark skinned and of course Leonard had known. In all the sketches of her, particularly the one in which she partially disrobed for the court and the one of the engagement scene, Alice's face and visible skin were shaded significantly darker than that of Leonard or the other principals.[6] Did the jurors see Alice this way? Did they share the *Mirror's* interpretation of Morschauser's instructions?

Morschauser ended his instructions with an echo of Davis's closing plea that the jury set aside racial prejudice in considering the Rhinelander Case. In what newspapers called a "plea for tolerance," Morschauser cautioned the jurors to keep all emotions and biases out of what should be an objective process:

> [I]f you allow yourself to be influenced by your sympathy or prejudices, you do the parties an injustice. Sentiment, passion and prejudices or other influences should not interfere with honest determination. An honest, courageous determination upon the evidence is required of you by your oath.[7]

Flanked by court security guards, the members of the jury silently withdrew to their task.

The crowds who stayed in and around the courthouse expected an early decision, as did most of the newspapers. Some of the jurors, however, seemed unprepared to enter their deliberations. They had asked, for example, to postpone hearing Morschauser's instructions from the previous afternoon to that morning. Foreman Clarence Pietsch told the judge that "all but one" were ready to hear them. Would that one hold out for a long embittered struggle?[8]

But the jury returned to the courtroom early on the afternoon of December 4, soon after beginning their deliberations. A hum of curiosity spread from the courtroom to the corridors and out onto the streets of White Plains. The jury was back! What was the verdict? Alice and her family had just left; Leonard had returned to his hotel with his bodyguards. Many others, however, had lingered on. People rushed inside, "pressing their way through the rain-soaked perspiring crowds in the lower halls."[9] The lawyers, of course, were still present, and a breathless crowd awaited the announcement.

The jury was indeed back, but with a question, not an answer. They had returned to ask for clarification on the testimony of Barbara Reynolds. A reporter for the *New Rochelle Standard Star*, she had testified in the last days of the trial. She recalled an interview with Leonard on November 14, 1924, the day after his and Alice's marriage was announced. Sent by her paper, she asked him if it was true that Alice was "colored." He replied, she testified, that yes, his wife was colored, and they were very happy. Davis argued that this clearly indicated that Leonard had known she wasn't white and certainly established that he had cohabited with her with that knowledge. The question now before the jury was, Had Leonard ever denied Barbara Reynolds's testimony? One juror thought he had, another was sure he hadn't. Judge Morschauser began to search the stenographer's transcript, a process the *Daily News* likened to looking for a needle in a haystack. The lawyers argued a bit and finally agreed that neither of them had asked Leonard to confirm or deny Reynolds's statement. All he had said was that he didn't remember being interviewed by her in particular.[10]

As the jurors withdrew again, reporters raced to submit the small flurry of excitement to their editors. Did this episode hint at the jury's progress? Barbara Reynolds's testimony could play a key role in the jury's consideration and spell trouble for Leonard. After this false alarm, the participants, onlookers, and reporters went back to waiting in the hallways, near phones, and in the streets. Deadlines came and went without a verdict, and each edition of the New York tabloids struggled to dramatize the lack of news. The front page of the next morning's *Daily Mirror* warned that the situation LOOKS DARK FOR KIP AS JURY PROLONGS BATTLE FOR VERDICT. A large photo of Leonard with a small photo of Alice's face pasted on his forehead noted that he would be "branded—win or lose. . . . His proud name will always be linked with that of dusky Alice Jones." And the boldface caption ended by exhorting readers: "Watch later editions of the Mirror for more news and a possible verdict."[11]

One way to feed public anxiety was to focus on the perceived and imagined feelings of the main characters. Both the *Mirror* and the *Evening Journal* printed nearly identical photos of Alice waiting at the courthouse the afternoon of the fourth, surrounded by attentive family members and a lawyer. While the accompanying text in the *Mirror* described her "wracked by suspense, nervously await[ing] her fate," the *Evening Journal* captioned the same picture: "Alice and Family

Confident of Winning." The *Daily News* reported that Alice and her mother were putting on a "brave front": Alice proclaiming her confidence and her mother adding, "[M]y daughter is right."[12]

Back in the courthouse, the hours were dragging on. After Alice's departure and the jurors' interest in Barbara Reynolds's testimony, the rest of the afternoon passed without event. The jurors reemerged only for their dinner break; they were followed across the street by reporters and photographers but, still under guard, paid them little attention. They appeared, said the *Daily Mirror*, a bit worn, like men facing a long hard job ahead. The departing Judge Morschauser told them he was going home for the night. If they reached a verdict before the evening's end, he directed that it be sealed and admonished them not to speak of it to anyone. Until the court reconvened to open it in the morning, the verdict should remain a secret. Morschauser's decision was a strong disappointment to the assembly of spectators who still packed the courtroom seats, having waited five hours for a verdict that didn't seem imminent.

The crowd thinned out, but as the evening wore on an estimated one hundred spectators still waited at the courthouse. After several more hours, these lingerers were finally rewarded for their endurance with tantalizing noises from the jury room. By late evening bystanders heard "loud arguments and banging of fists upon tables within, and the indications were that the jurors were hopelessly deadlocked."[13] Over the next few hours the noises continued, suggesting that considerable wrangling was under way.[14] The *Detroit Times* thought that "race prejudice was one of the stumbling blocks in the way of an early decision."[15] The *Philadelphia Inquirer* further reminded readers that the jury had to agree on answers to all six [sic] questions, yielding a mathematically accurate but otherwise improbable "seventy-two chances of disagreement."[16]

The suspense mounted, aided by dramatic and melodramatic press coverage. The *Mirror* closed their article with a highly imaginative description of Alice and Leonard worrying over the trial's outcome through the night.

> In her humble New Rochelle home, Alice Jones Rhinelander tore nervously at already broken and splintered finger nails, or tossed on her bed in a fever of suspense; . . . the last of the Huguenot

Rhinelanders walked the floor of his pretentious room in the
Gramatan Hotel in Bronxville, smoking cigarette after cigarette . . .
and facing—life, not with, but tied to a mulatto—or a life in which
he will be free to go out into the world and redeem the name he has
so besmirched.[17]

Both were in suspense here, but Leonard had the most to lose. For the
Daily News, however, it was Alice whose future swung most dramati-
cally between degradation and redemption. Their portrayal of her
tense night of waiting focused on her dilemma, not his. The awaited
verdict would decide "whether by morning she would again be plain
Alice Jones, daughter of a former New Rochelle bus driver, or whether
the dawn would find her the triumphant and undisputed possessor of
the great Rhinelander name." General opinion, furthermore, held that
Morschauser himself leaned toward Alice. He, after all, would make
the final decision, albeit based on the jury.[18]

Reported rumors and hints from the courthouse seemed to predict
overwhelmingly that Leonard's suit for an annulment of their marriage
would be denied. On the other hand, another source, with its own
interest in profiting from the Rhinelander Case, offered a very different prognosis. While the jury debated the case and Alice and Leonard
waited, New York bookies were reportedly doing brisk business on the
trial's outcome. By all accounts they set the odds at 5 to 1 that Leonard
would prevail. This expectation was based in large part on the assumption that the circumstances of the marriage and Leonard's class and
race position would overwhelm all other issues. As the *Detroit Free
Press* speculated, "[N]o jury would compel a member of the aristocratic Rhinelander family to live with the mulatto daughter of a taxi driver." This sentiment was repeated by others who could not imagine the
jury forcing the "white millionaire" to keep his "quadroon wife," whatever the weight of evidence against him.[19]

In fact these predictions had already started to pop up in the mainstream press a week earlier. On November 30, the *Hartford Courant*
pronounced "the end in sight," declaring that Leonard had "tied himself plainly enough and knew what he was about. The evidence that
he knew it has been produced in court and his own character has all
disappeared." Moreover, the editorial continued, Alice had clearly
"demeaned herself by marrying him."[20]

The black press tended to agree. Assessing the evidence as clearly on her side, African American editors nonetheless feared that the heavier weight of racism would prevail.

> From the very beginning of the famous and perhaps never-to-be-forgotten trial . . . , it was evident that Mrs. Rhinelander had in no way deceived her aristocratic husband about her race, as was the contestation. But even so, it was the consensus of opinion that race prejudice would dominate the decision of the jurors and wrest from this member of our group the dower right in a fortune of a leading aristocratic white family which approximates a hundred million dollars.[21]

Even African American editors who did not particularly identify or sympathize with Alice were concerned with the implications of the case for racism in the United States:

> Every intelligent Negro is following this notorious case with keenest interest, not that he has the least interest in or sympathy for any of the parties involved, but to see whether the courts in New York, where there is no civil distinction on account of race, will allow such sinister influences to operate in the back part of the judicial mind.[22]

Beneath the drama, behind the sensationalism, and embedded in the scandal lay the core of civil rights for African Americans: equal protection under the law. Where segregation was encoded in legal codes and public policy, civil rights activists fought to change the law. In places like New York, where discrimination lay more in social practice and prejudicial enforcement of race-neutral laws, a proponent of social equality could spend a lifetime in court suing restaurants, county clerks, theater owners, and others. A trial like the Rhinelander Case offered an extremely visible test of the ability of the New York State court system to render an impartial verdict.

But others feared that, whatever the outcome, the Rhinelander Case might be doing more to promote than to overcome race prejudice. Both Davis and Mills were criticized by the black press for feeding American racism in their arguments. The *Cleveland Gazette* also argued that white lawyers like Davis affirmed the permanence of racism when they invoked prejudice in defense of black clients. This editorial compared Davis's appeals with those of Clarence Darrow in the Sweet trial, which shared front-page headlines with the Rhinelander Case in the black press.

Sweet was a black Detroit doctor who had moved into a white middle-class neighborhood. Darrow had successfully defended Sweet against charges of murder for shooting and killing a white man while defending his home and family from a mob of white attackers. According to the *Gazette*:

> [P]rejudice is not so "deep-rooted," so hard to get rid of as both Messrs. Darrow and Davis impressed their hearers and thousands of others who read in the newspapers what they said. It is a thing people pick up and lay down as easily as one does his or her hat—when they want to do so. A case in point is Kip and Alice Rhinelander who would be living together today were it not for outside interference. He was prejudiced until he learned to love her. . . . Darrow's and Davis' prejudice-talk undoubtedly helped their clients in the Sweet and Rhinelander cases but did it help the race throughout the country?[23]

Here it was Davis's invocation of racism that bothered the writer. The attorney's concern that racism might sway the jury, that racism was behind the annulment itself, only served to give new life and power to such prejudices.

For most black journalists, however, it was Mills's racist assumptions that outraged. A monthly publication that ignored the day-to-day events of the case, *Opportunity: A Journal of Negro Life*, published an extended analysis in its January 1926 issue:

> There is an important angle of the Rhinelander annulment suit which no amount of clever editorial skirting, or summary disgust, or pity for the self-inflicted smirch upon the blazing escutcheon of a proud old family can overshadow. It is the implication upon which the suit itself rests, and which Judge Mills, trial lawyer for the plaintiff, with a last bold play to the passions of America, put in these words ". . . There isn't a father among you who would not rather see

his own son in his casket than to see him wedded to a mulatto woman. . . . There is not a mother among your wives who would not rather see her daughter with her white hands crossed in her shroud than see her locked in the embrace of a mulatto husband."[24]

Mills's closing had made explicit the reasoning behind the entire annulment suit and scandal: The Rhinelanders did not want their son to be married to a black or mulatto woman, regardless of the lack of legal sanctions against such marriages in New York State.

The *Broad Ax*, charging that Mills had made the trial into a race war, with Alice representing the blacks.

Isaac N. Mills did not look at Alice Rhinelander as an individual, but as a Race. He did not consider his case as a private affair between two persons, but as a fight between two races. His attitude was shared by the thousands of newspapers that poured columns and columns of filth into millions of homes daily during the past month. What was said of Alice Rhinelander (except the personal experience portions) could be said of any other girl of our Race who happened to find herself married to a white man.[25]

Mills drew on racial prejudices, the *Broad Ax* said, portraying Alice in ways that were familiar and stereotyped.

Further, the *Broad Ax* repudiated Alice's blackness. She was not, they emphasized, "representative of the Race we purport to champion." She was identified as black only by the circumstances of her marriage and trial, and the *Broad Ax* was interested only in the principles behind the case.

Information coming out of New York has acquainted us with the fact that she has always stood aloof from those with whom she knew herself to be identified. Our only interest in the case comes from the fact that what happened to her is happening to thousands of others of our Race in this country.[26]

Readers of black-published papers seemed similarly conflicted about the importance of such cases to themselves. A letter to the editor of the *Defender* thanked them for their "complete broadcasting" of the

Rhinelander and Sweet cases. Robert N. Crawford of Chicago wrote that he and others depended on the *Defender* for stories about "our Race, because the white press never prints anything about Negroes unless it is something to crush our standing." An anonymous letter from Arkansas City, Kansas, criticized front-page coverage in "our Greatest Weekly" for cases of amalgamation (racial mixing), arguing that those who amalgamated were disloyal to the race: "Amalgamation does not help the Race, for we don't want to join the other race, but surpass them and hold our own. Where our people are joining them shows unloyalty to the Race. So place these unloyal incidents on the back page."

Unlike most of the white-published newspapers, however, black newspapers in the 1920s were primarily weeklies published on Fridays. Most, therefore, did not have the chance to cover this interim waiting period. December 5 editions reported the last few days of testimony and the lawyers' closing statements. A few mentioned that jurors were expected to go into deliberations by the end of the week and return with a quick verdict.[27] (The next issues, on December 12, of course, reported the verdict.)

The *Jewish Daily Forward,* a leading daily Yiddish-language newspaper in New York City, published a commentary on the Rhinelander trial on December 3, as the closing statements were proceeding. Responding to a well-publicized lecture in which dramatist Channing Pollock condemned the publicity given to the case, the *Forward* defended the need for coverage. They agreed with Pollock that too much attention was given to sensational details, with the main motive of getting more readers. But the *Forward* editors asserted that the trial was of "great significance" because of the importance of the issues involved. While the editorial did not offer a prediction on how the jury would decide, it did emphasize that the case "had to do entirely with racial prejudice." In fact, they speculated that the reason the Rhinelanders had taken the case to court despite its obvious weaknesses was because they were convinced that the jury would "have enough prejudices against Negroes to release him from his Negro wife under any circumstances."[28]

Other observers' expectations that racism, not evidence, would determine the trial's outcome followed strong popular and institutional condemnation of interracial sex, particularly when legitimized by marriage. No matter their own position, they could not ignore the extent of white American hatred of interracial marriage. We do not know what the jurors thought of these issues and to what extent they were influenced by them as they sat and discussed the questions in that White Plains courthouse late into the night of December 4, 1924. They had reportedly had tears in their eyes on listening to Davis's closing description of Alice's fate—to be looked down on by whites and blacks alike—and Davis had also admonished the jury not to let race prejudice affect their decision. But, as we have seen, much of the evidence was based on assumptions about the relationship between race and behavior, and the testimony was confusing and contradictory. It was one thing to want to put aside racism, it was another, of course, to do so successfully, especially filtering through the subtle and not-so-subtle layers of the Rhinelander Case.

Although few papers reported it, there had also been incidents of interracial violence just as the trial was ending. The *Boston Globe* reported that the reason extra guards were posted around the courthouse as the jury went into seclusion was to prevent a repeat of the previous night, which had seen several fights between black and white men.[29] The threat of violence also operated more directly against the jurors. Just prior to the trial's end, the judge announced that many people involved with the case had received threats from white supremacists who wanted a verdict in Leonard's favor. Alice, Leonard, the judge, lawyers, and jury members had all received "many letters attacking the conduct of the case, threatening . . . physical violence and couched in abusive terms."[30] The threat of violence constantly lurked beneath the surface of discussions and events regarding interracial sex and marriage. The jurors, as well as most Americans, knew that organized white violence against parties seen as aiding intermarriage was a stark reality in the 1920s. They had sworn an oath to consider only the evidence presented in court while deciding their verdict. But they were under an extraordinary amount of pressure and may have feared reprisals if they refused Leonard's annulment suit.

And, as if these threats and fights were not enough pressure, one juror even claimed to have been approached directly in an attempt to sway the verdict. During the trial the jury had not been sequestered, although they had been given the usual warnings to completely avoid newspapers and conversations with family and friends regarding the case. In the American legal tradition, nothing and no one is supposed to be able to influence a juror except the evidence and arguments presented in the courtroom. To try to tamper with this process is a crime. Just a few days after the verdict was announced, Judge Morschauser asked the Westchester County grand jury to investigate charges of jury tampering. Juror Frederick D. Sanford of Yonkers claimed that Dr. J. C. Bennett, an eye specialist, was one of three respected men of the same town who had allegedly approached him regarding the case. (Sanford could not recall the names of the other two individuals.) Dr. Bennett, Sanford testified, had met him on the street on the second day of the trial and made comments against interracial marriages.[31] The grand jury did pursue the case but ultimately dropped it. Furthermore, although Sanford said he inferred that the three men were against interracial marriage, they had not directly told him how to vote or who they thought should win.[32] Nevertheless, having several community leaders express strong opposition to interracial marriages made enough of an impression on Sanford for him to come forward after the verdict was rendered.

Such experiences were no doubt in the jurors' minds as they sat discussing the questions throughout the afternoon and evening of December 4. Finally, however, their arguments were concluded. At 11:30 P.M., almost precisely twelve hours after they began deliberations, the jurors suddenly emerged from their room and announced not that they were breaking for the night, but that they were done. Though the verdict was decided, Judge Morschauser was long gone. And, according to his instructions, it could not be read until court reconvened the next day.

Morning newspapers, however, had deadlines long before the court's next session, and they needed headlines. But saying what? Rumors were flying around the courthouse, and mostly in one direction. Many papers managed to ignore them, reporting only that the questions had been turned over to the jury to decide.[33] While these papers told their readers they would have to wait for the reading of the verdict Saturday, others jumped to guess or even claimed already to know the contents of the sealed envelope. Several papers announced the "sealed verdict" in their headlines but speculated on its possible contents in the article.[34] The *Chicago Tribune* reported that all the rumors flying around the courthouse indicated that Alice had won.[35]

Just as many were willing to report these rumors, and even report them in headlines. MRS. RHINELANDER REPORTED WINNER IN JURY'S VERDICT the *Detroit Free Press* headlines pronounced.[36] The *Daily News* offered readers of its final edition the news that "Opinion Favors Alice As Jury Is Locked Up" with promises of complete coverage the next day. And the gossip continued to spread. In Atlanta the jury was reported to have favored the "quadroon wife" in a vote of ten to two.[37]

The *New York Daily Mirror* must have been particularly sure of this information. With the verdict still unread, its early editions proclaimed ALICE WINS in huge block letters across the front page. Smaller print noted that the verdict was still sealed and it was only "reports" that indicated what it said. Other journalists were confident—and insensitive—enough to go knocking on Alice's front door early Saturday morning before the family had left for court. The *New Rochelle Standard Star* set the scene and revealed the darkness of the hour.

"A light was burning in the humble Jones home in Pelham Road early this morning when reporters knocked at the door to bring tidings that Alice had won," the story began.[38] Elizabeth Jones answered the door and wearily began to turn away the reporters who had been besieging her family every day for the past few months. She looked, according to one brutally honest reporter, haggard and tired as she pleaded with them not to ask for interviews yet. But, they told her, they had "wonderful news." This gained them entry into the house, and Alice was called down to hear what they had to say: She had won. "The eyes of Rhinelander's bride seemed to light up and her arms went about a woman reporter's neck in a warm embrace. Tears rolled down her face as she sobbed. 'O God! What a wonderful message you have brought to me. Oh! I'm so happy! I'm so happy!'"[39] Alice then assured reporters that her family would be in court that day, "and I'll be there with my chin in the air."

Perhaps Leonard had received the same prediction. He did not appear in the White Plains courthouse that morning to find out if it was true. Premature headlines had been wrong before.

14

⤡

The Trial Ends

A tense and tightly packed gathering filled the White Plains courtroom on the morning of Saturday, December 6, 1924. "Men and women, debutantes and dowagers; white and black, all returned to rub elbows and witness the verdict's rendering."[1] The curious crowds who jammed the room were looking for Alice's reactions as much as they awaited the verdict itself. The excitement of the moment bound spectators and actors together in their tension. Surrounded, as usual, by her family, Alice sat calmly—or nervously, depending perhaps on the reporter's line of vision. From all angles, however, it was evident that Leonard had not appeared.[2]

At 10:00 A.M., Judge Morschauser arrived to begin the proceedings. His first order of business was to warn the waiting crowd to maintain a peaceful composure when the verdict was revealed. Anyone making the "slightest attempt at a demonstration when the answers were read" would be charged with contempt of court, the judge pronounced. "I want you to know this is no circus. . . . The court officers will see that no one moves when the questions have been read."[3] Morschauser then turned to the jurors to begin the familiar ritual of reading a verdict. He asked the jury if they had answered the six questions that framed their deliberations. Foreman Clarence Pietsch answered,

"Yes." The sealed verdict was then handed to Morschauser, who quickly read it to himself while those present held their breath. He then read the questions and their answers out loud.[4] Was Alice "colored"? Yes. Did she hide that fact from Leonard by silence? No. Did she conceal her race to get him to marry her? No. Had he married her thinking she was white? No. Would he have married her knowing she was colored? Yes.

The jury had answered all the questions squarely in Alice's favor.[5] Leonard had lost the suit to annul his marriage. The announcement was met with silence. The hushed courtroom then rippled with an audible sigh of exhalation from every corner. Correctly prepared, as it turned out, for this verdict in her favor, Alice also received the announcement calmly. She sat quietly with her eyes on the floor as the judge and jury continued the ritual by reading and answering each question individually. She showed no emotion when Mills offered the predictable request of a losing side that the judge set aside the verdict on the basis of the evidence.[6]

This obedient stillness was first broken by the rush of journalists running to report the outcome over telephones and telegraph wires. News of the jury's reckoning spread quickly. New York dailies printed extra editions with the verdict, and evening papers rushed to incorporate it into their afternoon printings. Having delivered the news of the verdict, journalists immediately set out to gather reactions. Reporters followed the key figures out of the courtroom to record their reactions and then roamed the streets of black and white neighborhoods for public opinion.[7]

The court rituals over, Alice and her family left the courtroom, closely followed, of course, by journalists and onlookers. The *New York Evening Post* described the scene:

Photographers fluttered in front of her [Alice]. A curious crowd closed about her. Mr. Jones became separated from the family in the rotunda of the court house, starting out one door while the other three headed for the main street exit. Mrs. Rhinelander darted fifty feet through the crowd, the photographers in hot pursuit, seized her father and dragged him, expostulating, back. The photographers raced back with them, beat her to the revolving street door and lined [up] in front as she emerged. Cameras clicked.[8]

Once outside the building, Alice and her entourage headed for attorney Lee Parsons Davis's office down the street, for what she undoubtedly hoped would be her final interview. Some thirty reporters followed them for a 1920s version of a press conference.

Described by one paper as her "last ordeal," this interview involved probing and extremely personal questions. Had she and Leonard really been in love? Yes. Would she go back to him? She couldn't say . . . no. Did she still love him? Yes and no. She showed bitterness toward Jacobs, who had deceived her and lured Leonard away from her, but seemed forgiving of Mills, although he had "flayed Alice and her mother as women are seldom attacked, even in a courtroom." She and her mother were planning a trip, perhaps to Florida. But then she would return to live in New Rochelle. Was she happy about the outcome? "Happy? Yes. But not too happy over the torture I've been through." She was deeply grateful to her family, "But I've always been close to my people."[9]

Since Alice had not testified, reporters took this opportunity to get her reaction to the trial. Alice herself did not seem interested in rehashing the previous events, but focused on the verdict and her current situation and feelings. When asked if she still loved her husband, Alice replied:

> I do love him—and I don't. Right now I'm happy over the result and I can forget some of the things that were done to me. I can forget some of the misery that came with the tortures of the past few weeks. I'd rather remember other things. I'd rather remember that Leonard's love and mine was a wonderful thing until they started to break it up.[10]

The *Birmingham Age Herald* summarized her interview: " 'I'm thankful for the verdict. I always loved Leonard. I'm too tired to talk any more at this time.' She added, however, in answer to questions, that she would never again live with her husband."[11] Davis ended the interview by requesting that journalists leave her alone "to rest and recover her health before the press again centers inquiries upon her."[12]

The sympathy New York tabloids encouraged for Alice reached a revealing height in the *Daily News* coverage of this interview. Overtly portraying Alice first as a polite child and then as an elegant "tropical beauty" who appeared "extremely Caucasian," the *News* heaped praise on the "dainty colored girl."

> Alice was a child—not a woman—as she sat beside her defender. As we looked at her, and heard her soft spoken replies, couched with the meticulous courtesy of a child showing respect for elders, it seemed incredible that here was the vampire, the lustful woman that Judge Mills had painted in court during progress of the annulment suit. . . . Her eyes glowed with feeling. Her voice was musical and low.

The *News*, then, tried very consciously to counter Mills's portrayal of Alice as a seductress, and furthermore as a dark seductress. This same passage, which described her as courteous, respectful, soft-spoken, and having a melodious voice, went on to emphasize pointedly how "white" she looked, albeit with the help of cosmetics:

> As she sat there, in a conventional oak office chair, wearing a water lily on the fur collar of her brown coat, one could easily imagine her as a girl that might captivate men, far more astute and worldly wise than the youthful scion of the Rhinelanders. Yesterday Alice looked extremely Caucasian as to skin. There was a deftly applied tint to her dusky cheeks and she had made generous but not vulgar use of powder. During the trial she seldom used makeup and the dark color of her face was more apparent. Those who saw her yesterday could understand readily that Alice with a backdrop of beauty and luxury in a setting different from the crowded little home in . . . New Rochelle might pass for a tropical beauty of pure Aryan ancestry.[13]

Even if one leaves aside the question of how a "pure Aryan" might also be a "tropical beauty," in the tortured logic of racialism, this passage aptly illustrates the complexity and confusion of white American ideas about race, behavior, appearance, and status. Although still described as "dark-skinned" by other reporters observing the same events, here Alice has become "extremely Caucasian" not only in appearance but also in dress, manner, and class. She was still, given the verdict, legally Mrs. Leonard Kip Rhinelander, belonging in a setting of beauty and luxury. She had been vindicated not only in court but in some of the popular press as well. Interestingly the reporter did not consider her apparent ability to make herself look white with carefully applied makeup a challenge to her defense that she had not tried to deceive Kip. She also grows during this passage from a "child" to a "girl that captivates men" to a "tropical beauty." Both childlike innocence and passive sexual allure hold an uneasy balance in this portrait of a woman redeemed.

But other papers saw and described Alice very differently. The *Detroit Free Press* described her the same day as "dark-skinned Alice" waiting for the verdict. And the *Cleveland Gazette* described her as "haggard and wan" during this same interview at Davis's office. "She slumped into a chair and her drawn face reflected her tiredness. But her eyes were alert and occasionally they sparkled."[14]

Quoted in many papers, with a few minor variations, Alice's postverdict expression of emotion and pain and her ambivalence toward her husband set the tone for coverage of her in the weeks to come. Newspapers continued to dog her footsteps and report rumors of Leonard's whereabouts with conflicting suggestions that a reconciliation was imminent and divorce proceedings were in the works.

Leonard's absence, of course, had not gone unnoticed by the press. They called seeking an interview at the Hotel Gramatan, where he had spent the night. All interviews were refused. Instead papers printed the prepared statement an anonymous spokesman gave over the phone. Leonard, he said, had received the news "stoically" and without comment. "He didn't say anything, . . . I guess we'll have lunch when the time comes and dinner when the times [sic] comes. Mr. Rhinelanders [sic] just hanging around."[15] Several papers further speculated that Leonard would be leaving the state and assuming a false identity to start a new life.

And of course the legal battle was likely to continue. Leonard's lawyers said they were already starting to prepare an appeal of the decision. And rumor had it that Alice would pursue a separation suit against Leonard, accusing him of abandonment. Additional speculation suggested she might also sue her father-in-law, Philip Rhinelander, and accuse him of coming between her and her husband. Such a legal charge, called "alienation of affection" was not unknown at the time. All of these rumored cases were based on the legal tradition that marriges should be difficult to end: Without a "no-fault" divorce, an individual wishing to end a marriage had to charge his or her spouse with some failing: abandonment, cruelty, adultery, and so on. Under this

*Alice, Elizabeth, and George, relieved yet aware
of the emotional costs of victory.*

structure, a third party who interfered in a marriage and caused or
contributed to its end could be found liable for damages. A husband
filing for divorce on the basis of adultery, for example, could also sue
his wife's lover for alienating her affection for her husband.[16]

For the moment, however, Alice had won, and she and Leonard
were still married. And there was much to find out about how the jury
had reached their decision, and what the responses of the supporting
characters and general public would be.

The twelve jurors were quickly interviewed and grilled about the
verdict and their perceptions of the case. In a formal statement, jury
foreman Clarence Pietsch described the influence of particular testimony on the jury:

> The filthy testimony that was introduced had very little to do with the
> finding of the verdict, or, I might say, in the answering of the ques-
> tions. We did not think very much of the testimony of the man

Chidester. . . . The testimony of Mrs. Reynolds was probably the greatest single factor in favor of the defendant. It was the testimony of Mrs. Reynolds that finally decided the jury on the answer to question No. 6. This question puzzled the jurors more than any other. We are tired and we are glad it is over. We decided the case on the evidence and we did not allow our personal views to sway us. Rhinelander was his own best witness. We consider Kip Rhinelander a normal being, as high a type as any of ourselves.[17]

The twelve had apparently made what one called a "gentlemen's agreement" not to discuss the specifics of their debate, how they reached their answers, or who held out longest and why. This restraint was reflected in Pietsch's careful statement, which did not contain many surprises. The sixth question, whether Leonard would have married her knowing she was "colored," was the key to his charge of misrepresentation. In order for misrepresentation to justify annulment it had to be about something that would have prevented the marriage. Barbara Reynolds's testimony had already been assumed to be an important issue when they interrupted their deliberations to question the record regarding just that testimony. Chidester's testimony, however, seemed to have impressed the media more than the jury.

Individual jurors, and some of their wives, did make statements regarding their own feelings about interracial marriage and racism. Several were quoted as claiming that race prejudice had "played no part" in their decision—that they had agreed to only discuss the case on the basis of the evidence and testimony. In fact the jurors' claim to racial objectivity was emphasized by many papers and provided the leading statement in a front-page article in the *New York World*: "Every one of the twelve white married men . . . believes personally that mixed marriages are not conducive to better feeling between the white and Negro races, or a source of happiness to the individuals who contract them."[18] Indeed, many of the jurors hastened to assert their strong disapproval of interracial marriage in the days after their judgment was rendered. As Henry Weil put it, "If we had voted according to our hearts the verdict might have been different."[19] Fellow juror Fred Sanford admitted that he had "a prejudice against marriage between the white and colored races, but my personal feelings had nothing to do with my answers to the questions." The wives of Weil and Sanford shared their husbands' feelings on interracial marriage and publicly disagreed with the verdict. "Of course Leonard Rhinelander should have been granted an annulment," Mrs. Sanford told the *World*, "It isn't right for a man of his standing to be tied to a girl with colored blood." She did think that Leonard should have been able to "see" that Alice was "colored," and that he had "made one big mistake" but that "he ought to have a chance to remedy it." Mrs. Weil also opposed her husband's decision, explaining that she sympathized with Leonard's tragic childhood and had hoped he would win his annulment.[20]

More details of the hours of seclusion emerged despite the gentlemen's agreement; the temptation to tell proved too irresistible to a few. It turned out that at the start of their deliberations, ten out of the twelve had favored a verdict against Leonard. Most of the twelve hours of deliberations were then spent trying to persuade the other two to change their votes.[21] According to the other jurors the main point of contention between the ten who favored Alice and the two who favored Leonard rested on the racial definitions used to describe Alice. One juror, Max Mendel, an exporter from Mount Vernon, held out by himself for five hours on the question of whether Leonard would have married Alice if he had known her to be colored. Mendel was apparently interpreting "colored" to be the equivalent of "negro" or "negress." His colleagues argued that the judge's question "did not concern a negress but a woman of color."[22] Much of the ensuing debate then focused on the definition of the word "colored" in the questions, an issue that was never directly dealt with during the trial. In fact, it was largely Davis's decision to concede that his client was colored that preempted the need to debate racial definitions.[23] In other words, while most jurors saw a clear distinction between "Negro" and "colored," Mendel did not.

Outside New York this aspect of the jury's decision was largely ignored. A few papers, though, could not overlook it. The *Baltimore Afro-American* ran its whole story on the verdict under the headline MRS. KIP NO NEGRO, COLORED SAYS THE JURY. With this unusual emphasis, the *Afro-American* went on to elaborate that the jury had found that her "colored blood" was "only twelve percent": She was 87 percent white. This particular formulation of Alice's racial identity is absolutely unique in the coverage. These percentages do correspond roughly to the blood quantum of an octoroon, a person of one-eighth black ancestry. Alice was occasionally called an octoroon, more often a quadroon, and mostly just "dark," "dusky," "black," "colored," "Negro," or "mulatto." Nevertheless the story continued, commenting that this decision "broke with tradition" by making a distinction between "Negro" and "colored." Citing legal definitions of Negro in several southern states, the paper argued that most such laws made a distinction between black and white but not black and colored.[24]

In fact, in an odd turn of events, an entirely new explanation for racial mixing and racial categories emerged to solve the jurors' dilemma. The question was: Did the term "colored" include someone like Alice, who had black ancestry but was not, by the reckoning of the recalcitrant jurors, truly black. The standoff was finally resolved when one juror turned to Mendel and explained that blackness was like whiskey. "Would a quart of clear water with a small glass of whiskey added be called whiskey?" he asked. Mendel had to admit it would not, nor was Alice a Negro. But she had admitted she was colored, so he promptly yielded.[25] Apparently for these jurors, the one-drop rule did not follow the simple logic of bartending.

When the jury turned in its quick negative verdict, newspaper editors and commentators across the country had a chance to analyze and explain the case. At least fourteen editorials were published on or soon after the day of the announcement, and many others revealed their perspective within the more traditional article format. Almost every newspaper reported on the verdict. These editorials and articles covered a great deal of thematic ground, falling into several categories. White-published southern papers tended to downplay the verdict, focusing on Leonard's plans to appeal and Alice's separation suit. The *Richmond Times Dispatch* led with the headline RHINELANDER WILL APPEAL; WIFE SUES FOR SEPARATION. Only in smaller print did they specify that the verdict was "Unqualifiedly Unfavorable to Rich New Yorker." The article went on to outline the events of the day, making no comment on the outcome.

In the North and Midwest there were two common themes. The first was that the jury had made the right decisions based on the evidence. The second was that in doing so they had rejected, or at least temporarily overcome, racial prejudice. Most commentators agreed with the *Reno Evening Gazette* that "nobody could expect different findings." The jury's findings were not only predictable, they were just:

"applauded wherever the dirty case has been followed and that seems to be everywhere."[26]

With all the clarity of hindsight, some editors hastened to assure readers that they had known all along what the outcome of this "most recent exposition of the drama of miscegenation" would be:

> During the trial it never seemed to us that there was any basis for the reported 5 to 1 betting odds among townsmen and spectators that Rhinelander would win an annulment. Such opinions must have been built upon the color line. They could not have been supported by the evidence.[27]

Another suggested that "from the very beginning of the famous and perhaps never-to-be-forgotten trial five weeks ago, it was evident that Mrs. Rhinelander had in no way deceived her aristocratic husband about her race." The jury's determination that she had never concealed her black ancestry from him was generally considered obvious from the fact that Leonard had visited her family often and seen his future father-in-law with his own eyes.[28]

In an editorial that was reprinted in several black newspapers, the *New York World* summed up the outcome as "A Just Verdict in a Sorry Case. . . . [T]he only verdict that could have been justified by the evidence." After a long trial with "morasses of unsavory details and three-day gales of needless talk," the case had finally found the "firm ground" of justice.

> The case should never have gone to trial. It was the duty of a lawyer, as an officer of the court, to warn the Rhinelander family of what has happened. Counsel should have informed clients that an annulment plea would open floodgates of nauseous testimony and that, upon the facts as known, it would have scant chance of success in a fair court before an honest jury.[29]

Avoiding a trial would have spared the Rhinelanders "much humiliation" as well as the legal scandal that had been inflicted on the public. Other editors agreed but pointed out that the reason the Rhinelanders had pursued an annulment was clear: They did not want a black woman to be able to use the Rhinelander name. Further, divorce involved alimony, and the Rhinelanders, as the editors of the *Reno Evening Gazette* suggested, may have chosen an annulment suit to avoid having to pay Alice alimony.[30]

In an article announcing that "Millionaire Rhinelander" had lost the verdict, the *Jewish Daily Forward* opined that "Rhinelander's pedigree, all his 'pull' with politicians, his millions" had been unable to save him. A woman of mixed race was able to beat him because the jury saw that she was in the legal right.[31] The *Rock Island* [Illinois] *Argus* suggested that Leonard must have expected the verdict because all the evidence favored Alice:

> There is no question but that Rhinelander made a grievous error in marrying an octoroon, but since he became a party to the contract with both his eyes open, and while in possession of his normal faculties, fair minded citizens will be pleased with the verdict of the jury. . . . The young woman is the one who should proceed further in the courts, inasmuch as Rhinelander should be compelled to support her as long as he is legally wedded to her.[32]

This editorial, reprinted in the *Chicago Defender*, reflected the jurors' stance that intermarriage was a "grievous error," but that Alice was in the right and should be the one to bring suit against Leonard and claim financial support.

WHAT DID THE Rhinelander verdict imply for the state of racism in the United States? Not much, according to some newspapers. One explanation was that the decision was specific to only small northern towns. Roscoe Simmons of the *Chicago Defender* even went so far as to claim that "this decision could have been reached in no other place in the United States than White Plains and other small northern towns where white people are free from graft and race-hatred." Noting the juror who said the verdict would have been different if they had followed their hearts, this writer praised the honesty of the jurors who overcame their own prejudices to settle this "weighty problem."[33] Similarly, Mark Whitmark of the *Amsterdam News* suggested that white racism did not flourish in upstate New York. "Crackers don't thrive on Westchester air. The cold breezes don't appeal to men accustomed to chew tobacco and run their mouths around the country store."[34]

Interestingly some black-published papers also emphasized class affinity in explaining the case and the verdict. Whitmark, for example, further explained the lack of race prejudice in the verdict by the class loyalties he felt connected the Joneses to their white peers. "There are but two classes of citizens in Westchester—those who work all the time and those who work when they want to or who have retired as a result of their own labors or the labors of their parents."[35] The *New York Age* also downplayed the racial implications of the case, claiming that the verdict indicated that class loyalties rather than racial divisions had moved the jurors.[36]

The decision also served to protect "womanhood in general and Negro womanhood in particular." Refusing the annulment suit, the *Amsterdam News* suggested, was a sign of moral progress: "In so many words it says that a man of means must not invade an humble home and carry off a beloved daughter, have sexual relations with her, give her his name, and then cast her into the gutter." Although in this case the attempted excuse was racial misrepresentation, the writer contended, it was the same verdict that a white woman would have received. Therefore, all women should hail it as a victory. On the other hand the case would hardly encourage others to form interracial relationships and marriages. Leonard's experience should prove a deterrent for white men whose intentions were not honorable, thus "curbing promiscuous miscegenation. Such interracial marriages as will then occur will not necessarily be conceived in immorality and iniquity."[37]

Editor Charles S. Johnson credited a brilliant defense and fair-minded judge and jury for the verdict, but pointed out it left many morals issues for people to consider. For Johnson, the most crucial danger was that facing black women who had no protections from predatory white men. Johnson quoted Booker T. Washington, often associated with acquiescence to segregation: "If your segregation wall will be high enough to keep us in, will it be high enough to keep the white man out?"[38] This harked back to the double standard the black press routinely identified and criticized in which black men could be lynched for the suspicion of involvement with white women while white men were able to force sexual relations on black women with little or no legal or social repercussions.

The black press was also very interested in the reactions of other papers and often republished selected editorials on the case. The *Cleveland Gazette* noted in its usual collection of editorial snippets that Alice's victory "certainly did not please New York City reporters. Their slurs since, ever referring repeatedly to her 'alley home' . . . show just how bitter was the pill they had to 'gulp down.' . . . Too bad, isn't it?"[39] If the verdict was a blow against the usual business of racism and interracial relationships, then it was a victory that all African Americans could share and bask in.

Several black-published journals that, as monthly publications, had not followed the trial's proceedings, used the occasion of the verdict to offer their perspectives on the significance of the case. In the January 1926 issue of *The Crisis*, Du Bois commented on the trial, emphasizing what he thought it revealed about white America:

> If anything more humiliating to the prestige of white America than the Rhinelander case has occurred recently it has escaped our attention. That high Nordic stream which produces super-men is here represented by a poor decadent descended from the best blood of white America.

Why Alice would have wanted Leonard, he proclaimed, is "more than we can fathom," but the real problem was not in their relationship but in the double standard white Americans used to judge interracial relationships.

> [I]f Rhinelander had used this girl as concubine or prostitute white America would have raised no word of protest; white periodicals would have printed no headlines; white ministers would have said no single word. It is when he legally and decently marries the girl that Hell breaks loose and literally tears the pair apart. Magnificent Nordic morality!

Du Bois concluded that it was "a fine thing" that Mills's "contemptible appeals to race prejudice" had not influenced the jury's quest for "the plain truth."[40]

THE AVERAGE MAN and woman on the street also occasionally got the chance to leave a published record of their opinions. Soon after the verdict was announced, reporters left the courtroom and hit the streets of New York City seeking public response to the trial and its outcome. The *New York World*, for example interviewed dozens of random passersby in City Hall Park. Their survey yielded only one objection to the verdict. The others agreed with Joseph O'Brien that "It didn't make much difference to him whether she was colored or not," and with George Jordan that "the jury was right." Jordan, however, added what others may have left unspoken: that he didn't think they should have married in the first place. Two other men agreed that Leonard "deserved" the verdict, while another deemed the case "so disgusting I haven't paid any attention to it."

Although the *World* reported that "Negroes were reluctant to discuss the case," they did print two responses from African American men. The first was J. M. Lee, a carpenter from Brooklyn. He explained: "I could tell you, right straight, my opinion, but I don't want to be balled up in it. If she knew she was colored she should never have married him. I think she thought she was too good for fellows like us." The second, songwriter Matthew Murphy, thought there was "no sense in keeping them tied together." The couple should get an annulment, but Alice should get alimony.

Four women, presumably white since no race was given, also responded to the survey. Miss Anna Schneider, a Brooklyn secretary, ignored race and declared the verdict "one of the few cases where a very poor woman won in a suit involving a rich opponent." Mrs. C. A. Schuettler seemed to agree. "I pity her," she said. "He's wealthy, and these wealthy men—" His status as a rich man courting a poor woman seemed to imply for Schuettler questionable behavior or morals. Jean Gordon, a clerk, agreed, elaborating: "He was entitled to no consideration, the way he dragged her into the mire." The fourth woman, typist Rose Grapin, said only that Alice should have won because "he knew she was colored. He saw her family and played cards with them." Only Grapin cited the issue of the trial: whether Leonard had known Alice was not white. For the other three white women, Alice simply represented poor women and wronged women victimized by rich, immoral men. Whether as a romantic tragic figure or a reminder of experiences they or friends of theirs had had, Alice stood for disempowered women in a way that both erased overt mention of her blackness and relied on it as part of her symbolic significance.

The dissenting opinion came from A. W. Mosier, a broker, who said that because he was from South Carolina he was "naturally . . . sore. I think he was stupid and not responsible, and she got a rope around his neck and tied him. No sensible jury would have done it."[41] The *World* deemed it quite self-evident why a southerner would be the one to object most strenuously to the verdict. Northern whites routinely projected racism as a southern province. In the issue of interracial marriage, however, they had some justification in the prevalence and relative harshness of anti-intermarriage laws in southern states.

A few days later, however, another self-identified southerner, A. K., wrote a letter to the editor of the *World* complaining about this assumption that "natural geographical prejudices" obliged southerners to disagree with the verdict. Although A. K. approved of laws that made intermarriage "properly. . . a crime," he or she believed that most southerners would have approved of the verdict in this particular case. The testimony about Leonard's knowledge of the Jones family and therefore his wife-to-be's racial status had, after all, gone unrefuted:

> His attempt to escape from his marriage by charging his wife with fraud was typical of the white man who would contract such a marriage and pursue such a social association. He should not be permitted to make his wife a victim of his change of view. The marriage should be annulled but the wife should bring the action and be amply compensated in alimony. That, I believe, is the average Southern viewpoint of this disgusting case. The average Southerner would not victimize a Negress for the sake of any white man who would first associate with her kind socially and marry her.[42]

Here it was Leonard's willingness to associate with and marry an African American that signaled for A. K. the young man's moral degradation and weakness of character.

As a well-known black New York City neighborhood, Harlem received a fair amount of attention after the trial. Like the rest of the country, Harlem residents had "kept up with the Joneses by minutely following the Rhinelander annulment suit." The *Chicago Broad Ax* reported that Harlem was stunned by the verdict. Even though most residents had thought that Alice should win, and would if the decision was made on the basis of evidence, they had not expected such an overwhelming victory. Few had believed a white jury capable of such an unbiased finding.[43]

White reporters also descended on Harlem to get the black community's reaction. Interviews in the *Daily News* concluded that the "General Opinion of Colored Folk" was that Leonard was paying the piper. Harlem was, the brief story read, very interested in the Rhinelander case and its outcome. Few Harlem residents called her "Mrs. Rhinelander," however. "To them she is just plain Alice Jones." The article quoted only four individuals but summed up the responses as accusing Leonard "of leading Alice into much sorrow." Having betrayed Alice and brought an unsupported suit against the woman he claimed to have loved, Leonard deserved to lose: The verdict was his just desserts.

U. S. Poson, a known author, theorized that the case indicated the inevitability of racial mixing between blacks and whites.

The Rhinelander case has proven a contention which I have adhered to for some time. It is that no two races influenced by the same environment and by the same examples of history can live side by side without miscegenation. It is not a matter [of] whether we like it or not. It is a fact. America is a melting pot, and in the process of melting it is only natural for the colored race to become part of the process. The trend in America is definitely toward racial homogeneity.[44]

Poson's assumption that Americans would one day be a single, fused race was not all that uncommon at the time. However, the dominant trend was to fear the results of such intermingling between blacks and whites.

The *Daily News* poll also queried Zora Hurston, now better known as Zora Neale Hurston, an anthropologist of African American and Caribbean culture and a writer, then studying at Barnard. She allowed that "[p]ossibly there was some deception on both sides," but that Leonard was not "as stupid as he pretended." When asked if the Rhinelanders could live happily together now that their marriage had not been annulled, she thought they should not live together again: "I do not believe that they would be happy." Similarly, teacher Roy

Lancastor thought that Alice's victory "shows that there is a great deal of justice being done for colored people." Could they live happily together again? "Yes . . . in Timbuctoo and no other place."[45]

Despite what they reported as overwhelming support for Alice and the verdict, the *News* found one black woman whom they quoted as disagreeing with the verdict. Kathryn Wise, a business manager, said that Alice should not have won the case. "She knew all along she was colored and should have taken the consequences. Still, Rhinelander should have seen for himself," she added.[46]

Although the *Daily News* cited Wise as an exception to Harlem's identification with Alice, the response to her published quote subsequently demonstrated the extent and depth of that identification. A few days after the *Daily News* article on Harlem, the New York–based black-published weekly, the *Amsterdam News*, reported that their offices as well as Wise herself had received many angry calls denouncing her criticism of Alice. The *Amsterdam News* agreed that if she had made the remarks reported in the *Daily News*, the callers' outrage was justified. But, they cautioned readers, they had investigated and found that several witnesses agreed that she had been grossly misquoted. Wise herself was so upset at the misrepresentation that she was now ill. The *News* stressed that Harlem was unanimously in support of Mrs. Rhinelander. The journalists, desperate for a different viewpoint, had exaggerated and perhaps even manufactured her words.[47]

Most important for the *Amsterdam News*, however, was what this incident revealed about black perceptions of the trial:

> This little sidelight is mentioned because it portrays the sentiment prevalent in Harlem as to the outcome of the Rhinelander Case. Harlem was for Alice without caring anything personally for Alice. It was for Alice because she stood as a symbol to Negro womanhood throughout the world. The price she paid was a high one, but the writer is tempted to record that the victory was worth it. Few women of any race would have paid so dear a price.[48]

Harlem, and by extension black America, supported Alice as a representative of African Americans and particularly African American women.

Finally, Alice reportedly received hundreds of congratulations inspired by sympathy, celebrity awe, and interest in the money many assumed she would soon receive from the Rhinelander estate. There was a constant stream of messengers and delivery boys to the door of her family home, carrying messages, invitations, and gifts. A New York City ward of the National League of Republican Women Voters sent "sympathy and heartiest congratulations on the outcome of your trial," while a University of Indiana student wrote, "Best regards and lots of luck. Thank heaven, justice still lives in New York City."[49]

Still competing for their readerships, New York tabloids bragged at their ability to scoop the news of the verdict. The *Daily Mirror* bragged about its scoop on the Rhinelander verdict, reproducing its ALICE WINS headline, and comparing it with the *Daily News* WHITE PLAINS COURT THRONGED READY TO HEAR VERDICT FOR ALICE. In the accompanying story the *Mirror* bragged about its "triumph in the important Rhinelander case," claiming that it had printed the verdict "long, long before any of our contemporaries, including the Snooze News, did."[50]

But the Rhinelander Case and the media frenzy were far from over. Would the couple reconcile? Would the verdict be overturned on appeal? Would she file for divorce? Would he? Would her suit against Philip Rhinelander be successful? Lest their readership fail to consider the many possibilities, the tabloids promised continued multiple editions covering the story, hoping for continued sensation and continued drama. Would the couple fade quietly back into history's shadows, or was this only the opening scene of their now public romance? The papers, quite adept at creating the illusion of news during lulls in the events of the trial, would continue to find stories and rumors to cover after the trial's end.

15

⤛⤜

SPOTLIGHTS ARE SLOW
TO FADE

AFTER A FEW days public reaction to the Rhinelander verdict settled down, and thoughts turned to what would happen next. Leonard's lawyers, of course, immediately announced their intention to challenge the verdict, while Alice's told reporters they were considering both a separation suit against Leonard and a charge of alienation of affection against his father, Philip Rhinelander. Leonard disappeared. Alice disappeared. Perhaps they had disappeared together. The American public and its self-appointed media representatives seemed reluctant to see the story end in separation. Backed by profit-conscious editors accustomed to selling papers by filling columns with details of the Rhinelander Case, reporters continued to stalk the families and neighbors for information on the tragic hero and heroine. Reports of Alice and Leonard's activities, and rumors of their imminent reunion, continued to appear regularly in local and national newspapers in the weeks and months that followed.

One of the odder happenings took place on December 7, the day after the verdict. A man claiming to be Leonard forced his way into the apartment of Grace Miller, Alice's sister, who lived with her husband next door to Alice and her parents. "Hello Grace," the man exclaimed, "I'm Leonard and I've come back to Alice!" Quickly arrested,

Theodore Dorm of Dumont, New Jersey, was determined to be suffering from dementia and was locked up.[1] Reports conflicted as to whether Alice herself had heard the man. According to the *Boston Globe*, not only had she been home, but the "False Kip" had upset her greatly. Apparently she had thought it was really her husband and came running, thinking he was back for her. Only when she saw the man did she realize it wasn't Leonard.[2]

The next day the *New York Sun* announced that Leonard Rhinelander and his wife had vanished. Not together, though: Alice and her mother had gone to Florida. Leonard's whereabouts were unknown. Reporters knew only that Leonard and Leon Jacobs had checked out of the Hotel Gramatan, where they had stayed for the duration of the trial. They left no forwarding address. Leonard, the *New York Times* reported, would be taking a long trip under an assumed name. If he could not be found to serve papers on, Alice's planned separation suit would be delayed.[3] Actually, with the Jones home still surrounded by a large crowd, Alice remained hidden inside for a day or two and then was thought to have slipped out secretly during the night, with her mother.

By midweek the black-published papers came out to report on the verdict and events of the last few days. These issues showed most interest in the larger issues of the case, but some did speculate on the couple's future. The *Chicago Defender*, for example, ran a side story claiming that Alice and Leonard had gotten back together. Their love, the *Defender* reported, had survived the trial, and reports from New York suggested that the two were reconciled.[4]

On December 15, new drama erupted over reports that the Ku Klux Klan in Florida had taken note of rumors of Alice's journey there. Klansmen had apparently organized to find her and were searching hotels and other locations. Both northern and southern papers reported that Alice was in Fort Pierce, Florida, although the Klan hunt had failed to find her yet. According to the *Detroit Free Press*, Alice and Leonard were together in Florida: A couple staying in a cottage there had been identified as the Rhinelanders. Other rumors spotted her in West Palm Beach; the Klan had formed committees there as well and was raiding local hotels and searching rented rooms.[5]

· · · ·

FLORIDA WAS AT an interesting point of its development in 1925. Only a few years into a real estate boom, Florida newspapers played to a national audience, trying to publicize its success and attract further investment. But of all the major city papers we examined across the nation, the *Florida Times Union* paid the least attention to the Rhinelander Case. It gave no attention to these Klan hunts, but on December 16, it ran an AP photo of Alice on the back pages. (All of the *Times Union*'s very few references to the case were buried on the back pages.) The timing of this photo publication, therefore, begs the question of its relationship to the unmentioned local fervor over Alice's possible presence in Florida. It is tempting even to speculate that this photograph might have been used by Klan members to help them identify Alice once they found her. At the very least it seems to be a response to rising local interest in the case. Further, the lack of an explanation of Alice's identity accompanying the photograph suggested, as did the few other articles and pictures of the case, that *Times Union* readers were quite familiar with the Rhinelander Case. (Perhaps the most intriguing example was an enigmatic cartoon spoofing the new fad of putting one's initials on one's property: It showed a young man inking the initials L. R. onto a woman's bared back.)

West Palm Beach hotels, however, announced that they would bar Alice Rhinelander if she did show up.[6] Within a day, however, the rumors that Alice was in Florida had been squelched by her attorney. Samuel Swinburne announced that she had never left New Rochelle. While the Klan searched Florida hotels, Alice was safe at home with her family. Swinburne also denied the rumors that Alice and Leonard were reconciled. The Klan's hunt provided more fodder for black editors, nonetheless, who denounced the organization as "the hooded realm of hundred per cent Americans." Black newspapers were also more willing than the white-published papers to spell out what Klan members would have done had they found Alice in Florida. The *St. Louis Argus* pointed out that white men routinely had mulatto children but were ready to lynch Alice Rhinelander. Rejoicing that Alice had fooled the Florida "Ku Kluxers," they also attached a story about a man in Virginia who was first thought to be black but then determined to be an Indian and therefore allowed to marry a white woman.[7]

The *Defender* was less sympathetic. They had warned Alice when she mentioned a trip to Florida, they reminded readers. America's

Southland was not the place for her to seek refuge. "There, where men are white and justice is unknown; where the mere mention of color is an invitation to the mob; where chivalry died when the Indians were bottled up and driven onto the reservation." There in the South there was no problem with white men "being with our women in the dark," but marriage was out of the question. Similarly the *Amsterdam News* suggested that the Klan focus its efforts on doing "missionary work among the 'Kips' who can see in the daytime, but who are stone blind at night." And the *St. Paul Echo* advised the Klan that it was too late to do anything about Alice. Instead it should focus on the "twenty or thirty thousand 'Kip Rhinelanders' of the South." Clearly the hypocrisy, racism, and violence of organizations like the KKK were of supreme importance to the black papers and their readership.[8]

Although not hunted by the Klan in New Rochelle, Alice was in hiding for good reason. When her sister, Grace, went shopping that same week, she was followed and harassed by curious crowds who mistook her for Alice or wanted information about Alice.[9] And, according to some reports, Alice and her mother did travel to Connecticut to stay with some of Elizabeth's relatives for a week or so. If they did, they were back in Westchester County before Christmas, throwing a celebratory party for friends and relatives. In contrast to her feelings at Thanksgiving, Alice was described as jubilant and joyful. One small story, however, in the *New Rochelle Standard Star* reported that a seat at the party was reserved for Leonard Kip Rhinelander. Left vacant by his absence, it was taken by a black guest. Indeed, Elizabeth told reporters, Alice had received no word from her estranged husband,[10] so why he would be expected is hard to understand. Nevertheless, whether true or not, this image of an empty chair probably represented Alice's continued feelings of loss, even in the midst of celebration. Leonard himself had completely disappeared from public view, amid rumors that he was planning to change his name and move west.

In January a new product of the "where's Alice" rumor mill surfaced in the Mid-Atlantic states. The *Baltimore Afro-American* got a scoop that Alice was in Richmond, Virginia. Once again the hunt was on for Alice, this time from presumably more friendly hunters. But once again Alice was nowhere to be found. The eagerness of reporters to speak to her is evidence enough, however, that the public obsession with following her story was not limited to the white-published New

York tabloids and their largely working-class white readership. What questions would these reporters have asked Alice? Would she have responded differently confronted by black interviewers? Given the specific interest of the *Baltimore Afro-American* in the issue of blood-quantum racial definitions, they would almost certainly have asked her whether she considered herself a Negro or not. It has never been determined if a reporter ever asked Alice this question after she had conceded that she had nonwhite ancestry for the purposes of the trial.

Meanwhile, the idea of a "Rhinelander Case" had come to take on a meaning of its own, defining any marriage or attempted marriage in which one party misrepresented his or her race in order to marry. These cases came to be referred to as "Rhinelanders," particularly in the black press. For several years both white and black papers referred to the Rhinelander Case when reporting on stories of interracial marriage, racial misrepresentation, and tests of racial identity in marriage or divorce cases. In rural Louisiana a white man sought to divorce his black wife, asking also that their children be made illegitimate. Like Leonard Rhinelander, the writer pointed out, this man wanted to avoid the economic and social responsibilities of marriage because his wife was black.[11] Similarly, New Orleans had a "Rhinelander Case" when a white man filed for divorce charging he had just discovered his wife was black. In Louisiana interracial marriage was invalid by law, and any amount of black ancestry would make a person legally black.[12] A widely reported "reverse Rhinelander" in New Jersey involved a white bride and colored groom who were denied a license. When they reapplied, this time listing the woman as colored, she was arrested for perjury.[13] The *Chicago Broad Ax* compared the Rhinelander Case to the Virginia Indian cases, in which a chemical test was reportedly being used to determine racial ancestry of mixed-blood self-identified Indians who wanted to be listed as Indian, not black.[14] In Missouri a judge refused to believe that a white-appearing woman married to a black man was herself black. Ignoring testimony that she had black ancestry, the judge told her to take off her hat and declared her white.[15]

On January 11 the *New York Times* reported that Rhinelander was preparing to sue Alice for divorce and had moved to Connecticut. In an unusually unemotional statement, Alice "declined to discuss her husband, saying it didn't make much difference to her where he was, as he had to pay her alimony just the same."[16] In March, Leonard was spotted in Ocean Springs, Mississippi, living under the name of Edward Johnson and still closely flanked by the ever-present Leon Jacobs. According to this story Leonard was sent there by his father after he learned that his son had taken Alice on a posttrial shopping trip.[17]

And so it went. The main characters studiously avoided the spotlights, but the critics kept writing the play. In March 1926 the *St. Paul Echo* noted that the Rhinelanders were "Gone But Not Forgotten." Case in point: Two conflicting stories had circulated that week. The first was that Leonard and Alice were reconciled and on their way to Italy. The second was that Alice had filed her separation suit. Neither was true. The *Echo* blasted such journalism based on conjecture and rumor: "If they succeed in effecting reconciliations after the unfortunate publicity which court trials have given them, let the stories wait until the reconciliation is indeed established fact."[18]

Still, the reconciliation stories did not end. In July 1926, Alice, now called "Alice Jones" by the *Standard Star* although she was technically still "Alice Rhinelander," made plans to sail for Europe. Although she repeatedly told reporters she was going to visit her mother's family in England, other papers repeatedly told readers that she was going to France to meet up with Leonard. Interestingly, even as they printed stories of rumors, some papers began to express their own fading interest in keeping the story alive. The *Houston Informer* duly noted rumors of a reunion in France with the opening assurance: "[N]ot that we are not tired of the whole affair."[19]

On the eve of her departure, Alice threw another party and was harassed once again by a stranger who had to be removed by the police. Louis George of New Rochelle initially claimed to be an author and barraged her with "personal questions" about why she and her husband had separated. After his arrest he said he was a cook, not a writer, and had been drinking. Alice did not press charges. Reporters and curiosity seekers followed her to the docks and learned that she was very happy, still loved her Leonard, and still denied that she had any plans to meet him in Europe. It was also noted that the trip was costing her—or someone—several thousand dollars, and she seemed to have acquired a new limousine. Although she also expressed the hope that the trip would take her away from reporters, Alice was fol-

Alice sails for Europe, 1926.

lowed aboard by a "small army of photographers and movie men [who] . . . pursued her all over the ship" before it set sail. Then she was hounded by "another battery of cameras" throughout the voyage. To avoid curious passengers and "camera fiends," Alice changed her cabin twice during the trip, before disembarking early and quietly at Cherbourg.[20]

Meanwhile the lawyers continued the legal process. On December 19, Isaac Mills had submitted his briefs asking the judge to set aside the verdict. In March 1926, Morschauser refused Leonard's plea for a new trial, upholding the jury's decision. The New York legislature had taken notice of the case as well. In the same month the state body proposed a bill that would ban marriages between blacks and whites. The black-owned *St. Paul Echo* commented dryly that "young millionaire social sportsmen can prepare for a season of legalized open hunting — that is, if the bill passes." Unable to retry the case in Westchester, in the meantime, Leonard's lawyers filed an appeal at the appellate court in August 1926. Leonard had already spent $50,000. It was estimated that the appeal would cost him another $50,000. (Approximately $2,500 of that went to copy the 2,500-page trial transcript from the Westchester trial.) At the same time Alice's lawyers were preparing both a separation suit and a suit against Philip Rhinelander for alienation of affection. These appeals and counterappeals also involved financial negotiations. Leonard was paying for Alice's lawyers (since she was still his wife) as well as his own. He was also paying her support. The amounts of each were constantly debated and cross-claimed by lawyers on both sides over the next few years.[21]

Perhaps convinced by the signs that Alice and Leonard were not reuniting in Europe, new rumors emerged, suggesting that one or both would be seeking a Paris divorce rather than a reconciliation.[22] But Alice returned to New Rochelle in October, neither divorced nor reunited. Soon thereafter, the appeal was heard at the New York Supreme Court, Appellate Division, in Brooklyn. The details of this hearing were granted relatively little media attention. Most coverage was brief, summarizing the issues, which were based in legal technicalities and offered no new information or surprises, certainly not any of the sensational variety anyway. The decision upholding the Westchester County verdict, handed down January 1927, cited one major issue charged by Isaac Mills: the lack of testimony from Alice or her father. Mills argued that this absence led jurors to assume that Alice and her father would have denied Leonard's testimony, when in fact (according to Mills) they would have corroborated some of it. The appellate court, with one dissenting judge, found that Alice's failure to testify regarding whether she had told Leonard she was not of colored ancestry did not create the presumption that she would deny she had.[23] In other words, they considered but ultimately rejected Mills's position on this matter. The dissenting judge did argue that it was an error for the judge to tell the jury not to assume anything from Alice's silence. (Morschauser had also told the jury to answer two of the questions in the affirmative.) This error was made more serious, the dissenting opinion held, when her attorney, by taking responsibility for keeping her from the stand, prejudiced the jury even further.[24]

When this decision was announced, the reporters appeared again at the Jones residence. Alice, of course, was pleased that the verdict had been upheld. Her mother had an appeal of her own. "We hope," she hinted gently to the assembled journalists, "that we can be allowed to continue life in our own quiet way." It had now been more than a year since the Westchester court's verdict, more than two years since the doomed marriage vows. No doubt the Joneses had long since had their fill of their celebrity status and the media attention it brought. Grace, who in the aftermath of the marriage announcement seemed to relish her role as family spokesperson, hadn't been heard from in quite some time. Neither had George. Alice was avoiding public appearances at all costs; the constant confusion over her whereabouts attested to that.

The papers, and their public too, were tiring of the case. Soon after Leonard's first appeal was denied, the *Baltimore Sun* printed a rather hopeful cartoon depicting the whole affair as "Passing Out of the Picture."

In this illustration a garbage man carries a trash can marked "Rhinelander Case" away from a crowd of onlookers with smoke and odor trailing behind.[25] Similarly a complaint to the *Chicago Defender* begged them to "keep Alice Jones Rhinelander off your front page, especially in those glaring headings." The writer appreciated that the paper supported her, but they really could not care much about the situation anymore and were concerned that young girls might misunderstand.[26]

Despite these complaints the coverage continued. One constant theme was the question "Where's Kip?" In November 1926 he was reportedly hiding out on Long Island; by January he was thought to be "leading a gay life" in New Orleans, preparing to divorce Alice from there.[27] In June 1927 he was rumored to be in Reno; in December he was supposedly spotted "somewhere in the South."[28] Even more popular were the continued rumors of a reconciliation. In commenting on the appellate court's decision, the *Chicago Broad Ax* noted that "Kip still has his beautiful mulatto wife."[29] The *Defender* was even clearer. They printed an interview with Alice in which she promised to "pick up the loose threads of our broken romance and start life anew," an oblique statement that did not specify whether she meant to renew a life with Leonard, or by herself. "I mean to vindicate myself. On the streets people of all races stare at me as if I was a haunted woman." And haunted she was. She had received a large arrangement of roses after the decision was announced. Although the caption of the photograph read "Kip Sends Roses," the text revealed that the sender was actually unknown. Nevertheless, the process of healing, in whatever sense, was aided neither by the continued court cases nor the accompanying media attention.

Meanwhile Leonard's lawyers were filing another appeal, this time to the highest New York State judicial level: the New York Supreme Court in Albany. And Alice was filing for more alimony. Both suits went forward in early 1927, as the New York and New Jersey state legislatures debated the antimiscegenation bills introduced the previous year. Both bills, perceived as partly inspired by the Rhinelander Case, failed to pass. Alice won more money for her lawyers, but not for herself. And, by the end of March 1927, the Albany court had joined the Westchester and Brooklyn courts in refusing Leonard Rhinelander's annulment suit.[30] This was the end of the line for an annulment. Wherever he was, Leonard would almost certainly be turning to the divorce courts to end his marriage.

THE REST OF 1927 was fairly quiet, until the very end of December, when Alice finally filed her separation suit against Leonard, claiming cruelty, inhuman treatment, and abandonment. Although Alice was still proclaiming her continued love for her husband, she had apparently given up all hope of a reunion. On a more practical level, this suit served to protect her legal and financial rights in the marriage, especially given the high probability that her husband would soon serve her with divorce papers. The abandonment charge suggested that she had not, in fact, seen or heard from him since the trial. The cruel and inhuman treatment, her lawyer Swinburne explained, were "suffered . . . throughout the wide publicity resulting from the annulment action brought by Rhinelander." The problem of where Leonard was, however, was now a legal one: Her lawyers had to find him in order to serve papers on him.[31] By February, Leonard still hadn't been found, but was rumored to have made Alice a sixty-thousand-dollar offer. The Joneses denied this rumor and assured reporters that they were not dropping the separation suit. April saw a return of reports that Leonard was in Ocean Springs, Louisiana, seeking a divorce. Perhaps the two were racing to see whose suit won first.[32] "Ho, Hum, Kip and Alice in Court Again," yawned even the intrepid *Chicago Defender* that month. But neither case was being heard yet: Leonard was not found in Ocean Springs after all, and Alice's suit was delayed.

In October 1928 reports surfaced again that Alice would drop her suit in exchange for an increased allowance.[33] Then all was quiet until June 1929, when Leonard was finally located, actually living in Nevada under an assumed name. He had also hidden his identity under a new moustache and twenty pounds of added weight. He hardly looked the same man, and certainly appeared aged beyond his twenty-seven years.

Disinherited by his father to protect the family fortune, Leonard had followed in the Rhinelanders' footsteps by successfully pursuing a career in real estate. He was reportedly "roughing it" in the not-yet-developed town of Las Vegas, living with only a bodyguard as company, cutting his own wood and carrying water from a mountain stream.[34] And he had indeed begun the paperwork to file for a Nevada divorce.

This new twist raised enough interest for the *Defender* to note that the case was still a topic of conversation for public gossip in upper- and lower-class houses in New York. But the stories, especially those in the *New York Times* and *New Rochelle Standard Star,* rarely warranted front-page coverage anymore. By July, however, Leonard had brought a suit for divorce in Nevada, and Alice responded with an alienation of affection suit against his father, Philip, long rumored but finally actualized. The divorce suit claimed that Alice

> took advantage of his youth and inexperience, dominated him and induced him to forsake his family and friends so that they became estranged from him and that he suffered humiliation and mental distress until his nervous condition became so acute that in order to prevent complete prostration he separated from her.[35]

Alice's alienation suit asked for five hundred thousand dollars in damages from the elder Rhinelander, blaming Philip for destroying Alice and Leonard's marriage.[36]

Both suits continued, accompanied by occasional short articles throughout August and September. There was little to report, other than the legal maneuverings. In an August interview Alice said she might just settle out of court because she was too busy to be bothered with a trial. And in September rumors arose that Alice and Leonard would be meeting face-to-face to discuss the situation, but they did not. In fact it seemed that Leonard himself hadn't spoken directly with his father in five years, according to one interview at a Kansas City, Missouri, meeting of lawyers and Leonard.[37]

In December 1929, Leonard was granted a divorce in Nevada, while Alice's suits went to court in New York. Apparently, under Nevada law, Leonard was able to win his case without Alice or her representation being present. Because of this, and because of other differences between Nevada and New York divorce laws, Alice was apparently under no obligation to recognize the Nevada court's decree. It was, according to the *New York Times*, "illegal and void."[38] By February a settlement conference between the parties' lawyers had been arranged. Alice began speaking to the papers again, repeatedly denying that she was looking for a settlement:

Leonard in Nevada a few years
after the annulment trial, 1929.

Money has never been my motive. I have a deep affection for my husband, and I have fought tirelessly and undergone unspeakable
anguish to hold him and to thwart efforts to part us. Now his spokes-
men, as a further humiliation, are treating our whole affair, which was
one of the heart, as though it were a mere commercial transaction.[39]

However, by April she had filed an annuity suit. She subsequently
turned down a reported offer of $100,000 cash, refusing to drop the sep-
aration suit and give up her interest in Leonard's real estate property.[40]

Finally, in July 1930, almost five and half years after Leonard first
filed his annulment suit, the legal marriage, and the story it spawned,
was over. Alice signed an agreement to accept the terms of the divorce
and drop both the separation suit against Leonard and the alienation-
of-affection suit against Philip. In exchange she received a $31,500 set-
tlement and an annuity of $3,600 for life. As part of the agreement she
promised never to use the Rhinelander name, a promise she kept.[41]
The details of the final terms were kept quiet, and for good reason. In
the agreement it was stipulated that because Alice was never served
and never appeared in the Nevada courts, the divorce was not binding
on her outside Nevada. Furthermore, what this document did was to
keep the divorce open: Alice could decide to submit a defense to the
Nevada courts (at her own expense, since Leonard refused to cover
any more lawyers' fees.) But if she challenged the Nevada divorce and
prevailed, Leonard consented to pay both the lump sum and a larger
lifetime annuity—$3,800 per year for life. However, at no time did
either party suggest that a victory in Nevada meant the marriage still
existed. It had ended years earlier.

Leonard trusted that he and Alice would move on with their respective lives. Too much had happened. So the agreement specified that as
long as Alice "shall remain the wife of [Leonard]," or not contest the
nonbinding divorce or bring further suit, she would receive $3,600 per
year in quarterly payments. Leonard and Alice agreed that they would
continue to live apart, and Alice relinquished all rights to property and
personal estate "and all other rights, interest or claims in any manner
arising or accruing out of the marriage relation now existing between
said parties." This was, in effect, a separation agreement, not a legal
divorce. Finally Alice not only agreed to use her birth name instead of
her married name, she promised not "in any way [to] use or make ref-

erence to the name of Rhinelander in connection with any appearance upon the stage or in connection with any writing or lecture."
Again, she kept this promise.[42]

ALICE AND HER family could probably never have returned to their
previous life. In October 1930 a speeding ticket returned Alice to the
pages of New York papers: "Kip's Ex-Wife Pays Fine for Driving
Fast."[43] But the Jones family and Leonard Rhinelander largely did disappear from the newspapers over the next decades. The other
Rhinelanders, of course, had always remained offstage, even during
the trial. Nevertheless, the 1930s were a terrible decade for Alice emotionally, although her annuity must have been a welcome financial
cushion against the economic hardships the nation suffered in the
Great Depression.

Three years after Alice finalized her separation from Leonard,
George Jones died. The *Standard Star* reported his death on the second page. The notice revealed that the Joneses were still living in the
same home on Pelham Road and still attending Christ Church in
Pelham Manor, where the funeral services were held. Grace and Alice
were also still living in New Rochelle (Alice with her parents), while
Emily, Robert, and Roberta were in nearby Pelham. This story was
picked up by a scattering of papers, including the *Chicago Defender*,
which reported simply that "Mrs. Rhinelander's Father is Dead."[44]
George had died suddenly of a heart attack and without a will, which
meant several years of legal paperwork to straighten out his estate and
papers. Ultimately everything was left to his wife, Elizabeth, who
promptly wrote her own will, no doubt hoping to spare her daughters
and heirs some of the pain and frustration George's unexpected death
had caused. George left a modest sum—enough to provide for
Elizabeth until her death. But Elizabeth was not to be the next loss
Alice would suffer.

LEONARD RHINELANDER HAD returned to New York after the
1930 divorce settlement, becoming an auditor of the family-owned
Rhinelander Real Estate Company. In 1936 he fell ill and moved into
his father's house on Long Beach, Long Island. He died in February of

pneumonia at the age of thirty-four. Both Leonard's work with the real estate firm and his presence at Philip Rhinelander's residence confirmed that the disinheritance had been primarily a financial maneuver. But whatever personal barriers the marriage and trial had brought between father and son seemed to have been overcome. Furthermore, unlike Philip's brother, who disappeared from the family record upon his wayward marriage, Leonard earned a permanent resting place in the Rhinelander vault at Woodlawn Cemetery in the Bronx.[45]

No information about any contact that might have taken place between Leonard and Alice between 1930 and 1936 has come to light. Certainly his return to the New York City area would have afforded them the opportunity to meet. According to the *Chicago Defender*, Alice had broken down and wept when told the news of his death. Weeping and talking for a half hour to reporters, she told them:

> "I always loved him, and he loved me. I believe he died of a broken heart. . . . If his family had not interfered," she asserted, "we would still be together. . . . He had been intensely unhappy since we separated and I have no sympathy with any parent who breaks up a marriage between two people who are happily married."

No one seems to have asked how she knew he was unhappy. It is quite unlikely that she mentioned anything about specific contact with Leonard in the years since their divorce. The *Defender*, always willing to believe stories of reconciliation, would hardly have omitted it if she had.[46] Furthermore, a Rhinelander family story recalls that among the few mourners at Leonard's funeral was a lone, veiled woman who sat in the back and was believed to be Alice, come to bid a final farewell to her former husband.[47] If she was there, however, she was not seen by the photographers who waited outside to shoot photographs of the mourners and noted her apparent absence. The years might have taught her how to avoid such notice.

Leonard's will, which Leon Jacobs had drawn up in 1925 after the Westchester County verdict, named his father, Philip, as the sole heir and Jacobs as executor. On his death in 1936, an appraisal of his personal property listed $1635.01 in assets and $1460.27 in debts and funeral costs. Among his personal affects were a Western saddle and harness valued at $25.00, an Essex Terraplane 1933 luxury sedan valued at

The funeral of Leonard Kip Rhinelander, 1936.

$250.00, a platinum watch chain with five seed pearls valued at $40.00, a sterling and fourteen-karat gold cigarette case with four small emeralds worth $75.00, and a collection of silverware with a total value of almost $300.00. Oddly enough, he had only $400.00 in his bank account.[48] No doubt Leonard had access to other, far more substantial resources. He was still paying Alice $3,600.00 per year in quarterly installments, payments that were taken over by Philip and Jacobs after Leonard's death.

Alice, still unmarried, still living with her mother, mourned the death of her beloved, or once-beloved, Len. Nestled in the embrace of her family, after the loss of her father, she still had her mother and sisters to support her through this difficult time. But in 1938 the final blow of the decade fell: Elizabeth Jones suffered a stroke and died in December at their Pelham Road home. As the one unmarried daughter, Alice had probably borne the greater weight of caring for her mother in her illness, aided by Grace and Emily, who were also still living nearby. Elizabeth's obituary also mentioned three sisters and brothers living in England. The text made no reference to the trial, but the caption said it all: "Alice Jones' Mother Dies of Stroke at 76."

PHILIP RHINELANDER DID not outlive his prodigal son by many years. In March 1940 he died in his Long Island home, leaving his sizable estate to his daughter, Adelaide, and two young nieces, daughters of Philip junior. Philip senior had continued to make annuity payments on behalf of his son's estate, as stipulated in Leonard's separation agreement. His estate, however, stopped the payments, and in 1941 Alice and the Rhinelanders were back in court, battling over the payments and the legality of the separation settlement. Lost in the events of World War II and the thickening mists of time, these new chapters received only brief mention in public records, except for court documents.

The *Chicago Defender* noted, "The skeleton in the closet rattled aloud again this past week" when the Nassau County surrogate judge upheld Alice's claim that Philip's estate should be paying her $3,600 per year. The *Defender* also outlined the case, now seventeen years stale.[49] Adelaide, not pleased, brought an appeal of the decision to the Brooklyn Appellate Division of the New York Supreme Court, now presided over by Judge Lazansky—the sole dissenter when the same court upheld the Westchester County verdict in 1926.

The Brooklyn court judged that the separation agreement "was a contrivance to make that appear to be legal which had an unlawful purpose, i.e., to develop an ineffective Nevada decree of divorce into one which bore the badge of general full faith and credit." The decision cited the fact that Alice made no effort to overturn the Nevada decree or present a defense—she added only the property agreement. There was, the Brooklyn court judged, "not the slightest proof that she had ever been guilty of cruelty to Leonard," although she had stipulated that in her presentation to the Nevada court. "All that was sought to be accomplished under the agreement in Nevada could have been done in New York, save the one all-important item—a full-fledged divorce for Leonard."[50] This severing of marriage ties without grounds, according to the court, was against the "public policy" of New York—and, they presumed, all states. This agreement was also, therefore, against public policy, particularly since the charges seemed specious.

The Brooklyn judges might have been responding in frustration to the rising number of "quickie" divorces coming out of Nevada. Reno was replacing Mexico as the divorce capital of the world, with relatively loose requirements. In fact Leonard was not the only Rhinelander to have taken advantage of such opportunities; both of his siblings did so too.

In fact the appellate court determined that the separation agreement was illegal and invalid, and certainly Philip was not bound by it, since he did not sign it. This was a win for Philip's heirs, but perhaps an uneasy one. If the agreement was illegal and the Nevada divorce unenforceable, Alice could not be bound to honor her promises either. Was she now Leonard's legal widow, with all the rights and implications that status would imply? Could she now, were it in her interests, embark on a nationwide speaking tour as forbidden by the agreement? Apparently these were not tempting options for Alice. She appealed the decision to the highest state level in Albany, where it was decided in 1943.

Once again, and for the final time in the New York court system, Alice won her case against the Rhinelanders. The New York Supreme Court overturned the appellate court's findings and upheld the legality of the document, and of the Rhinelanders' legal obligation to continue the annuity payments as long as Alice was alive and kept to her agreed terms as well. The Rhinelander Case was finally over.

Conclusion

～

The Last Word

MORE THAN FIFTY years after Leonard died, and nearly sixty years after Alice and Leonard said their final farewell, so did Alice. Save for the occasional news query or reference to the scandal-riddled fall in 1925 when her name (and Leonard's) became synonymous with race, sexuality, and class, she had faded into the shadows, little more than a footnote. Her death certificate stated simply that she died on September 13, 1989, of a heart attack brought on by a stroke caused by hypertension.[1] Her passing was not even noted by the local or city presses that had followed her trial for previous generations. What had happened in the decades between her unexpected emergence into the American public eye and her quiet, anonymous death in 1989? How had her life changed? How had the United States changed?

Very little is known about Alice's life after the trial. After the annuity suits of the 1940s, she dropped out of the media's sight. Details of Alice's last four decades of life remain obscure. She seems to have spent the remainder of her life living quietly in her parents' home in New Rochelle, avoiding the unwanted fame and notoriety that had been thrust upon her. Her phone number remained unlisted. She did not work outside the home. And, in all legal documents and public listings, she dutifully used her birthname, Alice Jones, according to the terms of her separation and divorce agreement. She buried her sister Emily in the sixties. Grace, in the meantime, had remarried and moved to California. So perhaps Alice found comfort in the company of her niece, Roberta, and Roberta's family, her closest living relatives.[2] If the death certificate is to be believed she never married again; instead she lived off of the money from the annuity—a paltry sum by 1989—and from income on several buildings left to her and her sisters by her parents.[3]

In the years between her forced celebrity and her decline, knowledge of the case also seemed to fade. In 1929 novelist Nella Larsen wrote one of her two novels on race and place in American life. Larsen, according to biographer Thadious Davis, struggled to reconcile her own desire for acceptance with her disdain for certain social conventions.[4] Writing at first became an outlet; it later became a hindrance. A recurrent theme of race and limits laced both of Larsen's novels, *Quicksand* and *Passing*. Illustrative is the following passage from *Passing*: "She was caught between two allegiances, different, yet the same. Herself. Her race."[5] Echoing Du Bois, Larsen's character struggled with the physical wherewithal to look and act white, while cognizant of the historical imperatives that linked her to "her race." In this instance the pronoun "her" showed ownership and a burden, with race functioning as the anchor or weight that dragged her back to not just race, but *her* race.

Three pages later Nella Larsen made oblique reference to a real case of a young woman who lived in the space formed by the overlapping worlds of black and white. While contemplating a situation in which a black woman was passing, married to a white man who did not know her ancestry, she worried, "What if Bellow should divorce Clare? Could he? There was the Rhinelander case."[6] The Rhinelander Case functioned as a fairly specific historical marker, especially for a late-1920s readership. It was such a trigger that just those few words conjured an event, a place, and a context. The phrase "There was the Rhinelander case" connected a fictional story and the historical event described in this book. In 1929 any American reader would have recognized the reference and understood its meaning.

By the 1980s, however, this historical memory had faded. In 1986, noted literary scholar Deborah McDowell admitted being puzzled by the reference to the case. In her notes on a reissue of *Passing* she thanked another colleague for telling her enough about the case to provide the following: "'Kip' Rhinelander, of a prominent New York family, married a black woman, but divorced her because of his family's disapproval."[7] In broad outline this reference is correct. However, Alice may have been colored, but it is not clear she ever consider herself a Negro. Even the 1925 jury drew a distinction between being colored and being Negro or black. Her death certificate left her race mysteriously blank. And, outside Nevada, Alice and Leonard never divorced. They reached a settlement for permanent separation. To highlight this fact, her death certificate simply stated she never married—a clear fiction or error. But by leaving her race blank and her marital status ambiguously incorrect, one of the last legal documents made it possible for her to evade being thrust back in time to a period when she was indeed of color and part of a national scandal.[8]

These details, while important, became lost in the sweep of time between the 1920s and the 1980s. So much so that even when African Americans in New Rochelle told their stories to historians, they made no mention of the Rhinelander Case. It had left no permanent mark on their lives and their histories. It wasn't that black residents of Westchester County lack a memory of the case. When questioned, for example, longtime resident Helen Tymes recalled in some detail aspects of the case. She in fact had come to know Emily, Alice's older sister.[9] Rather, the case faded in importance as larger battles played themselves out across the nation.

Much changed in the United States during the decades bounded by 1920 and 1980, especially concerning race, sexuality, and class. During the years in question the country went through a tumultuous decade and a half. Lasting from the mid-fifties through the late sixties, the world watched the nation and its citizens square off over basic civil rights for African Americans. By the mid-fifties the United States military had become integrated, the result of an Executive Order by President Harry S. Truman. And after several decades of momentous court victories, the NAACP had its greatest victory when the United States Supreme Court ruled that separate but equal was unconstitutional and thus illegal in school settings. A year later, in 1955, all eyes shifted to Montgomery, Alabama, and the inspiring act of courage of Rosa Parks and the stirring orations of a young, college-educated black Baptist minister named Martin Luther King, Jr. His words and the brave actions of countless others triumphed over segregated city transportation services. Very soon black college students took the lead, demanding fair and courteous service at lunch counters and the desegregation of interstate travel. In rapid succession the focus moved to direct action for racial integration, marches on citadels of segregation, and a demand for both civil and voting rights for black Americans.

Not since the end of the Civil War had the nation been forced to deal with matters of race so completely and so painfully. Race riots erupted in New York and Los Angeles by the mid-sixties, showing that the battle for civil rights could not be contained in the South. Emboldened by changes everywhere, new community organizations sprang up in cities and towns large and small, each demanding a range of new and better treatment. And while national figures such as King and Ralph Abernathy of the Southern Christian Leadership Conference (SCLC), Ella Baker of the Student Nonviolent Coordinating Committee (SNCC), James Farmer of the Congress for Racial Equality (CORE), and Roy Wilkins of the NAACP, among others, claimed a share of the headlines, more and more blacks at the grassroots level fought for local improvements in towns and cities large and small.

During this time the interest in racial ambiguities and the challenge posed by people of mixed ancestry took a backseat to these fundamental questions of civil rights. By the late sixties even interracial marriage became a matter of settled law and public policy. In a landmark decision in *Loving* v. *Virginia* (1967) the United States Supreme Court ruled that the Constitution prohibited legal barriers to marriage between two people just because they came from different races. While the Rhinelander Case hadn't addressed that particular question, clear resonances existed. Forty years earlier Isaac Mills appealed to base prejudices by arguing that marriage between blacks and whites violated the laws of civil society, nature, and family practice. The Virginia prohibition against such marriages, itself four decades old by the sixties, rested on a similar logic: Blacks and whites should never marry, period. The Court decided this was a private matter best left to those who were not state representatives.

Other traces of the Rhinelander Case persisted beyond the sixties, however. More than anything, Alice Jones's and her family's history raise the important question, What is race? What makes one person black and another white? A drop of black blood? Is that drop always perceptible? Is race always written on the body, as Davis suggested in having Alice disrobe?

With the growing generation of children of post–*Loving* v. *Virginia* interracial marriages and unions, these questions have begun to reenter the public debate on race and interracial identity in the United States. Should the one-drop rule still prevail? Should Americans be allowed to identify themselves as "multiracial" for legal and government documents? Answers to these questions animate conversations in academic halls, boardrooms, and lecture circuits, and on sidewalks. It is the rare person who has not caught him- or herself at some point playing the racial guessing game. That's when you look at someone of ambiguous lineage, pause for a second, and force-fit them into one of the designated racial boxes—black, white, Asian, Latino/Latina, Native American, or some combination. Or when you look at someone whose race seems quite clear, only to hear him or her speak, and then realize that skin color or other phenotypic characteristics amount to just a small sum of who they really are.

ALICE AND LEONARD'S story forces open a far more complex set of questions and answers. Alice's parents hailed from England. By all accounts her mother was unquestionably British and white; her father's mother was white; and his father a subject of one of the British colonies. As to George, raised some distance from London, Liverpool, or other sites of significant black populations, the question has to be what made him black? The easy answer in 1920s America: the one drop or more inherited from his unidentified father. By the twentieth century's end, however, this appears to be a really specious argument. It is quite as likely that George Jones grew up as a Briton until he moved to the United States. Race may not have been insignificant, but it need not have been the predominant way he had organized himself or constructed his identity.

If anything, George and Elizabeth Jones's American household exposed race for what it was to a certain extent—a fiction we tell one another. Echoing older perceptions, scholars note again and again that we create race by assigning more meaning to certain genetic features and characteristics than need be assigned. While we emphasize skin color, hair, lips, and other features to assess racial membership, we could use the same logic to group people into light- and dark-haired races, big- and little-feet races, and so on.

Through her actions Alice in fact attempted to challenge basic racial notions. She understood that people make up race in the same ways that Al Jolson became black without becoming African American. And despite a mixed-race background, at no time in early adulthood did Alice claim a social identification with African Americans primarily. She lived in a world inhabited by blacks and whites. Her level of intimacy stemmed from family and personal contacts. This enabled her to attend churches and other associations with a predominantly white membership, and yet form lasting bonds with family members whose race was less ambiguously black than hers.

At a glance, it might be said that Alice lived between the worlds of black and white. On reflection this fails to capture the Alice Jones described in this book, especially the one who married Leonard and in so doing became known around the world. That Alice appears to have constructed a social makeup, a sense of self, that refused to be pigeonholed. She lived less between and more with an ability to move other aspects of her identity to the fore when engaged in social interactions. Race, never completely removed or ignored, came after the midpoint in a list of ways of describing and thinking about herself.[10]

Of course Alice remained very much rooted in her times and the attitudes of those times. She understood the difference between black and white in American life. For almost a year she vigorously denied having any black ancestry. Reluctantly she admitted having some colored blood, without at any time calling herself black. She understood race as a descriptor but not necessarily a mark of identification. Perhaps that is why the racial category on her death certificate is blank. Thus this case anticipated much of the work in many academic disciplines that has examined race and its multiple meanings in twentieth-century America.

Furthermore, this case drew attention to questions of male and female relationships, especially sexuality. Without question Alice and Leonard had sex before marriage. Passé by the 1980s, such a revelation shocked 1920s America. Premarital relations were rare and seldom so brazenly discussed as the pair did in their love letters. They delighted in each other's company and obviously enjoyed each other physically. They experimented sexually and teased one another about the joys of those experiments. In effect they stood in sharp contrast to a more-restrained, fast-eclipsed Victorian Age.

Yet there is much we don't know. For instance we don't know what they did to avoid unwanted pregnancies. Mills considered it a blessing that the two had no children. The separation agreement made explicit reference to the lack of children, too. Alice would live long enough to see the introduction of the birth-control pill, which freed women to control their bodies and their sexuality in ways previously unknown. But the two knew enough to keep them blissful in the bedroom and out of the maternity ward—then again, that could have been the result of pure luck.

We also have no record of their innermost thoughts and worries during the weeks of the trial and the months that followed. We have glimpses. Glimpses, unfortunately, tell us very little about the hurt and sense of betrayal that Alice must have felt during the trial and the sense of loss she and Leonard may have felt in the months and years that followed the trial's end. Absent her own words, we have no accounting of how the disrobing settled into her psyche as she aged. What we have instead is a mature woman who eschewed public attention and willingly moved far off the public stage.

By the time Alice died at nearly ninety years of age, America's class structure had changed significantly too. After World War II, the United States had grown a large and bulging middle class. Men and women who could merely dream of moving up in the 1920s actually managed to do so in the fifties and sixties. They moved up from the working class into the blue- and white-collar middle classes.

In the 1920s Leonard's decision to marry Alice amounted to a hurdling of important class divisions. Men of wealth and standing seldom married young working-class women, despite Cinderella fables to the contrary. Yet this case required social viewers to ponder what class meant. Was class just about material well-being and resources, or did class have to do with a way of behaving in even the most trying of circumstances? The Rhinelander Case caught the public's eye because Leonard appeared so foreign to the majority of Americans who worked for wages on a daily basis. In Alice they saw a small part of themselves—marginally educated, striving, and willing to take a chance for advancement.

This case, as a result, may have faded in people's memories, except for the stray article, recent photographic retrospectives, and the spate of undergraduate theses and planned dissertations.[11] Still, it struck a chord with a 1920s audience because of both its scandalous contents and the questions it raised about race, sexuality, and class. Traces of its significance can be gleaned from any contemporary newspaper, magazine, or electronic story. In a nation in which the most populous state, California, will soon have a white minority, in a country prepared to debate the virtues of race-based affirmative action, in a country that changes its census racial categories every ten years, race not only matters, it counts. It counted for Alice Jones and Leonard Rhinelander too.

The story endured, however, for one reason: love. Many followed the details of the case because it was not just about race, gender, and sexuality, it was also very much about love. A basic human emotion, love allowed people who may have opposed cross-race and -class relationships at least to identify with the plight of Alice and Leonard. The interest in this love affair led some reporters and trial watchers to speculate wildly that the couple would reunite after the trial ended. Such attention may have simply reflected the observers' personal involvement and investment in Alice's and Leonard's love for each other. On the other hand, this very involvement and investment exposed the limits of dwelling solely on the many societal divisions: This story hinted at the possibility of overcoming differences and building relationships.

In a powerful rejoinder to a decision coerced in the 1930 settlement, after her death Alice told the world what she must have felt all along: She may have been forced to become Alice Beatrice Jones, denied the name she took on marrying Leonard. But her death apparently released her from that obligation.

So, as you make your way among the graves in Beechwoods Cemetery and your eyes dart from headstone to headstone, you will find no grave marker for Alice Jones. You will, however, find one for Alice J. Rhinelander.

With this simple gravestone, Alice got the last word. Ironically, in becoming Alice Rhinelander again, she thrust herself back into a time when questions of race, sexuality, and class made her well known and associated with the travails of placing love on trial. As Alice J. Rhinelander she joined Leonard in a scandal that confounded the meanings of black and white. As Alice J. Rhinelander, she also reclaimed her identity as Leonard's wife.

Afterword

༄

RESEARCHING AND WRITING
LOVE ON TRIAL

THIS BOOK HAD its beginnings more than seventeen years ago. At that time Earl, researching what became his dissertation, stumbled on a fascinating—and, memory had it, scandalous—love story in the *Norfolk Journal and Guide*. Aware that the story had little bearing on the project then at hand, he simply filed away the reference, inviting his students at the University of California at Berkeley and later the University of Michigan to follow the story as a possible undergraduate thesis or dissertation. For more than a decade, none did. When Heidi approached Earl about chairing her dissertation on interracialness in the first half of the twentieth century, he encouraged her to look up details of the story. She did, and although her dissertation took a different direction, she was nonetheless convinced that the story warranted further examination. In this decision a new collaboration was born, one that ultimately led to publication of *Love on Trial*.

Collaborative authorship in the field of history is still unfortunately uncommon. Among our colleagues, our joint venture has prompted almost as much interest in the process of researching and writing together as in the topic itself. The practicalities of writing together across long distances and incompatible computer systems have certainly brought some frustrations. But our collaboration has made this a far richer book than either of us would have produced alone. Our approach to writing was to divide up the chapters to write separate first drafts and then send them back and forth for editing and rewriting: Earl Lewis drafted 6–7, 9, 11–12, and 16. Heidi Ardizzone drafted 1–5, 8, 10, and 13–15. The rewriting and reorganization were often quite extensive, however, and we tried regularly to meet for a few days every few months to work together. The final product is truly a collective work, and one that involved the research and funding assistance of numerous individuals and organizations, detailed in the acknowledgments.

During the process of researching the Rhinelander Case, we came across several defining circumstances. The most significant was that one very crucial source was unavailable: the two-thousand-page transcript of the trial itself is missing from the Westchester County Courthouse archives. The higher courts do not keep such documents on site, and due to the passage of time, we were unable to locate other copies of this transcript. Fortunately several New York City and East Coast newspapers took it upon themselves to record the trial for their readers and reproduce what they thought were exact transcripts every day for their readers. During climactic events, other newspapers also offered this kind of detail. Dozens of papers reprinted full or partial texts of many of the letters written between the lovers. As a result the contemporary newspaper accounts of the events leading up to and away from this trial form our primary references. There are, of course, some variances among them, usually minor differences in wording or unmarked omissions in the dialogue. Working back and forth between these, we have produced a collective recounting of the trial, noting significant conflicts in newspaper accounts where relevant. In the process we reviewed more than five dozen newspapers and more than twelve hundred newspaper articles. Court papers, census data, and other public documents, as well as a few interviews and other personal accounts supplemented the newsprint.

However, due to the nature of some of the testimony, there were aspects of the case that no newspaper at the time could or would print in full. This means that we simply don't know the exact content of some of the letters and some of the questioning. In a way this put us in the position of the average reader of one of these newspapers—we had to read between the lines, follow the clues dropped by the different papers. Occasionally we were able to use other sources to figure out a missing piece. More often we relied on our training as scholars of history: We sorted the accumulated albeit incomplete evidence, reasoned judiciously, weighed alternative possibilities, and, where needed and appropriate, speculated.

There is another gap in our sources: We simply do not know how Alice Jones and her family perceived themselves, and how they lived in their community prior to (or for that matter after) the events discussed in this book. Our letters to her family's descendants were ignored, and we accepted their decision. The available evidence on how Alice saw herself and lived, then, is fascinating and conflicting. In fact, we have distinct, although not opposing, ideas about this topic. Did she try to live as white? Was she able to do so successfully? Did she and her family think of themselves in terms of white or black, or did they have another way of understanding themselves and their place in New Rochelle, New York, in the 1920s? Our divergent views on these questions made for a continuing conversation between us over the many layers and definitions of race and identity. At the same time the very fact that there are so many possibilities for the question of who Alice Jones Rhinelander was, how she perceived herself, how others perceived her, fed our fascination with this story. The lack of clear answers confirms our shared belief that racial identity and racial categories in the United States have always held multiple meanings, serving a variety of social, cultural, and individual purposes. As a result there are people who have lived as both black and white, as alternately black and white, and as neither black nor white. It is possible that over the course of a lifetime Alice and her family claimed all or none of the alternatives.

ENDNOTES

INTRODUCTION   TIL DEATH DO US PART

1. "Woodlawn: An Oasis of Art, History, Beautiful Ecology and a 'Hall of Fame,'" publication of Woodlawn Cemetery, Bronx, N.Y., founded 1863.
2. "Record of Interments," Woodlawn Cemetery.
3. Radio may have been an additional source in some areas. The Rhinelander Case caught the beginning of a radio boom in the United States. (The first commercial radio broadcasts did not develop until after 1920, and the major networks after 1926.) Most radio newscasts were read from newspapers. Stanley I. Kutler, et al., eds., *Encyclopedia of the United States in the Twentieth Century*, vol. 2 (New York: Simon & Schuster, 1996), 803–5.

CHAPTER 1   WAITING FOR LEONARD

1. *New York Daily Mirror*, 17 November 1925, 3.
2. *Detroit Times*, 9 November 1925, 2.
3. *New York Herald-Tribune*, 10 November 1925, 14; *New York Times*, 10 November 1925, 1.
4. *New Rochelle Standard Star*, 9 November 1925, 1.
5. *New York Herald-Tribune*, 9 November 1925, 28.
6. Ibid., 10 November 1925, 14.
7. Ibid.
8. *New York Evening Journal*, 10 November 1925, 2.
9. *Detroit Times*, 9 November 1925, 2.
10. *New York Evening Journal*, 10 November 1925, 2. In New York State the county courts are called "supreme courts." These county courts are overseen by the higher district and state courts, to which their verdicts may be appealed.

11. City of New Rochelle, Record of Marriages, 1924: 45810, Westchester County Historical Society, Elmsford, N.Y. (hereafter cited as WCHS).
12. *New York Evening Journal*, 14 November 1924, 1.
13. *New York Daily News*, 15 November 1924, 3.
14. *New York Evening Journal*, 14 November 1924, 1.
15. *New York Evening Journal*, 9 November 1924, 1.
16. Specifically, the Rhinelanders were known as sugar merchants, which tied them to the institution of slavery—Cathy Mason, *Merchants and Empire: Trading in Colonial New York* (Baltimore: Johns Hopkins University Press, 1998), 178–79; *New Rochelle Standard Star*, November 14, 1924, 1.
17. The naming could also have reflected Adelaide Kip's own desire to establish her name and lineage on all her children.
18. *New York Daily News*, 14 November 1924, 2.
19. Ibid., 15 November 1924, 3.
20. *New York Herald-Tribune*, 14 November 1924, 2; *New York Times*, 15 November 1924, 6.
21. *Detroit Free Press*, 15 November 1924, 3.
22. *New Rochelle Standard Star*, 13 November 1924, 1. The paper did not name any sources other than the marriage license itself.
23. *New York Evening Post*, 13 November 1924, 1.
24. *New York Times*, 14 November 1924, 1.
25. *Poughkeepsie Evening News*, 14 November 1924, 1.
26. *Boston Daily Globe*, 14 November 1924, 1. See also *Hartford Times*, 14 November 1924, 12: "Rhinelander's Bride Is Cabman's Daughter," and *Natchez Democrat*, 14 November 1924, 3: "Rich Man's Son Marries Cab Driver's Daughter," which also says that "details of the wedding were meagre."
27. Our survey of national media is based on a meticulous reading of every major New York City daily available and a cross-section of major city papers representing every region of the country.
28. *Poughkeepsie Evening News, Boston Daily Globe, Hartford Times, Natchez Democrat, New York Times, New York World*, 14 November 1924.
29. *Philadelphia Tribune*, 22 November 1924, 1.
30. "Rhinelander Family Tree," Vertical Files, "Rhinelander," WCHS.
31. "Follows Uncle's Footsteps," *Detroit Free Press*, 26 November 1925, 1–19; *Chicago Tribune*, 26 November 1925.
32. *St. Louis Globe-Democrat*, 26 November 1925, 4.
33. Quoted in *Chicago Daily Tribune*, 26 November 1925, 17.
34. *Chicago Defender*, 21 March 1925, part 1, 1.
35. *Detroit Free Press*, 25 November 1925, 3.
36. *Richmond Times Dispatch*, 28 November 1925, 6. For a history of this pattern of interracial relationships see Glenda Gilmore, *Gender & Jim Crow* (Chapel Hill: University of North Carolina Press, 1996), 63–71.
37. *New York Daily News*, 15 November 1924, 3; *New York Evening Journal*, 14 November 1924, 1.
38. Although a few papers quoted Leonard as saying that he had told his father, most quoted him that Philip did not know, and he was worried that he would read it first in the papers. *New York Evening Journal*, 14 November 1924, 2.
39. *New York Daily Mirror*, 17 November 1924, 3.
40. *New York Daily News*, 15 November 1924, 1.

41. *New York Evening Journal*, 14 November 1924, 1.
42. *New York Daily News*, 15 November 1924, 3.
43. This was the same William Rhinelander Stewart responsible for the arch over the entrance to Washington Park, one of many such philanthropic and civic projects he helped to organize and fund.
44. *New York Daily Mirror*, 17 November 1924, 3.
45. Ibid., 15 November 1924, 3.
46. *New York Daily News*, 15 November 1924, 1.
47. Ibid., 15 November 1924, 5.

CHAPTER 2   WHO WAS ALICE JONES?

1. *Philadelphia Tribune*, 22 November 1924, 1.
2. See "Afterword" for a discussion of the newspaper research, availability, and coverage of the case.
3. *Richmond News Leader*, 15 November 1924, 1.
4. *New Orleans Times-Picayune*, 18 November 1924, 1; *Birmingham Age-Herald*, 14 November 1924, 1; *New York Herald-Tribune*, 14 November 1924, 2.
5. "Adventures of a Near-White," *Independent* 75, 14 August 1913, 375. See also "When is a Caucasian Not," editorial, *Independent* 70, 2 March 1911, 478–79. These and other examples are cited and discussed in Heidi Ardizzone, "Red-Blooded Americans: Mulattoes and the Melting Pot in Early-Twentieth-Century Racial and Nationalist Discourse" (Ph.D. diss., University of Michigan, 1997).
6. *St. Louis Argus*, 21 November 1924, 1; *New Orleans Times-Picayune*, 18 November 1924, 1.
7. *Detroit Times*, 14 November 1924, 11.
8. *Chicago Defender*, 22 November 1924, 1.
9. *New York Daily News*, 14 November 1924, 1; *New York World*, 13 November 1924, 1; *New York Herald-Tribune*, 14 November 1924, 1 (same in *Washington Post*, 14 November 1924, 1); *New York World*, 15 November 1924, 13.
10. *Jewish Daily Forward*, 15 November 1924, 16.
11. Readers should keep this in mind when viewing the photographs reprinted in this volume, as well as the problem of using seventy-five-year-old prints and the range of shades that differential elements in lighting, exposure, developing, aging, and the process of reproduction can create.
12. *New York Daily News*, 14 November 1924, 1.
13. *Washington Post*, 14 November 1924, 1; *New York Herald-Tribune*, 14 November 1924, 1; *New York Daily News*, 15 November 1924, 1.
14. Helen Lefkowitz and Kathy Peiss, eds., *Love Across the Color Line* (Amherst: University of Massachusetts Press, 1996), 58.
15. *Baltimore Sun*, 14 November 1924, 1.
16. *New York Daily News*, 14 November 1924, 1. Unless otherwise noted, all citations of the *Daily News* and *Daily Mirror* are from the early editions. Articles were almost always carried over from edition to edition, usually with just the headlines changing. When events during the day led to a new article in the evening editions, they were always reproduced in the next morning's paper as well.
17. *Des Moines Register*, 14 November 1924, 1.

18. See Walter White, *A Man Called White: The Autobiography of Walter White* (New York: Viking Press, 1948) for a description of White and the power of color on him and others policing the racial divide.

19. Indeed, in *The Birth of a Nation*, the blockbuster historical film about the Civil War and Reconstruction period, which premiered in 1915, it was the mulatto characters who sought the destruction of white unity and threatened the nation with racial equality. The "true" blacks in the film were content with their lot, loyal to their former owners, but as easily swayed by the lies and promises of the mulatto Silas Lynch, as was the northern white senator by his mulatto mistress, Lydia Brown. On the broader theme of mulattoes in American history, see Joel Williamson, *New People: Miscegenation and Mulattoes in the United States* (New York: Free Press, 1980) and William B. Gatewood, *Aristocrats of Color: The Black Elite, 1880–1920* (Bloomington: Indiana University Press, 1993), 69–138.

20. Judith Berzon, *Neither White nor Black: The Mulatto Character in American Fiction* (New York: New York University Press, 1978), 8, and Werner Sollors, *Neither Black nor White Yet Both: Thematic Explorations of Interracial Literature* (New York: Oxford University Press, 1997), 3–30, 220–335. Ardizzone, 107–25.

21. For a discussion of color differences among people of African descent, see Gatewood, *Aristocrats of Color*, 7–95; Bernard E. Powers, *Black Charlestonians: A Social History, 1822–1885* (Fayetteville: University of Arkansas Press, 1994), 120–60. For a history of shifts in the meaning of "Creole" in Louisiana, see Virginia Dominguez, *White by Definition: Social Classification in Creole Louisiana* (New Brunswick, N.J.: Rutgers University Press, 1980). For New Orleans see John Blassingame, *Black New Orleans, 1860–1880* (Chicago: University of Chicago Press, 1973), 173–202.

22. On anti-Asian sentiment, review Ronald Takagi, *Strangers from a Different Shore* (Boston: Little Brown and Company, 1989), 79–131, and Edward L. Ayers, *The Promise of the New South: Life After Reconstruction* (New York: Oxford University Press, 1992), 132–49.

23. See Charles Lofgren, *The Plessy Case* (New York: Oxford University Press, 1987); Andrew Kull, *The Color-Blind Constitution* (Cambridge, Mass.: Harvard University Press, 1992), 124; Donald G. Nieman, *Promises to Keep: African-Americans and the Constitutional Order, 1776 to the Present* (New York: Oxford University Press, 1991), 105–13; A. Leon Higginbothom, Jr., *Shades of Freedom* (New York: Oxford University Press, 1996), chap. 9; *Plessy v. Ferguson* 163 U.S. 537 (1896).

24. The ten states were South Dakota, Utah, West Virginia, Arkansas, California, Colorado, Delaware, Idaho, Nevada, South Carolina, and Wyoming.

25. Information compiled from *The Claude A. Barnett Papers* (Frederick, Md.: University Publications of America, Inc., 1985, from the holdings of the Chicago Historical Society), Part Three, "Subject Files on Black Americans, 1918–1967," Series I: "Race Relations, 1923–1965," Folder 378-1, "Correspondence, 1928–1962," 07:00697–00736; and Albert Earnest Jenks, "The Legal Status of Negro-White Amalgamation in the United States," *American Journal of Sociology* (1914), in Ardizzone, *Red-Blooded Americans*.

26. Michigan was the one state that had a legal definition of "Negro" but no law against intermarriage. The definition was found in the state constitution.

27. *New York Evening Journal*, 15 November 1924, 3.
28. *New York Daily News*, 15 November 1924, 3. Mayor Scott never commented on the event, although it was pointed out that he had known George Jones for a few years.
29. Gilbert Osofsky, *Harlem: The Making of a Ghetto* (New York: Harper & Row, Publishers, 1966), 42. *New Rochelle Standard Star*, 10 November 1925, 1. Morever, some of that state's most prominent citizens of color managed such affairs, even during the nineteenth century. See Maria Diedrich, *Love Across Color Lines: Ottilie Assing & Frederick Douglass* (New York: Hill & Wang, 1999), which offers a probing analysis of the quite public relationship between Assing and Douglass that ended in her suicide.
30. *New York Evening Journal*, 14 November 1924, 1–2; *New York Herald-Tribune*, 14 November 1924, 1, 4.
31. *Chicago Broad Ax*, 22 November 1924, 1.
32. *Los Angeles Times*, 15 November 1924, 1.
33. *New York Daily News*, 14 November 1924, 1, 3–4.
34. Ibid., 15 November 1924, 5.
35. *New York World*, 16 November 1924, 3.
36. *New York Evening Journal*, 15 November 1924, 3.
37. *New York Daily News*, 15 November 1924, 1.
38. *New York Evening Journal*, 15 November 1924, 3.
39. *New Rochelle Standard Star*, 15 November 1924, 1–2.
40. Caroline Bond Day, *A Study of Some Negro-White Families in the United States* (Westport, Conn.: Negro Universities Press, 1970), 4–5, 108–10.
41. Wade Hall, *Passing for Black: The Life and Careers of Mae Street Kidd* (Lexington: University of Kentucky Press, 1997), 41. See also Elaine Ginsberg, ed., *Passing and the Fictions of Identity* (Durham, N.C.: Duke University Press, 1996), 1–18; Becky Thompson and Sangeeta Tyagi, eds., *Names We Call Home* (New York: Routledge, 1996), introduction.
42. Matthew Frye Jacobson, *Whiteness of a Different Color* (Cambridge, Mass.: Harvard University Press, 1998), 82–85.
43. *New York Daily News*, 16 November 1924, 4.
44. *New York Daily Mirror*, 17 November 1924, 3.
45. David Fowler has documented a marked increase in American writings about miscegenation and mulattoes in the first decades of the twentieth century. David H. Fowler, *Northern Attitudes Towards Interracial Marriage: Legislation and Public Opinion in the Middle Atlantic States and the States of the Old Northwest, 1780–1930* (Ph.D. diss., Yale University, 1963; University Microfilms Inc., Ann Arbor, Mich.). Paul Spickard discusses the shift from focusing on black-white mixing to foreign-born/native-born mixing in the 1920s, *Mixed Blood: Intermarriage and Ethnic Identity in Twentieth-Century America* (Madison: University of Wisconsin Press, 1989). Ardizzone's research further documents the peaking of American interest in the mulatto during the 1910s and 1920s.

CHAPTER 3   BROKEN PROMISES

1. *New York Evening Journal*, 22 November 1924, 1–2.
2. "Affidavit and Notice of Motion," December 29, 1924; "Affidavits in

Opposition to Motion," December 29, 1924, Document A, Statement of Leon Jacobs, Signed December 18, 1924, *Leonard Kip Rhinelander, Plaintiff, vs. Alice Beatrice Jones, Defendant,* New York Supreme Court, Westchester County, 1924, Westchester County Clerk's Office, Index #3910–1924, Vol. 96: 423 (hereafter cited as *Rhinelander v. Rhinelander,* 1924).

3. *New York Daily Mirror,* 21 November 1924, 3.
4. *New York Daily News,* 24 November 1924, 3.
5. *New York Daily Mirror,* 29 November 1924, 2.
6. "Affidavit and Notice of Motion," December 29, 1924, *Rhinelander v. Rhinelander,* 1924.
7. *New York Herald-Tribune,* 22 November 1924, 1.
8. *New Rochelle Standard Star,* 25 November 1924, 1.
9. *New York Evening Journal,* 26 November 1924, 1–2.
10. Ibid., 1.
11. *New York Times,* 25 November 1924, 3.
12. "Affidavit and Notice of Motion," December 29, 1924; "Affidavits in Opposition to Motion," December 29, 1924, Document A, Statement of Leon Jacobs, signed December 18, 1924, *Rhinelander v. Rhinelander,* 1924.
13. *New York Daily Mirror,* 27 November 1924, 1.
14. *New York Daily News,* 28 November 1924, 2–3.
15. *New York Evening Journal,* 26 November 1924, 2.
16. *New Rochelle Standard Star,* 25 November 1924, 2.
17. *New York Daily News,* 27 November 1924, 3.
18. *New York Herald-Tribune,* 28 November 1924, 5; *New York Evening Journal,* 28 November 1924, 3.
19. *New York Daily Mirror,* 29 November 1924, 3.

CHAPTER 4   THE VAMP AND THE DUPE

1. *New York Daily Mirror,* 10 November 1925, 3.
2. *New York Herald-Tribune,* 10 November 1925, 14.
3. *New York Times,* 10 November 1925, 1, 8; *New York Herald-Tribune,* 10 November 1925, 14.
4. *New York Evening Journal,* 10 November 1925, 1.
5. Ibid., 10 November 1925, 1.
6. Ibid., 2.
7. Ibid., 9 November 1924, 1.
8. *New York Daily Mirror,* 10 November 1925, 3.
9. Ibid., 1 November 1925, 1.
10. *Philadelphia Inquirer,* 10 November 1925.
11. *Hartford Courant,* 10 November 1925; *Los Angeles Times,* 10 November 1925, 2.
12. Lary May, *Screening Out the Past: The Birth of Mass Culture and the Motion Picture Industry* (New York: Oxford University Press, 1980), 106.
13. Joanne J. Meyerowitz, *Women Adrift: Independent Wage Earners in Chicago, 1880–1930* (Chicago: University of Chicago Press, 1988), 114–16, 124–25.
14. Jacqueline Dowd Hall, "The Mind That Burns in Each Body: Women, Rape and Racial Violence," *Southern Exposure,* 12(6), 1984: 61–71; Darlene Clark

Hine, "Rape and the Inner Lives of Black Women in the Middle West: Preliminary Thoughts on the Culture of Dissemblance," *Signs* 14(4), 1989: 917–19.

15. *New York Evening Journal*, 11 November 1925, 3.
16. *New York Times*, 10 November 1925, 1.
17. *Florida Times Union* (Jacksonville), 15 November 1925, 22.
18. *New York Evening Journal*, 10 November 1925, 3.
19. *Chicago Tribune*, 10 November 1925, 10.
20. *New York Evening Journal*, 10 November 1925, 3.
21. *Norfolk Journal and Guide*, 14 November 1925, 1.
22. *Baltimore Afro-American*, 14 November 1925, 11.
23. *Amsterdam News*, 13 November 1925, 3.
24. *New York Age*, 14 November 1925, 1.
25. *New York Evening Journal*, 10 November 1925, 3.

CHAPTER 5   CONCESSIONS OF RACE

1. Davis cautiously pronounced Alice not white without fully calling her black. In effect, he left open the meaning of race—that is, what Alice considered herself to be may have differed from what society considered her. *Philadelphia Inquirer*, 11 November 1925, 1.
2. *New York Daily News*, 11 November 1925, 2.
3. Upon her death, the "nearly black" niece would be listed as white on her death certificate. *New York Daily Mirror*, 11 November 1925, 4. Neither Mills's nor our researchers could find birth records or other evidence in England to determine if George's father was East or West Indian.
4. *New York Evening Journal*, 11 November 1925, 2; *New York Daily Mirror*, 11 November 1925; *Hartford Times*, 11 November 1925, 8. Another version reads, "If they want slime I'm going to meet their slime with the same article and they will find out that their kettle is just as black as our pot." *New York Daily Mirror*, 11 November 1925, 3.
5. *Richmond Times Dispatch*, 11 November 1925, 2.
6. *New York Evening Journal*, 11 November 1925, 1; *New York Daily Mirror*, 11 November 1925, 3.
7. Ibid.
8. *New York Evening Journal*, 11 November 1925, 1; *New York Daily Mirror*, 11 November 1925, 3.
9. *New York Daily News*, 11 November 1925, 4.
10. *New York Daily Mirror*, 11 November 1925, 1–3.
11. *New York Evening Journal*, 11 November 1925, 2; *New York Daily Mirror*, 11 November 1925, 1–3; *Hartford Times*, 11 November 1925, 8.
12. *New York Times*, 11 November 1925; *St. Louis Argus*, 13 November 1925; *New Rochelle Standard Star*, 10 November 1925; *New York Sun*, 10 November 1925; *Reno Evening Gazette*, 10 November 1925, 1; *San Francisco Chronicle*, 10 November 1925, 1; *Chicago Tribune*, 11 November 1925, 3.
13. *New York Herald-Tribune*, 9 November 1925, 28; *New York Evening Journal*, 9 November 1925, 1.
14. *Houston Informer*, 21 November 1925, 8.
15. New York Supreme Court, Westchester County (hereafter cited as "NYSC-

WC"), Index #3190–1924, Item 11-A, "Summons and Complaint," November 26, 1924, *Rhinelander v. Rhinelander, 1924.*

16. "Answer," December 29, 1924, *Rhinelander v. Rhinelander, 1924.*

17. *Leicester* [England] *Mercury*, 24 November 1925, 7; *New Rochelle Standard Star*, 25 November 1924, 2.

18. Peter Fryer, *Staying Power: The History of Black People in Britain* (London: Pluto Press, 1991), 228–36.

19. *New York Evening Journal*, 28 November 1924, 3; *New York Herald-Tribune*, 28 November 1924, 5, same article verbatim.

20. Ian F. Haney López, "*Ozawa* and *Thind*," in *White by Law: The Legal Construction of Race* (New York and London: New York University Press, 1996), 79–109. For a fuller discussion of the efforts enlisted to define whiteness and the conflicted court renderings that followed, see Matthew Frye Jacobson, *Whiteness of a Different Color* (Cambridge, Mass.: Harvard University Press, 1998), chap. 7.

21. Isaac N. Mills, "Affidavit in Opposition to Application for Additional Counsel Fees," July 13, 1926, *Rhinelander v. Rhinelander, 1924.*

22. "Affidavit in Opposition to Motion for Additional Counsel Fees," October 27, 1925, *Rhinelander v. Rhinelander, 1924.*

23. *New York Daily Mirror*, 29 November 1924, 4; *New York Daily News*, 29 November 1924, 4.

24. Higginbotham, *In the Matter of Color*, 19–50.

25. *New York Times*, 29 November 1924, 15.

26. *Chicago Defender*, 13 December 1924, 1, 12.

27. *Houston Informer*, 21 November 1925, 8.

28. *Chicago Defender*, 15 November 1925.

29. *Chicago Defender*, 6 December 1924, 2, 1.

30. *Richmond Planet*, 2 December 1924, 4.

31. *Richmond News Leader*, 28 November 1924, 8.

32. *Philadelphia Tribune*, 6 December 1924, 4.

33. "Amended Complaint," November 30, 1925, *Rhinelander v. Rhinelander, 1924.*

CHAPTER 6   JUST A COMMONPLACE LOVE AFFAIR

1. *New York Daily News*, 12 November 1925, 2; *Boston Evening Globe*, 12 November 1925, 19; *New York Times*, 12 November 1925, 1; *New Rochelle Standard Star*, 11 and 12 November 1925, 1.

2. *New York Evening Journal*, 11 November 1925, 1.

3. *New York Times*, 11 November 1925, 1, 14.

4. *Des Moines Register*, 27 November 1925, 4.

5. *New Rochelle Standard Star*, 27 November 1925, 1.

6. *Reno Evening Gazette*, 14 November 1925, 1, 3.

7. *New York Daily News*, 12 November 1925, 2, 4; *New York Times*, 12 November 1925, 1; *Atlanta Journal*, 12 November 1925, 4; *Poughkeepsie Evening News*, 12 November 1925, 1.

8. *Philadelphia Inquirer*, 12 November 1925, 1, 4; *New York Times*, 12 November 1925, 1.

9. *New York Evening Journal*, 12 November 1925, 1; *New York World*, 12 November 1925, 1; *New York Daily News*, 12 November 1925, 2, 4.

10. *New Rochelle Standard Star*, 12 November 1925, 1, 3; *Arizona Republican*, 13 November 1925, sec. 11:9; *Chicago Tribune*, 12 November 1925, 1.

11. *New York Daily Mirror*, 12 November 1925, 2.

12. There seems to have been a phone in Alice's home, or at least one near enough that the two were able to call each other on occasion. Alice and her family did not list a number in any New Rochelle phone books, however. For a discussion of the earlier courtship, see *New York Times*, 12 and 13 November 1925, 1; *Philadelphia Inquirer*, 12 and 13 November 1925, 1, 4, and 1–2, respectively. On phone use see Claude Fisher, *America Calling: A Social History of the Telephone to 1940* (Berkeley: University of California Press, 1992).

13. *New York Daily News*, 18 November 1925, 3.

14. Ibid., 3, 4.

15. *Detroit Times*, 12 November 1925, 3. We have chosen not to highlight Alice's divergences from standard spelling and grammar with the corrective "*sic*'s."

16. *New York Daily News*, 12 November 1925, 3; *New York Daily Mirror*, 12 November 1925, 2.

17. *New York Daily News*, 12 November 1925, 3; similar to *New York Daily Mirror*, 12 November 1925, 2, except that the *Mirror* started the greeting with the correct spelling of Leonard's first name.

18. *New York Daily Mirror*, 12 November 1925, 1.

19. Ibid., 11 November 1925, 1; *Philadelphia Inquirer*, 12 November 1925, 1, 4.

20. As quoted in *New York Daily News*, 13 November 1925, 1, 2, 4; similar to *New York Daily Mirror*, 13 November 1925, 3.

21. *New York Daily Mirror*, 13 November 1925, 3.

22. *New York Daily News*, 13 November 1925, 2, 4.

23. *Detroit Times*, 13 November 1925, 3.

24. *Detroit Free Press*, 13 November 1925, 1.

25. *San Francisco Chronicle*, 12 November 1925, 1; *Detroit Times*, 14 November 1925, 3; *New York Evening Journal*, 17 November 1925, 3.

26. *New Rochelle Standard Star*, 16 November 1925, 1, 11.

27. *New York Times*, 13 November 1925, 1–2; *New York World*, 18 November 1925, 12, 13; *New York Sun*, 18 November, 1925, 1–2, 15.

28. *New York Daily Mirror*, 20 November 1925, 3; *Des Moines Register*, 20 November 1925, 5.

29. *Detroit Times*, 12 November 1925, 3.

30. *New York Times*, 12 November 1925, 1.

31. *New Rochelle Standard Star*, 12 November 1925, 1, 13.

32. John D'Emilio and Estelle B. Freedman, *Intimate Matters* (Chicago: University of Chicago Press, 1997), 239–40, 256–74. See Pamela S. Haag, "In Search of the Real Thing," in John C. Fout and Maura Shaw Tantillo, *American Sexual Politics* (University of Chicago Press, 1993), 161–70.

33. Kathy Peiss, *Cheap Amusements* (Philadelphia: Temple University Press, 1983), 98.

34. Scholars such as George Chauncey, David Nasaw, and Roy Rosenzweig provide important details about the nature of socializing, especially in New York and New England. See George Chauncey, *Gay New York* (New York: Basic Books, 1994); David Nasaw, *Children of the City* (Garden City, N.Y.: Anchor Books, 1985) and *Going Out* (New York: Basic Books, 1993); and Roy

Rosenzweig, *Eight Hours for What We Will* (Cambridge, England: Cambridge University Press, 1983) and *The Park and the People* (Ithaca, N.Y.: Cornell University Press, 1992).

35. *New York Daily News*, 12 November 1925, 4. See also *Philadelphia Inquirer*, 12 November 1925, 1.

36. *New York Daily News*, 13 November 1926, 6.

37. *New York Daily News*, 13 November 1925, 1, 36.

38. *New York Daily Mirror*, 12, 13, 14 November 1925, 1, 2; *New York Times*, 13, 14 November 1925, 1.

39. *New York Daily News*, 13 November 1925, 6; *Detroit Free Press*, 13 November 1925, 1.

CHAPTER 7   ON THE FACE OF IT

1. *New Rochelle Standard Star*, 14 November 1925, 1; *Detroit Times*, 14 November 1925, 3.

2. *New York Daily News*, 18 November 1925, 3.

3. *Philadelphia Inquirer*, 18 November 1925, 4; *New York Daily News*, 18 November 1925, 3; *New Rochelle Standard Star*, 17 November 1925, 1.

4. *New York Daily Mirror*, 18 November 1925, 3. On a very personal level, the trial may have also reminded Jolson of the fragility of love, especially under the pressures of public life and media scrutiny. Hopelessly preoccupied with his own career, he had frequently neglected his first wife, Henrietta Keller; that marriage had ended in divorce after thirteen years in 1919. Within a few years he married Ethel Delmar, his wife at the time of the Rhinelander trial. Was their marriage undergoing the same strains? His continued references to his wife's reactions to the controversy could be read as a furtive commentary on the obstacles to love or a professional playing for laughs—or both.

5. *New York Daily News*, 18 November 1925, 3.

6. *New York Daily Mirror*, 18 November 1925, 4.

7. *New York Daily News*, 18 November 1925, 3; *Philadelphia Inquirer*, 18 November 1925, 4.

8. *New York Daily News*, 18 November 1925, 3.

9. *Philadelphia Inquirer*, 18 November 1925, 4.

10. *New Rochelle Standard Star*, 17 November 1925, 1.

11. *New York Daily News*, 18 November 1925, 3.

12. The *New Rochelle Standard Star*, 14 November 1925.

13. The *Hartford Courant* (20 November 1925, 15) did quip that "at the present rate of denials of acquaintanceship . . . it may be that Alice Beatrice Jones didn't know any man besides Leonard Kip Rhinelander."

14. Louis Fremont Baldwin, *From Negro to Caucasian, or How the Ethiopian is Changing His Skin, A Concise presentation of the manner in which many negroes in America, who, being very fair in complexion, with hair naturally or artificially free from kink, having abandoned their one-time affiliations with Negroes, including their own relatives, and by mingling at first commercially or industrially, then socially with caucasians, have ultimately been absorbed by the latter. Prepared and published at the request of the Society for the Amalgamation of the Races, New York, Paris, London.* (San Francisco: Pilot Publishing Co., 1929).

15. Caleb Johnson, "Crossing the Color Line," *Outlook* 158, 26 August 1931, 526; "When is a Caucasian not," Editorial, *Independent* 70; 2 March 1911, 478–79. These documents are cited and discussed further in Heidi Ardizzone, *Red-Blooded Americans*, 13–15, 244.

16. W. E. B. Du Bois, "Rhinelander," *The Crisis* (January 1926), 112–13.

17. In fact, having both been immersed in the research and writing of this project for several years, we each have somewhat different speculations on how Alice and her family perceived themselves in racial terms, how their community perceived them, and how these perceptions affected their experiences and daily lives.

18. Interview with Helen Tymes, 2 January 1997, Westchester County, New York.

19. Earlier versions of sections of this chapter were presented at the University of Kentucky, 14 February 1997 and the University of Pennsylvania, 25 February 1998. Alain Locke, *Race Contacts and Interracial Relations*, edited by Jeffrey C. Stewart (Washington, D.C.: Howard University Press, 1992); W. E. B. Du Bois, *Dusk of Dawn: An Essay Toward an Autobiography of a Race Concept* (New York: Harcourt, Brace & World, Inc., 1940; reprint, New Brunswick, N.J.: Transaction, 1995) and *Darkwater, Voices from Within the Veil* (New York: Harcourt, Brace & Howe, 1920), 30.

20. Reginald Horsman, *Race and Manifest Destiny: The Origins of American Racial Anglo-Saxonism* (Cambridge, Mass., and London: Harvard University Press, 1981), 116–38, 187–297.

21. *Birmingham Age-Herald*, 13 November 1925, 6.

22. Frederick Jackson Turner, *The Frontier in American History, 1861–1932* (New York: Holt, Rinehart & Winston, 1962), 2–3.

23. A century later it is generally agreed that Turner was only partially correct. Indeed, the settling of the West and the pacification of the native peoples did signal the end of a period in American history. Yet American expansion did not come to an abrupt end in 1893. Americans simply redefined the frontier. In so doing, through the 1890s into the first years of the twentieth century, they pursued expansion with great vigor. Expansion in race relations, communication, business, consumerism, population, and foreign affairs obviously were not the frontiers that Turner had in mind. Nor could he have anticipated how interconnected these areas of human affairs would become.

24. Jacobson, *Whiteness of a Different Color*, 119–22; chap. 5.

25. Herbert G. Goldman, *Jolson: The Legend Comes to Life* (New York: Oxford University Press, 1988), 3–17. Some biographers have suggested that his mother's death played a profound role in young Asa's career choices. This resonates with the strong effect the death of Leonard's mother had on his life, although if his lawyers were to be believed, the effect was entirely negative.

26. Michael Freedland, *Jolie: The Story of Al Jolson* (London: W. H. Allen, 1985), 35.

27. By the nineteenth century, meanwhile, audiences in America had taken refuge in an easy read of this powerful play, concluding oftentimes as had John Quincy Adams in 1836: "[T]he intermarriage of black and white blood is a violation of the law of nature. That is the lesson to be learned from the play." Quoted in Lawrence W. Levine, *Highbrow, Lowbrow: The Emergence of Cultural Hierarchy in America* (Cambridge, Mass.: Harvard University Press, 1988), 39.

28. Eric Lott, *Love and Theft: Blackface Minstrelsy and the American Working Class* (New York: Oxford University Press, 1993), 8.
29. Ibid.; Ann Douglas, *Terrible Honesty: Mongrel Manhattan in the 1920s* (New York: Noonday Press, 1995) 354–62; and Michael Rogin, *Black Face, White Noise: Jewish Immigrants in the Hollywood Melting Pot* (Berkeley: University of California Press, 1996), especially sections on Jolson.
30. Douglas, *Terrible Honesty*, 354.
31. These points have been made in several recent texts, see, among them, Walter LaFeber, *The American Search for Opportunity, 1815–1913* (Cambridge, England: Cambridge University Press, 1992) and Nell Painter, *Standing at Armageddon* (New York: W. W. Norton, 1987).
32. Eileen Southern, *The Music of Black Americans: A History* (New York: W. W. Norton, 1983), 307–36; Douglas, *Terrible Honesty*, 354–61.
33. Ibid., 359.

CHAPTER 8 A MAN OF STANDING

1. The *Arizona Republican* identified this as the Salt River Valley School, a preparatory boys' school drawing students from many wealthy eastern families. 13 November 1925, sec. 2, 9.
2. *New York Daily News*, 17 November 1925, 3.
3. *Philadelphia Inquirer*, 18 November 1925, 4.
4. *New York Daily Mirror*, 19 November 1925, 5; 18 November 1925, 3.
5. *Philadelphia Inquirer*, 18 November 1925, 4.
6. Trial details for this section are gleaned from a number of newspapers, among them the *Philadelphia Inquirer, New York Daily News, New York Evening Journal, New York Mirror, New York Times, New Rochelle Standard Star*, 18 November 1925.
7. *New York Daily News*, 19 November 1925, 4.
8. *New York Times*, 19 November 1925, 6; *New York Daily Mirror*, 19 November 1925, 3; and *Houston Informer*, 21 November 1925, 8.
9. *New York World*, 19 November 1925, 1.
10. Ibid.
11. For a general review of changing perceptions of manhood, see Anthony Rotundo, *American Manhood* (New York: Basic Books, 1993), particularly chap. 6, 8, 9, and 10. As the issue applies to Victorian America, see Thomas J. Schlereth, *Victorian America* (New York: Harper Perennial, 1992), especially chap. 6. On the critical question of masculinity and manhood discussed in this section, see Gail Bederman, *Manliness and Civilization* (University of Chicago Press, 1995), 1–44.
12. Bederman, *Manliness and Civilization*, 17, 232.
13. In several other cartoons Powers played with the word "Kip," drawing Leonard as a "kippered fish" being grilled by Davis or caught on a fishing pole by Alice. *New York Evening Journal*, 28 November 1925, 14; *New York Daily Mirror*, 12 November 1925, 2.
14. On the sociohistory of race and lynching in the South, see Joel Williamson, *A Rage for Order* (New York: Oxford University Press, 1986), especially 82–95, 120–26.
15. For an account of Wells's activism against lynching, see Alfreda M. Duster,

ed., *Crusade for Justice: The Autobiography of Ida B. Wells* (University of Chicago Press, 1970); Ida B. Wells-Barnett, *On Lynchings* (New York: Arno Press, 1969).

16. W. E. B. Du Bois was one of the first to raise this issue most poignantly. See Du Bois's *Dusk of Dawn: An Essay toward an Autobiography of a Race Concept* (New York: Harcourt, Brace and Co., 1940), 51–58, 67. For an elaboration on this theme, see Thomas C. Holt, "The Political Uses of Alienation," *American Quarterly* (June 1990), 301–23.

17. *Philadelphia Tribune*, 21 November 1925, 1.

18. *Baltimore Afro-American*, 10 January 1925, 2.

19. Here see Thomas F. Gossett, *Race: The History of an Idea in America* (Dallas: Southern Methodist University Press, 1963); Ashley Montagu, *Man's Most Dangerous Myth: The Fallacy of Race* (New York: Columbia University Press, 1942); Stephen Jay Gould, *The Mismeasure of Man* (New York and London: W. W. Norton & Co., 1996); William A. Ripley, *The Race of Europe* (1899); John R. Commons, *Races and Immigrants in America* (New York: Macmillan Co., 1907); and Madison Grant, *The Passing of the Great Race, or the Racial Basis of European History*, 4th ed. (New York: Scribner's Sons, 1921).

20. *Houston Informer*, 21 November 1925, 8.

21. *Baltimore Afro-American*, 28 November 1925, 9.

22. Du Bois, *The Crisis* (January 1926), 112.

23. *Hartford Times*, 27 November 1925, 10; *Des Moines Register*, 26 November 1925, 8.

24. *Philadelphia Inquirer*, 19 November 1925, 12.

25. *Des Moines Register*, 17 November 1925, 6.

26. *New York Evening Journal*, 24 November 1925, 2.

27. *Hartford Times*, 27 November 1925, 10. *Richmond Times-Dispatch*, 18 November 1925, 3; *Atlanta Journal*, 19 November 1925, 5; *Birmingham Age-Herald*, 19 November 1925, 3.

28. *Richmond Times-Dispatch*, 28 November 1925, 6.

CHAPTER 9   THE FALLEN PRINCE

1. *New York Evening Journal*, 20 November 1925, 2.

2. *New Rochelle Standard Star*, 20 November 1925, 1–2.

3. *Philadelphia Inquirer*, 20 November 1925, 4.

4. *New York Daily Mirror*, 29 November 1925, 3; *Philadelphia Inquirer*, 21 November 1925, 8.

5. *New York Evening Journal*, 23 November 1925, 1.

6. *New York Times*, 24 November 1925, 1.

7. *New York Daily News*, 24 November 1925, 3.

8. *Philadelphia Inquirer*, 24 November 1925, 6, 8; 23 November 1925, 1; *New York Evening Journal*, 24 November 1925, 2.

9. *Philadelphia Inquirer*, 24 November 1928, 8; *Baltimore Afro-American*, 28 November 1925, 1.

10. *New York Daily News*, 24 November, 1925, 3.

11. Frank B. Gilbert, *Criminal Law and Practices of the State of New York: The Penal Law, The Code of Criminal Procedure, The Inferior Courts Act, and the*

Parole Commission Law for First Class Cities, 8th ed. (Albany, N.Y.: Matthews, Bender & Co., 1925), 222.

12. *Philadelphia Inquirer*, 24 November 1925, 6, 8.
13. Ellen Chesler, *Woman of Valor* (New York: Anchor Books, 1992), 67–70, 157–60, 295–97, and 397–90.
14. Pamela S. Haag, "In Search of 'The Real Thing': Ideologies of Love, Modern Romance, and Women's Sexual Subjectivity in the United States, 1920–40," in John C. Fout and Maura Shaw Tantillo, eds., *American Sexual Politics* (University of Chicago Press, 1993), 170–80.
15. Jesse F. Battan, "'The Word Made Flesh': Language, Authority, and Sexual Desire in Late-Nineteenth-Century America," in John C. Fout and Maura Shaw Tantillo, eds., *American Sexual Politics* (University of Chicago Press, 1993), 101–22; on Comstock, 117–21.
16. *New York Evening Journal*, 24 November 1925, 30; *Hartford Courant*, November 1925, 14.
17. *San Francisco Chronicle*, 3 December 1925, 24.
18. *Philadelphia Inquirer*, 24 November 1925, 6, 8.
19. *New York Daily Mirror*, 19 November 1925, 3; Pamela S. Haag, "In Search of 'The Real Thing,'" 180–83.
20. *New York Evening Journal*, 20 November 1925, 2.
21. *Detroit Free Press*, 18 November 1925, 1.
22. Jane Yolen, "America's Cinderella," in *Cinderella: A Folklore Casebook*, edited by Alan Dundes (New York: Garland Publishing, 1982), 296. The origins of the Cinderella story are, of course, European, not American. For an analysis of the historical development of the tale in the context of industrialization and capitalist societies, see Elizabeth Panttaja, "Going Up in the World: Class in 'Cinderella,'" *Western Folklore* 52 (1993): 85–104.
23. *Reno Evening Gazette*, 16 November 1925, 4.
24. Ralph Williams, "Modern Cinderellas," *The Claude A. Barnett Papers* (Frederick, Md.: University Publications of America, Inc., 1985, from the holdings of the Chicago Historical Society), Part Three "Subject Files on Black Americans, 1918–1967," Series I: "Race Relations, 1923–1965," Folder 382-2, "Newsclippings," 07:00810–12.
25. *Philadelphia Inquirer*, 18 November 1925, 4. The *Inquirer* was reporting on Davis's cross-examination of Leonard here. The perspective, therefore, may be more Davis's than the newspaper's, but as far as we have seen, Davis himself never referred to Alice as a Cinderella.
26. *New York Herald-Tribune*, 15 November 1925, 19.

CHAPTER 10   THE LAST VEIL LIFTED

1. Sander Gilman, *Difference and Pathology: Stereotypes of Sexuality, Race, and Madness* (Ithaca, N.Y.: Cornell University Press, 1985); Robert Rydell, *All the World's a Fair: Visions of Empire at American International Expositions, 1876–1916* (University of Chicago Press, 1987), discusses the 1893 World's Columbian Exposition in chap. 1, 6.
2. *Philadelphia Inquirer*, 24 November 1925, 1, 6; *Richmond Planet*, 5 December 1925, 4.
3. *Richmond Planet*, 5 December 1925, 4.

4. *Philadelphia Inquirer*, 24 November 1925, 6.

5. *New Rochelle Standard Star*, 18 November 1925, 2–3.

6. *Leicester Mercury*, 24 November 1925, 1. This article also noted that Alice's father was said to be from Leicester but that research had not been able to confirm this or identify any family in the area.

7. NYSC-WC, #3190-1924, Item 9, Isaac N. Mills, "Affidavit in Opposition to Application for Additional Counsel Fees," July 13, 1926, *Rhinelander v. Rhinelander*.

8. The *Baltimore Sun* proved an exception. In a matter-of-fact manner the paper reported that Alice suffered too when she had to disrobe for the benefit of the jury and others, noting that "Alice was in tears and shaking with sobs." *Baltimore Sun*, 21 November 1925, 8.

9. *Philadelphia Inquirer*, 18 November 1925, 4.

10. *New Rochelle Standard Star*, November 18, 1925, 2–3.

11. *Detroit Free Press*, 24 November 1925, 1. This article was attributed to Grace Robinson, a regular writer for the *New York Daily News*.

12. *Detroit Free Press*, 16 November 1925, 1.

13. *New York Daily Mirror*, 24 November 1925, 1, 3–4.

14. *Philadelphia Inquirer*, 24 November 1925, 1, 6, 8.

15. "White, But Black, a Document on the Race Problem," *Century* 109 (February 1925), 494. Cited in Ardizzone, *Red-Blooded Americans*, 248. Other supposed signs included dark shading of the backbone or aureoles, or of the skin under the eyes.

16. *Chicago Broad Ax*, 9 January 1926, 2.

17. Roi Ottley, "White Negroes," *Ebony* (March 1948), 28. It is interesting to note that this article, twenty years later, emphasized Alice's breasts as the presumed gauge of racial identity. At the time skin color was the most-often-cited physical evidence, with the exception of veiled remarks concerning the sexualized, voyeuristic aspect of the scene.

18. *Chicago Defender*, 13 December 1924, 14.

19. *Chicago Defender*, 12 December 1925, 2, 10.

20. *St. Louis Argus*, 27 November 1925, 6. The *Argus* did devote multiple columns to reprinting several of Leonard's letters and to describing the context in which they were read in court that day. This followed the pattern set by white southern papers' coverage of that day's events.

21. *Cleveland Gazette*, 28 November 1925, 1.

22. *Dallas Express*, 5 December 1925, 1.

23. *Houston Informer*, 28 November 1925, 8.

24. For discussions of these images see Deborah Gray White, *Ar'n't I a Woman? Female Slaves in the Plantation South* (New York and London: W. W. Norton and Co., 1985) and Donald Bogle, *Toms, Coons, Mulattoes, Mammies, and Bucks, An Interpretive History of Blacks in American Films* (New York: Viking Press, 1973).

25. Tyler Stovall, *Paris Noir: African Americans in the City of Light* (Boston and New York: Houghton Mifflin Company, 1996), 52–53.

26. Ibid., 54.

27. Maurine H. Beasley and Sheila J. Gibbons discuss the emergence of the "girl reporter" in *Taking Their Place: A Documentary History of Women and*

Journalism (Washington, D.C.: American University Press, 1993), 111–22, 131–38.

28. Ibid., 111.
29. *Los Angeles Times*, 29 November 1925, sec. 2, 4. Gethesemane was the biblical location of Jesus' agony and betrayal by Judas.
30. Ibid. This article does not identify the author or source of the description cited. Only three female reporters were said to be in the room at this time, and two were certainly Grace Robinson and Margery Rex, both of whose write-ups of the disrobing are discussed here. Alma Sioux Scarberry, of the *Daily Mirror*, may have been the third, although she was credited with only a few articles on the case.
31. *New York Daily News*, 24 November 1925, 4.
32. Ibid., 3.
33. *Norfolk Journal and Guide*, 28 November 1925, 1.
34. *New York Evening Journal*, 24 November 1925, 2.
35. *New York Daily Mirror*, 24 November 1925, 3; *Baltimore Afro-American*, 28 November 1925, 1.
36. Ken Kobré, "Positive/Negative," online column in *Photoplex*, www.gigaplex.com, 1995.
37. *Evening Graphic*, n.d.

CHAPTER 11   REVELATIONS

1. *New York Times*, 25 November 1925, 3.
2. *Philadelphia Inquirer*, 25 November 1925, 4.
3. *New Rochelle Standard Star*, 24 November 1925, 1–2.
4. *New York Times*, 25 November 1925, 3.
5. Davis mocked Rich's testimony: "[W]ait a minute, you say Jones was of English descent and he dropped his h's?" To which she fired back, "Well, he was of Spanish-English descent." *New Rochelle Standard Star*, 24 November 1925, 1–2.
6. Ibid.
7. *Philadelphia Inquirer*, 25 November 1925, 4.
8. Ibid.
9. Encounter recalled in *New York Daily Mirror*, 26 November 1925, 3.
10. *Philadelphia Inquirer*, 25 November 1925, 4; *New York Times*, 25 November 1925, 3.
11. *Philadelphia Inquirer*, 25 November 1925, 4.
12. *Los Angeles Times*, 26 November 1925, 3; *Philadelphia Inquirer*, 26 November 1925, 4; *New York Daily News*, 26 November 1925, 3–4.
13. *New Rochelle Standard Star*, 25 November 1925, 1–2.
14. *New Rochelle Standard Star*, 25 November 1925, 2; see also *Philadelphia Inquirer*, 26 November 1925, 4; and *New York Times*, 26 November 1925, 3.
15. *Philadelphia Inquirer*, 26 November 1925, 4; Chicago Tribune, 26 November 1925, 17; *New Rochelle Standard Star*, 25 November 1925, 2.
16. *Philadelphia Inquirer*, 26 November 1925, 4; *New York Times*, 26 November 1925, 3; *Chicago Tribune*, 26 November 1925, 17; *New Rochelle Standard Star*, 25 November 1925, 1–2.
17. *Philadelphia Inquirer*, 26 November 1925, 4.

18. Ibid.
19. Ibid. Unfortunately what Chidester actually said was not specified.
20. *Los Angeles Times, Chicago Tribune, New York Daily News, Philadelphia Inquirer, Birmingham Age-Herald, Detroit Free Press,* 26 November 1925.
21. *Atlanta Constitution,* 27 November 1925, 4.
22. *New York Evening Journal,* 27 November 1925, 3.
23. *New York Daily News,* 26 November 1925, 1; *New York Daily Mirror,* 27 November 1925, 3.
24. *New York Daily News,* 25 November 1925, 3.
25. *New York Daily News,* 2 December 1925, 17.
26. *New York Evening Journal,* 27 November 1925, 3.

CHAPTER 12   BEFORE GOD AND MAN BE FAIR

1. *New York Times,* 27 November 1925, 3; *New York Daily News,* 27 November 1925, 4.
2. *New Rochelle Standard Star,* 30 November 1925, 1.
3. *New Rochelle Standard Star,* 27 November 1925, 2; *Philadelphia Inquirer,* 26 November 1925, 2.
4. *New York Times,* 1 December 1925, 12.
5. *Philadelphia Inquirer,* 1 December 1925, 2.
6. Ibid.
7. Ibid.; 2 December 1925, 2; see also *New York Times,* 2 December 1925, 3; *New Rochelle Standard Star,* 2 December 1925, 1–2; and the *New York Daily News,* 2 December 1925, 3–4.
8. Events and quotes taken from *New York Times,* 3 December 1925, 3, and 4 December 1925, 3; *Philadelphia Inquirer,* 3 December 1925, 2, and 4 December 1925, 2; *New Rochelle Standard Star,* 3 December 1925, 1–2, and 4 December 1925, 1–2; *New York Daily News,* 3 December 1925, 3–4, and 4 December 1925, 4; *New York Daily Mirror,* 3 December 1925, 3–4, 6, and 4 December 1925, 3–4; and *New York Evening Journal,* 3 December 1925, 3–4, 6, and 4 December 1925, 3–4.

CHAPTER 13   AWAITING THE VERDICT

1. *New York Daily Mirror,* 5 December 1925, 3.
2. *Detroit Times,* 4 December 1925, 2.
3. "Issues to be Submitted to the Jury," December 29, 1925, *Rhinelander v. Rhinelander.*
4. Morschauser's decision to tell the jury that this final question had been answered was a major point of contention in subsequent appeals and later trials.
5. Annulment cases were not always heard by a jury. In this case the process was that Morschauser would make a recommendation based on the jury's findings.
6. *New York Daily Mirror,* 5 December 1925, 5.
7. *Philadelphia Inquirer,* 5 December 1925, 6.
8. *New York Daily Mirror,* 5 December 1925, 3.
9. Ibid.
10. *New York Daily News,* 5 December 1925, 3; *New York Daily Mirror,* 5 December 1925, 4. Reynolds had been one of several reporters interviewing the young cou-

ple that day. The *Chicago Tribune* suggested it was a "slight indication" that they were "leaning in Mrs. Rhinelander's favor." The *New York Daily Mirror* observed that the question had caused a "visible flurry in the Rhinelander counsel" and certainly indicated that the jury thought Reynold's testimony was important. Perhaps, they intimated, this was why the Rhinelander lawyers hurried off to their hotel that night for a conference.

11. *New York Daily Mirror*, 5 December 1925, 1.
12. *New York Evening Journal*, 4 December 1925, 2; *New York Daily News*, 5 December 1925, 3.
13. *Chicago Tribune*, 5 December 1925, 1.
14. *Richmond Planet*, 12 December 1925, 5.
15. *Detroit Times*, 5 December 1925, 1–2.
16. *Philadelphia Inquirer*, 5 December 1925, 1.
17. *New York Daily Mirror*, 5 December 1925, 4.
18. *New York Daily News*, 5 December 1925, 3; *New York Evening Journal*, 5 December 1925, 10.
19. *Detroit Free Press*, 29 November 1925, 1. See also *New York World*, 6 December 1925, 19; *Hartford Times*, 28 November 1925, 1.
20. *Hartford Courant*, 30 November 1925, 12.
21. *Chicago Defender*, 12 December 1925, sec 2, 10.
22. *Baltimore Afro-American*, 12 December 1925, 11.
23. *Cleveland Gazette*, 12 December 1925, 2.
24. *Opportunity*, January 1926, 4. It should be noted that the exact wording of Mills's appeal to the jury as parents is not exactly the same in this source as in that quoted above. This is a typical example of the lack of precision in reporters' notes or newspapers' citations of the trial record. At the same time, however, it serves to illustrate the general agreement among newspapers on the content.
25. *Chicago Defender*, 12 December 1925, sec. 2, 10. The *Defender* routinely capitalized the word "race" when using it as a synonym for blacks, as in "those of our Race."
26. Ibid.
27. Ibid., 5 December 1925, sec. 1, 1–2.
28. *Jewish Daily Forward*, 3 December 1925, 1. Translation by Libby Garland. The *Forward*, edited by Abraham Cahan, was published in New York City. In 1924–25 the paper's circulation probably approached 250,000.
29. *Boston Daily Globe*, 5 December 1925, 10.
30. *Detroit Times*, 2 December 1925, 1.
31. *Cleveland Gazette*, 12 December 1925, 1; *New Rochelle Standard Star*, 9 December 1925, 1.
32. *Boston Daily Globe*, 10 December, 1925, 11.
33. *Minneapolis Journal*, 4 December 1925, 26.
34. *Boston Daily Globe*, 5 December, 1925, 1; *Detroit Times*, 5 December, 1925, 1.
35. *Chicago Tribune*, 5 December 1925, 1.
36. *Detroit Free Press*, 5 December 1925, 1.
37. *Atlanta Constitution*, 5 December 1925, 1.
38. *New Rochelle Standard Star*, 4 December 1925, 1.
39. Ibid.

CHAPTER 14 THE TRIAL ENDS

1. *Detroit Free Press*, 5 December 1925, 2.
2. *New York Daily News*, 6 December 1925, 3.
3. *New Rochelle Standard Star*, 5 December 1925, 14. The *New York Evening Journal* reported a slightly different warning. "'This is not a circus,' [Morschauser] declared, 'This is a court. I want the attendants to report anybody who makes any demonstrative move, and I want all of you distinctly to understand that.'" *New York Evening Journal*, 5 December 1925, 10.
4. *New York Evening Journal*, 5 December 1925, 10.
5. Although technically the judge could still decide against the jury's recommendation, he was not expected to and in fact did not. In the reporting and for all practical purposes, the jury's answers were the verdict.
6. *New York Evening Journal*, 5 December 1925, 10; *New Rochelle Standard Star*, 5 December 1925, 14; *Birmingham Age-Herald*, 6 December 1925, 2.
7. *New Rochelle Standard Star*, 5 December 1925, 14.
8. *New York Evening Post*, 5 December 1925, 10.
9. *New York Daily News*, 6 December 1925, 3.
10. *Cleveland Gazette*, 12 December 1925, 1.
11. *Birmingham Age-Herald*, 6 December 1925, 2.
12. *Cleveland Gazette*, 12 December 1925, 1.
13. *New York Daily News*, 6 December 1925, 3.
14. *Cleveland Gazette*, 12 December 1925, 1.
15. *New York Evening Post*, 5 December 1925, 10; *New York World*, 6 December 1925, 1.
16. *Chicago Tribune*, 6 December 1925, 1.
17. *New York World*, 6 December 1925, 2.
18. Ibid., 1.
19. *Chicago Defender*, 12 December 1925, 2. The *World* rendered this quote as "If we had voted according to our hearts, it would have been a different story."
20. *New York World*, 6 December 1925, 1.
21. The two dissenters were identified as Max Mendel, an exporter from Mount Vernon, and Simeon Brady, a farmer in Somers. Brady reportedly conceded to the majority before 6:00 P.M., while Mendel held out until 11:15. *New York World*, 6 December 1925, 1.
22. *New York Evening Journal*, 7 December 1925, 2.
23. *New York World*, 6 December 1925, 1.
24. *Baltimore Afro-American*, 12 December 1925, 11.
25. *New York World*, 6 December 1925, 1; *New York Evening Journal*, 7 December 1925, 1. The *Journal* refered to this as a "happily conceived analogy between diluted whiskey and mixed negro and white blood."
26. *Reno Evening Gazette*, 5 December 1925, 4.
27. *New York Daily News*, 6 December 1925, 19.
28. *Chicago Defender*, 12 December 1925, 1. See also *Reno Evening Gazette*, 5 December 1925, 4.
29. *New York World*, 7 December 1925, 12.
30. *Reno Evening Gazette*, 5 December 1925, 4.
31. *Jewish Daily Forward*, 6 December 1925, 1.
32. *Chicago Defender*, 16 January 1926, sec. 2, 8. (The *Rock Argus* editorial is

reprinted in this issue of the *Defender* under the heading "Other Papers Say.")

33. *Chicago Defender*, 12 December 1925, sec. 2, 10.
34. *Amsterdam News*, 9 November 1925, 1.
35. Ibid.
36. *New York Age*, 12 December 1925, 4.
37. *Amsterdam News*, 9 December 1925, n.p.
38. *Opportunity*, January 1926, 4.
39. *Cleveland Gazette*, 26 December 1925, 2.
40. *Crisis*, January 1926.
41. *New York World*, 6 December 1925, 2.
42. Ibid., 8 December 1925, 16.
43. *Chicago Broad Ax*, 12 December 1925, 1.
44. *New York Daily News*, 6 December 1925, 9.
45. Ibid.
46. Ibid.
47. *Chicago Broad Ax*, 12 December 1925, 1.
48. *Amsterdam News*, 19 December 1925, 1.
49. *Baltimore Afro-American*, 12 December 1925, 1; *New York Daily Mirror*, 7 December 1925, 3.
50. The *Mirror's* headline in later editions on December 5 read simply ALICE WINS in large bold capitals. *New York Daily Mirror*, 7 December 1925, 3.

CHAPTER 15　SPOTLIGHTS ARE SLOW TO FADE

1. *New York Times*, 7 December 1925, 29.
2. *Boston Daily Globe*, 7 December 1925, 22; *Boston Evening Globe*, 7 December 1925, 16; *New York Times*, 5 December 1925, 54.
3. *New York Sun*, 7 December 1925, 3.
4. *Chicago Defender*, 12 December 1925, sec. 1, 2.
5. *Boston Daily Globe*, 15 December 1925, 1, 10; *Natchez Democrat*, 15 December 1925, 1; *Detroit Free Press*, 15 December 1925, 1; *New York Times*, 15 December 1925, 1; *St. Louis Globe-Democrat*, 15 December 1925, 1.
6. *Florida Times Union* [Jacksonville], 16 December 1925, 26; *New Rochelle Standard Star*, 15 December 1925, 1.
7. *St. Louis Argus*, 18 December 1925, 1, 8.
8. *Chicago Defender*, 19 December 1925, sec. 2, 10; *Dallas Express*, 26 December 1925, 1; *Amsterdam News*, 23 December 1925, 1; *St. Paul Echo*, 26 December 1925, 2; an editorial from Oklahoma in *Chicago Defender*, 2 January 1926, sec. 2, 8.
9. *New Rochelle Standard Star*, 16 December 1925, 1.
10. Ibid., 26 December 1925, 1; *New Rochelle Standard Star*, 20 December 1925, 1; *New York Times*, 21 December 1925, 20; *St. Louis Argus*, 25 December 1925, 1; *Chicago Broad Ax*, 2 January 1926, 4.
11. *Houston Informer*, 19 December 1925, 8.
12. *Baltimore Afro-American*, 26 December 1925, 3.
13. Ibid., 1; *Dallas Express*, 26 December 1925, 1.
14. *Chicago Broad Ax*, 9 January 1926, 2.
15. *Philadelphia Tribune*, 30 January 1926, 1.

16. *New York Times*, 11 January 1926, 3.
17. *Chicago Defender*, 20 March 1926, sec. 1, 1.
18. *St. Paul Echo*, 6 March 1926, 2.
19. *New York Times*, 16 July 1926, 2; 18 July 1926, 2; *Houston Informer*, 17 July 1926, 8.
20. *New York Times*, 18 July 1926; *Amsterdam News*, 21 July 1926, 1; *St. Louis Argus*, 23 July 1926, 1; *Norfolk Journal and Guide*, 24 July 1926; *New York Times*, 24 July 1926, 11.
21. *New Rochelle Standard Star*, 19 December 1925, 1; *St. Paul Echo*, 27 March 1926, 2.
22. *New York Times*, 8 September 1926, 17.
23. The *Times* quoted Swinburne as saying, "[W]e were somewhat surprised that the plaintiff's attorneys did not contend at the outset that their client was blind, or at least color blind, instead of 'brain-tied.' " *New York Times*, 11 November 1926, 13.
24. 219 New York Supplement Supreme Court, Appelate Division, Second Department 189, 4 January 1927, *Rhinelander* v. *Rhinelander*, 548–50.
25. *Baltimore Sun*, 6 December 1926, 12.
26. *Chicago Defender*, 27 March 1926, sec. 1, 8.
27. Ibid., 27 November 1926, sec. 1, 1.
28. *New York Times*, 18 June 1927, 14; *New Rochelle Standard Star*, 30 December 1927, 1.
29. *Chicago Broad Ax*, 15 January 1927, 1.
30. *New York Times*, 30 March 1927, 11; *New York Age*, 26 March 1927, 1, 4.
31. *New Rochelle Standard Star*, 30 December 1927, 1; *New York Times*, 30 December 1927, 9.
32. *New York Times*, 28 April 1928, 21.
33. Ibid., 18 October 1928, 20.
34. Ibid., 13 June 1929, 31; 20 July 1929, 6.
35. Ibid., 18 September 1929, 32.
36. Ibid., 6 July 1929, 14; *Chicago Defender*, 13 July 1929, sec. 1, 3.
37. *Chicago Defender*, 24 August 1929, sec. 1, 2; *New York Times*, 14 September 1929, 20; *New York Times*, 15 September 1929, 24.
38. *New York Times*, 22 January 1930, 12.
39. Ibid., 9 February 1930, 22.
40. Ibid., 4 June 1930, 13.
41. Ibid., 18 July 1930.
42. "Proof of Claim" filed 5-18-40 in "Citation and Affidavits of Service" Nassau County Surrogate's Court, *in re* Estate of Philip Rhinelander.
43. *Chicago Defender*, 25 October 1925, sec. 1, 11.
44. *New Rochelle Standard Star*, 23 November 1933, 2; *Chicago Defender*, 2 December 1933, sec. 1, 1.
45. *New York Times*, 21 February 1936, 17; *New York Times*, 23 February 1936, sec. 2, 11.
46. *Chicago Defender*, 29 February 1936, sec. 1, 4.
47. Louise Rhinelander Doyle, Personal communication with authors, October 12, 1997.
48. Probate Court, Long Island 27391, Book 69, "Leonard Kip Rhinelander," 4 March 1936, 493.

49. *Chicago Defender*, 15 November 1941, sec. 1, 2.
50. 36 New York Supplement Second, 264 Appellate Division, Supreme Court, Second Department, July 6, 1942, *In re* Rhinelander's Will. *In re* Rhinelander et al.

CONCLUSION   THE LAST WORD

1. Certificate of Death, Alice Jones, 13 September 1989, file no. 1989-2932. See Alice Jones Estate, File #2932-89, Westchester County Surrogate Court.
2. Because these relatives have not responded to our attempts at correspondence, we are assuming they do not wish to be identified, and we have chosen to honor that.
3. Certificate of Death, Alice Jones, 13 September 1989, file no. 1989-2932. See Alice Jones Estate, File #2932-89, Westchester County Surrogate Court; Roberta Carlos Estate, File #1151-1993, Westchester County, Surrogate Court.
4. Thadious M. Davis, *Nella Larsen: Novelist of the Harlem Renaissance* (Baton Rouge: Louisiana State University Press, 1994), introduction.
5. Nella Larsen, *Quicksand and Passing*, edited by Deborah E. McDowell (New Brunswick, N.J.: Rutgers University Press, 1986), 225.
6. Ibid.
7. Ibid., 245.
8. Race was not altogether ignored. The certificate did indicate that someone did hand-check that Alice was not of Hispanic origin. It should be noted, however, that such forms are as likely to be filled out by medical personnel as by family members, and items such as race may simply not be considered important at a time of death.
9. Marion R. Forstall, "Voices and Profiles of New Rochelle's Rich, Color-Full History," 5 January 1981, in the Public Library of New Rochelle, New York. Also, *300 Years: Blacks and New Rochelle (Glimpses of History)*, New Rochelle Public Library. Interview with author December 1996.
10. In more academic parlance, Earl has called this ordering and reordering of the components of one's identity "multipositionality." By "multipositionality" is meant the need to view individuals as not just racial, gender, and class beings. Rather, individual identity is defined by all the parts of a person—sexual, age, gender, and so on—that make them whole. Moreover, the self is constructed in time and space. So those things that may best define what a person presents of him- or herself in a church, workplace, or courtroom may differ. Surely this was true of Alice and Leonard. See Earl Lewis, "'To Turn as On a Pivot,'" *American Historical Review* (June 1995), 782–84.
11. Insofar as we know, junior or senior theses on the case have appeared at Princeton and Harvard Universities, and students at Rutgers and the University of Virginia have dissertations in progress. See also Mark J. Madigan, "Miscegenation and 'The Dicta of Race and Class': The Rhinelander Case and Nella Larsen's *Passing*," *Modern Fiction Studies* 36, no. 4 (Winter 1998), 523–28. Phillip Brian Harper, *Are We Not Men? Masculine Identity and the Problem of African-American Identity* (New York: Oxford University Press, 1996), 132–39. Moreover, the story has appeared in other New York publications in recent years, including Marc Ferris, "One Block," *Avenue Magazine* (November 1999), n.p.

ACKNOWLEDGMENTS

THE FORMULATION, RESEARCH, and writing of this book have been a true collaboration, not only between us as coauthors but involving the assistance and support of numerous individuals and organizations. This project began in 1995 with a University of Michigan Rackham Research Partnership grant cofunded by the Horace H. Rackham School of Graduate Studies and the Office for the Vice President for Research. The Research Partnership Program was designed to encourage collaborative work between faculty and graduate students. On completing the initial research funded by the grant, we coauthored the article "A Modern Cinderella: Race, Sexuality, and Social Class in the Rhinelander Case" in *International Labor and Working Class History* (Spring 1997). Work on this article confirmed our sense that we had enough material for the book you have just read, as well as enough compatability in writing and analytical approaches to weather a much longer undertaking together. Over the years our work has been supported by the University of Michigan's Office of the Provost, College of Literature, Sciences and the Arts (LSA), Institute for the Study of Women and Gender, Center for Afroamerican and African Studies (CAAS), Summer Research Opportunity Program, and Program in American Culture.

The task of compiling our sources was an immense one. For their aid in compiling and transcribing newspaper articles and supporting documents we would like to thank Marya Smith, Marisela Martinez, Kate Masur, Hajj Womack, Nsenga Lee, Libby Garland, Adrian Burgos, and Alexis Stokes. For helping us locate and follow leads in Great Britain we thank Julia Drake and Aimee Unze. For their hospitality and assistance during numerous research trips Heidi would like to thank Dora Ardizzone, Jason and Jeni Ardizzone-West, Larissa Swedell, Leslie Paris, Caroline Danielson, and the staffs of the New York Public Library, New York Historical Society, Westchester County Historical Society, Westchester County Clerk's Office, New Rochelle Public Library, New Rochelle Beechwoods Cemetery, and the Nassau County Clerk's Office. The University of Notre Dame's American Studies Department provided additional support for travel in the final stages of writing. Earl is indebted to the assistance provided by colleague and Westchester County native James Grossman and his mother, Adele, and longtime resident Helen Tymes.

A number of people deserve special thanks. We are especially appreciative of the aid provided by Earl's secretary Carolyn Amick, who unscrambled disks, sent attachments, reformatted endless drafts, and cleared and coordinated schedules so that we might finish this book. On numerous occasions others at the Rackham School of Graduate Studies helped, too. Thanks to Rhonda Kandow, Susan Fitzpatrick, Doug Heady, and Lynne Dumas. At a critical point Law School librarian Margaret Leary, director of the University of Michigan's Law Library, came to our aid, as did Michael Awkward, Carol Smith Rosenberg, and Sonya Rose, with help we truly value. Assistance from CAAS staff Geraldine Brewer, Tammy Davis, and Camille Spencer also helped tremendously.

In addition a long list of colleagues either listened to one or both of us talk about the book for more than five years, or they provided settings for us to discuss some aspect of the project. Earl wishes to acknowledge the following institutions for inviting him to speak: the History Department at the University of Pennsylvania, the Social Theory Seminar on Whiteness at the University of Kentucky, the American Studies and History Department at William & Mary College, the Newberry Library, Camp Michigania, the University of Michigan's LSA Visiting Committee, the Seminar on Race sponsored by the Center for Political Studies in the Institute for Social Research and the seminar for fellows in the Michigan Journalism Fellows Program. We both benefited from participation in CAAS's African Peoples in the Industrial Age Project colloquium, and are indebted to colleagues and students at the University of Michigan. Heidi is also grateful for the comments, challenges, and interest provided by the participants in the Women's Studies Forum at Plattsburgh State University in New York State; my students and colleagues in the Plattsburgh's Women Studies Program and members of the Center for Womyn's Concerns and Organization of Women of Ethnicity; students and colleagues in the American Studies Department at the University of Notre Dame; and participants in the annual meeting of the American Studies Association, Pittsburgh, in November 1995 and the Brown Bags Series in American Culture and CAAS at the University of Michigan.

Our editor, Amy Cherry, supported this project from the first time Earl mentioned it. Remarkably, she listened patiently when he announced, before any writing had begun, that we had a book for Norton. She encouraged us to develop our idea, and then convinced others that this project could become a book. More than anything she proved to be the editor we had imagined: devoted, sensitive, exacting, critical, encouraging, professional, and a real friend. As is often the case but often goes unstated, this is our collective work. Thanks, too, to her assistants Nomi Victor and Anne White, for their steady hand through the writing and production phases.

And we are both eternally grateful for the patience and support of colleagues, family, friends, and significant others.

FOR THEIR INTELLECTUAL and spiritual support, Heidi would like to thank Betty Bell, Crisca Bierwert, Elsa Barkley Brown, Jessica Chalmers, Ben Giamo, Graciela Hernandez, Susan Johnson, Carol Karlsen, Joseph Moreau, Susan Ohmer, Leslie Paris, Rebecca Poyourow, Tom Schlereth, Bob Schmul, David Scobey, and Margaret Washington, who inspired me to be a historian. Alexis Stokes sat in my living room to make me work, talked me through some rough spots, and put up with my cats. Robin Balthrope, Wendy Gordon, Ed Guenther, Alexandria Lafaye, Don Mayer, Erin Mitchell, and Amy

Mountcastle helped me barbecue by the lake and watch the moon rise. Welcome, Chet. Stacy and Sasha Serwicki have always offered shelter, shoulders, and shopping as therapy. Michael Adam Perry and Diane Sampson have both provided long-term support, criticism, and reassurance in my writing and my life. Friendships like these are the reason we are here. And to Roderick Earl White, who gave me so much during the final stages of writing and editing: You have all my faith and hope.

For my mother and father, Rich and Wendy Ardizzone, who crossed some lines of their own when they married, I thank you for the cross-ethnic upbringing and the endless love and support you give me. Matt Ardizzone and Jason Ardizzone-West grew somehow from annoying kid brothers to trusted and treasured friends. Among the many gifts they've given me were two wonderful sisters. Rachel Lauber and Jeni Ardizzone-West: Things are happening; we need to talk! And a special thanks to Michael Webster and Leone Buyse, whose sojourn in Ann Arbor at just the right time provided me with home-cooked meals and family nearby.

This book is dedicated to the memory of three of my grandparents, two of whom passed away while I was writing the final chapters. And to my grandma Dora Ardizzone, who still tells me stories about where I came from, sends money, and gives me prayers and love over the phone. From all of them I've learned that creativity is as necessary as sunlight, that historical memory lives in us all, and that we never stop learning and growing.

EARL WOULD LIKE to thank his many graduate students, who listened and questioned, as well as colleagues and collaborators Michael Awkward, Elsa Barkley Brown, Nancy Burns, Fred Cooper, P. Gabrielle Foreman, James Grossman, Tom Holt, Tera Hunter, Robert Jefferson, Robin D. G. Kelley, Diedra Harris Kelley, Don Kinder, Lawrence Levine, George Lipsitz, Monica McCormick, Peggy Pascoe, George Sanchez, Gay Seidman, Stephanie Shaw, Dana Takagi, Joe Trotter, and Rafia Zafar. To Cheryl Hurley, who became intrigued by the book and what it promised to say from the outset, many thanks for your words of encouragement.

To my mother, Virginia Lewis Carr, and brother, Rudolph Lewis, sister-in-law Rosalind, and nephews Damon and Desmond, I say thanks for reminding me of who I am. Your unstinting love has meant much. This project has spanned two important phases in my personal life. When it began I was married to Jayne London. While our marriage has ended, we remain friends and dedicated parents to our children, Suzanne and Max. In different ways each of them knows what it means to have someone in their lives who is both a full-time administrator and faculty member as well as a scholar and writer. I appreciate their forbearance and love. In the last year I have learned anew the power and joy of love. To my new partner, Susan Whitlock, a fine editor, beautiful person, and dear love, I say thank you for reminding me that not only was this book possible but also so much more. I look forward to our future, together.

I wish to dedicate this book to my children, and all others who live on the fault line between racial absolutes. With one parent in the social, historical, and cultural nomenclature of our time white and the other black, Suzanne and Max symbolize for me the power of race on the social imagination of the United States. Each has had the experience of having others perceive them differently when in my company or that of their mother. Nor is this true just in the United States. More than once, on a recent trip to Mexico strangers began conversations in Spanish with the two, only to revert to English when I appeared alongside them. Sometimes it was my more audible English that placed us as Norte Americanos. In other instances it may have been my dress, body language, color, or bearing—who knows? Strange and universal is the need to know, to categorize, and to place.

So if that impulse is strong and enduring in postsegregation North America, imagine the pull on Alice and her family in the 1920s. It is little wonder, then, that Americans watched this case in utter fascination. Still, little did Alice and Leonard know that their actions, nearly eight decades ago, would have something to say to the grandchildren and great-grandchildren of their contemporaries. We have both been reminded through this work of both the vast distance between our world and theirs, and the wide bridges that connect them.

INDEX

Page numbers in *italics* refer to illustrations.